LIBRARY BUILDERS

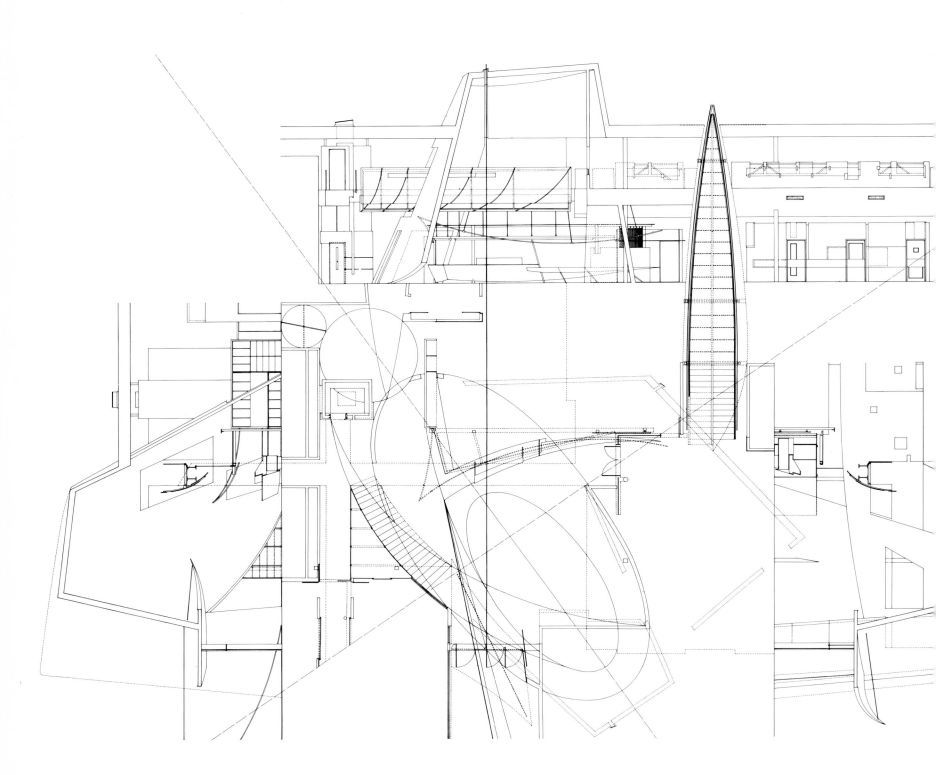

LIBRARY BUILDERS

A.D. ACADEMY EDITIONS

Acknowledgements

We would like to express our appreciation for the enthusiasm shown by all of the contributors and for their assistance in providing material for this publication.

Photo credits:
All photographs are courtesy of the architects unless stated otherwise: Arup Associates p33; James Austin p31; Javier Azurmendi pp108, 110, 112, 114, 138, 140-41, 152-54, 219; Jan Roger Bodin p116; Mario Bettella p7; Michael Brawne p46; Richard Bryant/ARCAID pp200-201; Peter Cook pp32, 34, 36, 62, 64, 70, 72-74, 202, 204-05, 217, 218 (centre); M Denancé/Dominique Perrault pp158 (above left); John Donat pp208, 210-213; J Dow pp148, 150; Steven Evans p56; Georges Fessy/Dominique Perrault pp156, 160 (above right, below), 162-63; Dennis Gilbert pp58, 60-61, 66, 68, 76, 78-79; Jeff Goldberg/ESTO pp100, 102-03; Bjørn Harstad pp118/119; Craig Hodgetts pp92, 94; Timothy Hursley pp136-37, 165-67, 180-81, 186, 188-89, 192-194, 196-97, 214; Mr Kida pp168, 170; Antti Luutonen pp144 (below), 146 (below); Peter Mandelkorn pp184-85; Malcolm Parry p8 (above); Perrault Projets p218 (above); Mandy Reynolds p171; Irene Rhoden p209 (below); Christian Richters pp38, 40, 42-44, 80, 82-83, 120, 122-26, 128-29,132-33; Timothy Soar pp88, 90; Stüwing/HLTa/s pp104-07; Jyrki Tasa pp144 (above), 146 (above); Jussi Tiainen pp84, 86-87; Bill Timmerman cover, pp48-54, 218 (below); Tohru Waki pp96, 98-99

Illustration credits:
Henri Labrouste, Bibliothèque Nationale on p8 (below) from Kenneth Frampton, *Studies in Tectonic Culture*, courtesy MIT Press; Perrault Projets p218 (above)

Cover: Phoenix Central Library, Phoenix, Arizona, bruder DWL architects
Frontispiece: John J Ross – William C Blakely Law Library, Arizona State University, Tempe, Arizona, Scogin, Elam and Bray

First published in Great Britain in 1997 by
ACADEMY EDITIONS

An imprint of

ACADEMY GROUP LTD
42 Leinster Gardens, London W2 3AN
Member of the VCH Publishing Group

ISBN: 1 85490 484 1

Distributed to the trade in the United States of America by
NATIONAL BOOK NETWORK, INC
4720 Boston Way, Lanham, Maryland 20706

Printed and bound in Italy

CONTENTS

INTRODUCTION

Michael Brawne

■ Libraries are at a cusp: poised uneasily between the legacy of Gutenberg and the byte of the digital age. There might indeed be those who would argue that the idea of an information store within a building is an anachronism and that what this volume shows is therefore no longer relevant. I believe that the libraries presented here prove this view to be both premature and unfounded.

Moreover, the important issue as far as architecture is concerned is what impact changes in information transfer may have on the organisation and appearance of the places where transfer occurs. What has been created for this purpose in the last decade is likely to be of some significance, perhaps both as pointer and as warning. Many of the examples shown here are thus architectural explorations of the problem of the new – or possibly transitional – library. They cover a wide range in terms of size, function and location and certainly no single example could be said to be definitive.

Two primary functions occur in libraries: the storage of the information source – books, journals, maps, recorded music, CD-ROMS, and so on – and the opportunity of having access to that information by individuals at a time of their choosing. That this is a matter of a direct and individual relationship is crucial, and of primary design significance. In many other media, the cinema or the theatre for instance, the communication is addressed to a particular group at a specified time; in other media, such as radio or television, it is transmitted to an unknown number but at a stated and controlled time. The library – and the museum – allows for individuals to decide when they need access and equally to determine what information they want. This freedom of choice, within the constraints of availability, is of paramount importance to any concept of the freedom of information.

If this analysis is correct, one would expect libraries to contain spaces which in some way delineate the activity zones of individuals. The carrel associated with the monasteries of the Middle Ages provides an early and important example for it provided a personal space within a larger whole. In some ways it was analogous to the niches on the west front of cathedrals that sheltered the statues of saints and gave each one a defined *aedicule*.

A celebrated and now iconic image of the carrel occurs in the painting by Antonello da Messina (*c*1430-79), now in the National Gallery in London, of *St Jerome in his Study*. A scrutiny of the shelves reveals that St Jerome had something like thirty volumes within reach and room for more. Although a monastic library of the second half of the fifteenth century would have housed a much greater collection than this, it seems likely that these thirty books satisfied the saint's needs for a considerable period of study and indeed could have dealt with a sizeable part of the then available knowledge. Storage, accessibility and expansion had thus simple and direct solutions; in fact, they hardly existed as problems.

Antonello painted *St Jerome in his Study* only a few years after Johann Gutenberg (*c*1397-1468) printed his first Bible using movable type in 1445. In 1450 the library of Lincoln Cathedral listed one hundred and seven works in its catalogue; in 1338 even the Sorbonne in Paris had only one thousand, seven hundred and twenty-two codices. Since then a vast increase in the size of the information store has dramatically altered the problem and the solutions. Local public libraries might now have fifty thousand to a hundred thousand volumes, university libraries nearly a million, and national libraries count their stock in tens of millions. It is of course this great explosion in the amount of published material – and a corresponding increase in the number of readers – which makes so desirable forms of access which are able to scan the store rapidly.

This huge quantitative leap does not however alter the essential personal relationship between book and reader. Although libraries often agglomerated users into large reading rooms, the more imaginative solutions tended through the design of furniture to create desks which in some way defined a territory. In Sydney Smirke's circular Reading Room (1854-56), in the central courtyard of the British Museum, for example, the radially arranged desks had upstands and adjustable sloping book rests which helped to individualise each reader's place. A more recent and ingeniously elaborated solution occurs in Louis Kahn's library for Phillips Exeter Academy in New Hampshire where half-enclosed desks are placed near windows which have a small glass area related to the desk. Each reader is able to adjust a wooden sliding shutter to control the amount of light falling on the page. Yet every reader is part of the larger space and also in contact with the outside world, just as St Jerome was in Antonello's painting.

Architecturally the interesting question is whether the substitution of an electronic source for the book alters the person-to-information relationship in a way which would affect design. If St Jerome faced the screen of a computer and the shelves held compact disc containers, would the space suddenly become inappropriate? I believe not. Because the information source – whether book or computer – is relatively small and has only to be associated with a single person, the aedicular nature of the space remains entirely appropriate. The important consequence is that even if that source were to change to some new form as yet unknown, it is highly likely that the essential characteristics of the space would remain largely intact.

Nothing in the argument that there is an essential one-to-one relation between individual and source presupposes that the information exchange needs to occur in a library. On the contrary it enables it to happen much more freely than when a medium is tied to cumbersome equipment, as in the cinema. In fact every time we borrow a book from a lending library, we probably read it in our living room. When that book or its equivalent can be transmitted electronically, we need not even go to the library; the library has come to our living room.

Through links to the World Wide Web, the size of that library has increased vastly in quantity, if not necessarily equally in quality. There has been a simultaneous increase in both users and creators of information; frequently they are one and the same person or institution. This has meant that responses to the information can be exchanged rapidly and the information store grows continually by accretion. Very little of this, however, has architectural implications on the design of either libraries or living rooms.

All designers create from an awareness of what exists. A book such as this is interesting in that it shows the roots of many of the designs and these in turn are sure to have an influence on what will be designed in the future. This is likely to be the case even though information technology has changed dramatically in the last ten years and is certain to change in the next ten. The existing libraries will act as models to be criticised, amended and developed.

Many of the projects are based on ideas of flexibility and the resultant creation of large flat floors capable of taking either stacks or readers. The regular spacing of lines of book stacks and the librarian's nervous concern about supervision has tended to create great open areas to be filled with furniture. As architects have often had to accept that furniture was purchased by the institution under a separate contract, their control over this vital small-scale part of the design tended to be weak. The resultant undifferentiated spaces have not always celebrated the act of reading and study. St Jerome with either a book or a computer on his desk would not necessarily feel comfortable.

Other more overtly architectural sources can also be discerned. The circular central space, derived from Asplund's wonderful drum at Stockholm's Public Library and the earlier round Reading Room of the British Museum, is clearly in evidence. However, Kahn's ability to create a 'family' of spaces, allowing for the

FROM ABOVE: St Jerome in a modern day mock-up of the British Library study carrels, at the Venice Biennale; Antonello da Messina, St Jerome in his Study, c1475, oil on lime, 45.7×36.2cm (reproduced courtesy of the Trustees of the National Gallery, London)

small within a larger whole, seems particularly apposite to the design of libraries and has been explored fruitfully in several schemes. It is place-making through structure, levels, materials and degrees of openness and enclosure.

The introduction of computers makes the creation of such differentiated spaces easier. Information can now come down the wire and thus there is no longer the need for flat floors as book trolleys are no longer a necessity. For example, the kind of stepped reading terraces which Alvar Aalto created in the library of the University of Jyväskylä, reminiscent of Boullée's design of 1784 for a vast Bibliothèque du Roi, become at once more feasible. Aalto's manipulation of the section in many of his libraries produces subtly defined areas for readers which are yet part of the total volume of the building. They are as much models for the library of books as of disks.

As reading is so crucially dependent on light, the control of light and particularly daylight has been a fundamental concern of library design for a long time. The relation of desks and shelves at right angles to tall windows in medieval and Renaissance libraries stems from the need to provide efficient side lighting. As libraries grew ever larger, light from above became important and the ceiling an element which was to be explored and elaborated. Labrouste's Reading Room at the Bibliothèque Nationale (1862-68) continues to be an inspiration. It demonstrates how important the overhead plane is in a space where small-scale objects such as shelves and desks predominate.

A further look at the buildings in this volume would reveal two additional insights. The first and more obvious is that the libraries exhibit various stylistic languages of the present; it could not be otherwise. In fact the wide range of the editorial selection indicates that it has not been driven by stylistic considerations alone. The second and much more important insight would be that, as in all buildings, design considerations go beyond those that have to do with the main function of the building. One of the frequently described concerns is with siting and context. Libraries are not only places of information storage and transmission but also buildings in particular places; that they are libraries may make their contribution especially significant. We thus see public libraries in suburbia, for example, taking on characteristics of a heightened domestic architecture.

It would be impossible to divorce a symbolic aspect from the library building. It enshrines our belief in knowledge as an essential element of our culture; indeed many aspects of our culture are held within the library. Symbol and reality become

FROM ABOVE: Study carrels in Louis Kahn's Phillips Exeter Academy Library; Henri Labrouste, Bibliothèque Nationale

enmeshed. This may in fact be one of the reasons why we continue to construct libraries.

Clearly there are others. We have a vast accumulated store of books which numbers millions. These are unlikely to be transferred in the near future into digital form. Even if they were, we are at present not certain how long such electronic forms will last. We know that books will survive centuries without their content being affected in any way. The deterioration of electronic data and the relative ease with which it can be altered are both matters of serious concern. It is vital that we are able to hand down an untrammelled legacy. This does not mean that libraries will not change in their functions; the material they make available will probably become extended and already the addition of spaces for exhibitions is almost routine. It has also been suggested that libraries will not only store information but will actually create it, possibly both in electronic and printed form.

There is also of course something about the book as an object which is unlikely to make it obsolete for a long time to come. This is not just historical conditioning. No other form is quite so handleable, so easily used under all sorts of conditions from lying in bed to sitting on a mountain top, or so independent of any support systems such as telephone lines. In any case the book continues to be produced in great quantities each year. A new form of communication does not necessarily supplant previous ones; it may simply widen the possibilities.

We should perhaps also remember that we are social animals. Although the book or the computer provides us as individuals with information, that search may still at times be a social act. We may want to be where the pursuit of knowledge is celebrated. And that celebration may well show itself through architecture; through the manipulation of space, the control of light and sound and movement, and the creation of meaning, achieved by the thoughtful use of materials. These have been the traditional pleasures of architecture; I believe they will continue to be pursued no less strenuously in the digital age.

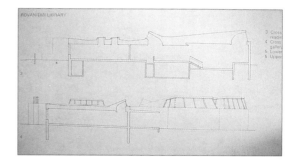

Alvar Aalto, Rovaneimi Library: interior view and sections through reading room

THE ART OF READING

John Olley

THE BOOK AND THE BUILDING

'This will kill that. The book will kill the edifice.' Victor Hugo has the archdeacon assert in *The Hunchback of Notre-Dame*. '. . . Printing will destroy architecture.'[1]

■ In the recent past, the architecture of the library has been diminished by the printing press. In turn that building type has rounded on the book for revenge, reducing it to an inert object. The sheer quantity of volumes coagulated the categorisation and locational systems, convoluted the access and retrieval procedures and converted security and preservation into paranoia. Libraries are being ossified into tombs of tomes.

The result: the joy of reading is dimmed almost to extinction in some recent repositories of literature. Where is that vitality of the act of reading and the centrality of books to discovery, scholarship and creation which has so often been portrayed in many a painting from Antonella da Messina's *St Jerome in his Study* to Degas' portrait of the writer Edmond Duranty? Should not making or finding a place to study, think and write, surrounded by an atmosphere of books, be fundamental to the building type? For Louis Kahn it was:

> A library building should offer a system of spaces adaptable to the needs in time; the spaces and their consequent form as a building should originate from broad interpretations of use rather than the satisfaction of a program for a specific system of operation . . . A library designed around the incipient influences of a standardized book storage and reading devices could lead to a form with two distinct space characteristics – one for people, one for books. Books and the reader do not relate in a static way.[2]

Now the book itself is under attack from another technology, the computer. And with it comes yet one more threat to the intellectual setting, that beloved environment of books. The information technology industry has the capacity to bare the bookshelves and to ensnare the reader in its *inter*minable *net*.

At a recent book launch in Dublin, the Minister of Culture spent the duration of his congratulatory speech with the said volume in hand. Often flicking it open to refer to the text or reinforce a point he concluded by articulating in words what was already so apparent to the eyes of his audience – it was an object whose size and weight he obviously enjoyed. The book is transportable, easily cross-referenced, reassessed and *scrolled* (to use the jargon of the cumbersome computer). And likewise there is the traditional delight in the book-lined place for reading, an ark to sail the seas of words and rechart their meaning. What is to be the fate of the book, this identifiable actor in the theatre of knowledge, and the building block, both metaphorically and literally of the architecture of the library until the recent past? What opportunities exist for creating a place, engendering a sense of wonder at what the word might reveal and feeling at ease with the activity of reading and study, when the shelves are bare and the tables expand to house the computer monitor and its demanding flicker?

THE BOOK BUILDS THE LIBRARY

In the past, the book built the library and its architecture catalogued knowledge. A type with medieval origins was a long shed-like space, into which was introduced a rhythm, illuminated by the regular pattern of windows, structured from above by the bay articulation of trusses or beams, and spatially defined below by book stacks as they enclosed a scholar's cell. Each of these book-lined bays or carrels was a room within a room, a library within the library and so easily a category within the expanse of knowledge. This elegant coincidence of structure, daylight, functional space and discipline division has been at the heart of a persistent typological framework for the architecture of the library, fading and re-emerging over the centuries. But alas, in its more recent history a formalist approach has shed the responsibility to seek a symbiotic relationship between the architecture of knowledge and the articulation of space.

The medieval form *par excellence* can be seen in the present configuration of many an Oxbridge library. In the Bodleian in Oxford, Duke Humfrey's library of 1480, with its later alterations to the furniture, is a fine example. Parading down its central aisle, the ends of the stacks present a text, the pages of the catalogue made spatial. However, at either end of this library, in 1610 and in 1640, the so-called Arts End and Sheldon End, formed transverse arms, turning the books to become the display of the library as they line the walls and are stacked in galleries to form a rival typology, a theatre of knowledge. The spectator/actor on the floor is presented with the panoramic view of the assembled and ordered knowledge, a parallel to Camillo's Memory Theatre. The books become the architecture.

Much later, this second typology is presented in grandiloquent form in Boullée's famous project for the reading room of the Bibliothèque du Roi. An imperious statement theatrically presenting the power embodied in knowledge as the authority for the collector of the books to dominate. The user is there merely to complete the tableau, dwarfed by this *vast amphitheatre of books*, constantly visible for surveillance, and allowed no niche for study. But before Neo-Classical austerity depersonalised and cooled the environment for scholarship, the theatre of books reached dazzling heights in the Baroque monastic libraries of Stift St Florian and St Gallen. The sensuous line of the wall of books sculpt the space, bulging forward into structural piers, sometimes separating to frame a flood of light, but all merging into the vaulted ceilings with painted iconography. The library in form and content becomes a cosmology. The book-clad piers, pillars of wisdom support the heavens – the universe as spatial text. This was a supreme synthesis of representation, architecture, books, space and knowledge made articulate and legible. Unlike the compartmentalisation of knowledge, created and confirmed by the bay structure of medieval building, the Baroque library liberated these divisions between disciplines to provide for a spatial dialogue across the arena of knowledge.

It is as if the Baroque period sought to liberate the singularity of classification of knowledge enforced by the architecture of the library to allow a plurality of correspondences. It might provide an architectural exit from the librarian's dilemma, as expressed by Leibniz: 'one and the same truth may be put in different places according to the terms it contains'.[3] The linear arrangement of books upon a run of shelving is akin to the sequential reading of a text. However, the possibility of the simultaneous apprehension of objects in space allows the linear catalogue to fold back on itself, establishing correspondences and coincidence.

But could this cerebral conceit of symmetry between spatial organisation of books and a model architecture of knowledge continue in the face of a burgeoning quantity of volumes and the ever-increasing divisions within disciplines? Warehousing and retrieval became the alternative. A book was ordered, not found. It was finally read under the supervision of a watchful eye in a vast room which was not the location of the volume. However, this reading room could still aspire to that grandiose vision of a compilation of knowledge. For instance, the Round Reading Room at the British Museum, Smirke's theatre of learning, was a reference library, a kind of indirect catalogue of the wisdom stored out of sight, and of course, more recently, out of site. Nearer the centre of the space, another tighter ring was formed by the cabinet containing the card index of the total collection. And at the focus of this arena of books beneath its celestial dome was not the scholar but the librarian, a privileged position to scan the panorama of wisdom but also a post of vigilance. The Benthamite panopticon was here made real as the centralised geometry of Smirke's rotunda distributes the reader down the radial sight-lines of surveillance. The librarian becomes an intermediary who determines the organisation of knowledge, replacing its spatial map with an inert numerical code, loaded of course with the priorities and proclivities of the profession. Before, you were your own librarian, pacing the floor, browsing the theatre of books, remapping the catalogue's sterile sequential logic on to space by the trace

of your movement from stack to stack, from shelf to shelf, all accessible. You can shape your own vision of the world, full of illuminating chance encounters, assembling a personal library as you dance the labyrinth of learning. Alas, knowledge is now mediated by the middleman. The librarian becomes a keeper of books rather than disseminator of wisdom.

But if by necessity the library was reduced to only its catalogue for the reader by the ever-increasing stock of volumes, the same was true where resources or circumstance limited acquisition. Alternatives were explored. In the seventeenth and eighteenth centuries *bibliothèques* were produced, not a 'gallery, building full of books' but 'a collection, a compilation of several works of the same nature or of authors who have compiled all that can be on the same subject'.[4] This, a condensed version of the British Museum Reading Room, might take another form where the library was no more than a catalogue, a single volume which listed and located each literary work, not in a single building but distributed through the collections of the globe. In this way, 'the closed world of individual libraries could be transformed into an infinite universe of books noted, reviewed, visited, consulted and eventually, borrowed.'[5] If this idea has a long history, its origins rooted in the sixteenth century, it now has a new reality with the impact of computers. The ideal of the Internet, where not only catalogues of other libraries can be accessed and searched, but the material seen and read from the screen or printed out. Now the library as a place melts into cyberspace, its location immaterial. All that is left is a lonely monitor on a table and a connecting cable.

CATALOGUING THE SPATIAL CONTENT

With large holdings, the logistical problems of book handling fossilised the form and function of the library and the methodology of its management. The growing number of volumes separated the reader from the location of the book and developed a cataloguing system which was numerical and linear rather than spatial. The universal adoption of this strategy became a force to shape any library, irrespective of size or disciplinary bias. The disconnection of a system of cataloguing from a spatial presence did much to create banality within library architecture and to confirm the separation of the reader from the stacks.

The architecture of the library is the architecture of the catalogue. Each library is particular in form and in the composition of its holdings. Even the blandest warehousing system perverts the linear mentality of the numerical cataloguing system. It has edges, an entrance, sources of light, each facilitating or frustrating access to certain sections of the stock. The most used subject classification might break rank from its sequential stacking to locate itself close to the door. Furthermore, no collection is constant; it grows, the emphasis shifts, new disciplines emerge, others coalesce or expire, yet it still has to be accommodated within the particular space of the building. The librarian has to be the architect of the collection, creatively assembling and spatially organising the material for the inspiration and convenience of the reader.

With future acquisitions being more in cyberspace than having a bodily presence on the shelves, the nightmare of organising and managing a massive collection fades. Furthermore, with the dissolving boundaries of traditional disciplines and the demands for a complexity of interconnections between the divisions of knowledge, the spatial analogue becomes more compelling. The librarian needs to be more architect than compiler of catalogues.

THE ARCHITECTURE OF THE TEXT
In *The Order of Books*, Roger Chartier discusses the impact of the presentation of the text upon the process of reading and comprehension. The organisation of the words on the page, its format and font, along with the marginalia, have the potential to shift the interpretation of the content.

> If texts are emancipated from the form that has conveyed then since the first centuries of the Christian era – the codex, the book composed of quires from which all printed objects with which we are familiar derive – by the same token all intellectual technologies and all the operations at work in the production of meaning will be modified. 'Forms effect meanings', DF McKenzie reminds us, and his lesson, which should be taken to heart, warns us to be on guard against the illusion that wrongly reduces texts to their semantic content. When it passes from codex to the monitor screen the 'same' text is no longer truly the same because the new formal devices that offer it to its reader modify the conditions of its reception and its comprehension.[6]

The backdrop against which the text is read and received can be further shaped by its location in the catalogue of disciplines, and how these are then distributed about the shelves of the library. The spatial architecture of knowledge might be revelatory or limiting through juxtapositions and correlations.

The reception of a text might further be conditioned by the physical and psychological environment in which it is read. In the recent past many a library conceived the user as a machine for reading located in a factory of instruction, that given a diet of sufficient lumens for the ocular mechanism to operate and to reduce other undetectable environmental attributes – sound and thermal – to neutrality, midway between shiver-

ing and sweating, would create that numbing condition called 'comfort'. With these materials to create a building, the result is likely to join the increasing register of *non-places* sandwiched between launderette and motorway. The resulting space may be physiologically warm but it is psychologically cold and, above all, intellectually barren – a sterile environment. In strict contrast to this, a library needs to establish a human-centred environment, rich in choices which appeal to the senses and psyche.

What can compete with the tactile experience of a book held in the hand or set on a wooden table, warm to the touch, and positioned in a rich variety of locations each with a boundary of books. You can engage in the act of reading, by the light, with a view, away and beyond the activity to escape to a distant landscape, or to survey the interior with its lining of books and the assembled fellow travellers in search of enlightenment. Alternatively you can be enclosed, isolated and insulated in a world of books, or removed to an inert space with only the text before you. The preference might be absolute or variable over time. And all this variety should be in the natural provision of the architecture and the physical environment it creates.

THE TEXT OF THE ARCHITECTURE
The value attached to the library by the institution, king or culture and its collection, and the building's architectural and decoration programme can condition the will to study and choreograph the movements of the mind.

The medieval library and its Renaissance successor were accommodated in an unpretentious non-specific container. Its repeating constructional unit, reinforced by the light falling from a rhythm of windows provided the only articulation to the space enclosed by the humble shed-like structure. It was the life and richness of the activity installed which elaborated the interior to give functional definition. By the time the Enlightenment arrived, expense had run ahead to create grandiose edifices where ideas of self-conscious representation became more important than housing the human activity.

Notes
1 Victor Hugo, *The Hunchback of Notre-Dame*, trans WJ Cobb, New American Library (New York), 1965, pp174-75.
2 Louis I Kahn, 'Space Form Use: A Library', *Pennsylvania Triangle*, vol 43, December 1956, p43.
3 GW Leibniz, *New Essays Concerning Human Understanding*, trans AG Langley, Macmillan (New York), 1896, p623.
4 Furetière, *Dictionnaire*, 1690, quoted in Roger Chartier, *The Order of Books*, trans LG Cochrane, Polity (Cambridge), 1994.
5 Roger Chartier, op cit, p70.
6 Ibid, p90.

WHITHER://MULTI-MEDIA.(CYBER).LIBRARIES?

Paul Lukez

■ The library has traditionally served as a repository of knowledge, or as a 'place, room or building containing books and other materials for reading, study or reference'.[1] Yet, the digital revolution, compressing time and space, making our public and private experiences increasingly aspatial and asynchronous, challenges the very definition and role of libraries. Increasingly affordable computing power combined with the spread of on-line services gives the web-literate public access to international libraries and databases direct from home or the office. What then will become of the library typology and its civic role, if, as Massachusetts Institute of Technology's Dean William Mitchell claims 'every node [on the infobahn] is potentially both a publication and consumption point, and such centralized concentrations of activity will be supplanted by millions of dispersed fragments'?[2] The non-hierarchical nature of new information technologies has also altered the role of library users (that is, information consumers can be publishers) and blurred the definition of institutions (libraries can become editors and publishers of material). How will information technologies redefine libraries, and what kind of challenges do designers encounter attempting to create 'place' in the ether of 'cyberspace'?

LIBRARIANS AS EDITORS AND PUBLISHERS

Nicholas Negroponte, director of MIT's Media Lab, predicts in *Wired* magazine that libraries, a product of the industrial revolution, will fall out of use, but 'librarians will not disappear'.[3] Indeed, John Browning in *Wired* suggests that, increasingly, librarians will serve as editors and quasi-publishers.[4] They will catalogue the enormous flow of information generated every day. Not only will they be instrumental in pulling an appropriate source out of a vast sea of information, they will also have the capacity to download this information and, in effect, publish books on demand. Book printing, once the protected domain of publishers, will be within reach of the public.

The new technologies will make it more economical for libraries to produce, distribute and share or sell new publications, which in turn raises some important questions: if libraries charge for the information that they output, would they 'disenfranchise people from information', as John Browning asserts. If, on the other hand, librarians disseminate their electronic publications for free, would they 'put publishers out of business with free competition'?[5]

INFORMATION 'HAVES' AND 'HAVE-NOTS'

This new class of the information-disenfranchised, left behind by a society dominated by information technology, will be well served by libraries; libraries will empower them by continuing to provide open archives for books and digital information. But access to *on-line* libraries, fast becoming the primary source of information (and, therefore, knowledge), will be limited to those who can afford the computer hardware and software. While the cost of on-line services continues to decrease (commercial services levy a low charge per hour plus a monthly fee), hardware still requires a substantial investment, an initiation fee that can remain out of reach for many segments of society. Will the information age fulfil Thomas Jefferson's ideal that libraries be free and accessible to all? Or will the information revolution perpetuate class distinctions by widening the gap between the information haves and have-nots? Sony, IBM and Oracle have at least started to address these issues by developing low-cost computers designed solely to access the Internet. The limited power of these machines to store and process information will turn their users into consumers of information services, not processors of information.

HARD AND SOFT LIBRARIES:
THE ARCHITECTURAL CHALLENGE

William Mitchell argues that with the emergence of the virtual or digital 'soft library', there 'is nothing left to put a grand facade *on*',[6] while Rem Koolhaas counters that real libraries serve a significantly symbolic role 'that responds to the persistent desire for collectivity'.[7] Despite our transference from physical to virtual realities, we are social creatures who need to belong (and be seen to belong) to groups and communities. Virtual simulations cannot meet all of our interpersonal communication needs. The architectural challenge is to design libraries that synthesise both the real and the virtual worlds while still meeting the constantly changing demands of technological developments.

Three speculative proposals, by Toyo Ito, Bernard Tschumi and Rem Koolhaas, take up this challenge by exploring the architectural and tectonic potential of the new multimedia programme. In Boston, Massachusetts, four multimedia centres interpret components of the library programme for a computer research centre, cafe, hardware and software resource centre and marketplace. The final multimedia project, Peter Droege's proposal for a 'Kawasaki Information City', explores the possibilities contained in 'City as Library'.

But first it will prove useful to browse the web and introduce the reader to the on-line resources currently available; only then can we predict how future technological developments will affect library design.

VISITING TODAY'S ON-LINE LIBRARY

The Internet already provides access to a plethora of on-line libraries throughout the world. One of the most information-rich web sites is the San Francisco Public Library from which one can access hundreds of other libraries. The San Francisco Public Library (SFPL), under the direction of Kenneth Dowlin (author of *The Electronic Library*, 1984), has developed an electronic platform that supports the library's resources located in its central branch and thirty supporting branches. Thanks to a $30 million fund-raising effort (supported by sixteen thousand San Franciscans and several Silicon Valley technology companies) the library was able to buy eight hundred terminals to provide on-line access to its regional patrons.[8] Special multimedia terminals give users access to custom-designed multimedia files created by the library's research staff. By digitising and linking its rich photographic, audio and text archives, the 'multimedia librarians' have created these files on such topics as San Francisco's history, gay and lesbian issues and so on.

This information is not only available to local patrons but to anyone hooked onto the World Wide Web. The library's home page guides browsers through a variety of options that in turn are 'hyper-linked' to the library's catalogues, archives, reference materials, community events, 'search engines' and other literary resources. One can also link with hundreds of other networked libraries around the world. Among the best on-line libraries are the Swedish Karolinska Institute, the University of the Internet Public Library, and of course the Library of Congress. CR Associates' web site lists an extensive catalogue of international libraries, including the European Common Market's 'Telematic Library' network.

The SFPL home page also has a number of 'search engines', including *Lycos*, *Yahoo* and the *Web Crawler*, that allow users to identify sources throughout the World Wide Web by simply calling out keywords based on subject or author. Also located on the SFPL's home page is the 'Bookwire' hyper-link, which provides free access to five hundred libraries, six hundred publishers, three hundred booksellers and over one hundred other resources, including access to the CIA's World Intelligence Report, Slovene-English Dictionaries and Oxford University Computing Service's archive of classic literary works in Greek and Latin. In addition, this service allows you to download any of the one hundred and eighty books that have been electronically filed.

While most of the on-line libraries noted provide an abundance of resources, the amount of digitised information is only ten per cent of all text.[9] Any search for reference material will reveal a rich array of Internet-based resources published after 1991, but it will be less bountiful for sources published earlier. The French address this issue by digitising 100,000 of the twentieth century's greatest works.[10] As nearly 80,000 books are lost each year, as estimated by Joseph Price, the Library of Congress recognises the importance of digitising texts. But according to Browning, digitising still requires 'a few gigabytes worth of information', indicating that the conversion of the twenty-six million volumes of the Library of Congress and the fifteen million of the British Library is still a long way off.

THE BOOKS AND LIBRARIES OF TOMORROW

The book is the unit by which a library measures its resources; but as Bill Gates notes in *The Road Ahead*, the very definition of a book will be radically altered as electronic technologies are miniaturised.[11] The electronic book (E-book), Gates predicts, will be an affordable and durable source of information that will eventually replace the printed book as we know it. At about the same size as a conventional paperback, it will allow you to 'thumb through' its pages by using voice commands. Its high-resolution screen will show vivid graphics with optional audio. The E-book will be able to receive files remotely, so that, in essence, it could become a user's personal multimedia library.

Nicholas Negroponte states in *Being Digital* that digital multimedia is just another word for 'co-mingled' bits of data, video and audio[12] – where these bits share a common electronic stream, they can be mixed and linked in infinite combinations. Gates notes that while the linearity of the novel will always have a secure future among its readership, the creative possibilities inherent in multimedia will allow authors and artists to develop new forms of interactive works. Hypermedia, or highly linked hypertext files, allow readers/users to move through a virtual book in a non-linear and non-hierarchical flow. In interactive multimedia productions, the reader is free to make alterations to the sequence or content of the story so that the very meaning of the original work and its authorship come into question. As a result, the identity of the author and the meaning of the narrative are constantly in flux. As the technologies allow each consumer of information to become a producer of information, the role of the reader, author and publisher becomes fluid and interchangeable.

Multimedia productions will not be limited to a two-dimensional screen as advancements in virtual reality technologies will increasingly simulate physical reality. Information technologies will eventually become integral to our bodies and their immediate physical environments. 'Netware', now being developed by Chris Hawley of the Media Lab,[13] will seamlessly weave electronics into the fabric of our clothing. This will link our clothing/bodies to the space/information field that surrounds us. Negroponte, an architect by training, contends that architectural spaces will be prewired and electronically preconfigured so that individuals moving through space will be in a kind of electronic/spatial symbiosis.

These admittedly optimistic predictions suggest that as information technologies continue to miniaturise, the library could become mobile and integral to the space we inhabit. As 'ubiquitous computing environments' become the tectonic norm,[14] the need for libraries with 'grand facades' diminishes.[15]

PROTOTYPICAL CYBER-LIBRARIES

The following examples illustrate the programmatic and architectural potential of multimedia libraries of the future and their associated economic and social issues. The first three proposals present evocative images of the spatial and tectonic potential inherent in this new programme. As distinctions in building types will continue to be blurred by overlapping programmatic requirements, the next four examples suggest combined uses that a library could serve: as a research centre, cafe, resource centre and marketplace. Finally, Peter Droege's proposal for a Kawasaki Information City will be considered in the framework of a 'City as Library'.

Library as Fluid Space: Toyo Ito

The Sendai Multimedia centre designed by Toyo Ito, the result of a competition held in 1995,[16] is due to be completed in the year 2000 and houses an art gallery and extensive audio-visual collections. Like Ito's 'Egg' project in Tokyo with its ever-changing projected facade, this design represents the architect's attempts to create spaces that are light, fluid and gravity-defying – spaces that respond to the forces shaping a twenty-first-century society. The organisation of the six-storey, forty-eight-square-metre building defies the classic hierarchical architectural orders and blurs the distinction between interior and exterior worlds.

Organisation is based on three sets of components; tubes, platforms and building skins. Twelve irregularly-shaped, tube-like, steel structures support the habitable platform and carry all of the building's services (including elevators, electrical, mechanical, sound and information systems). The open, cage-like tubes reveal all their contents while providing a light source through an integral prism system. The glass prisms capture exterior light and filter it deep within the building, creating changing internal light patterns. To enhance further the ambiguous definition between interior and exterior worlds, the double layer of glass is laced with discontinuous bands of aluminium that, like a foliage pattern, are more transparent at the lower levels and opaque at the levels above. The double-walled southern elevation provides heat during the winter months and air circulation for summer cooling.

Ito's project clearly evokes architectural imagery that coincides with the programme. By considering the technical and use parameters within a fully integrated tectonic and spatially configured building, Ito has transformed conventional library building typologies.

Library as Message: Tschumi's Karlsruhe ZKM

If the media is the message, then the electronically charged skin of Tschumi's Karlsruhe ZKM (Centre for Art and Media) is the message. Tschumi's digitised facade reminds us that if 'once upon a time, architecture generated the appearance of stable images, today it may reveal the *transience of unstable images*'.[17] The building's exterior uses 'a photo-electronic computer-animated double-glazed skin that can react to external light and sound variations'. This electronically animated skin is suspended between two parallel movement systems, railroad tracks and a boulevard bounding the old baroque city. The building's bifurcated plan is seamed together with a public spine, or 'line of exchange'. The spine is crossed by several bridges whose skewed geometry (in the x, y and z axis), according to Tschumi, help to activate the space, along with 'giant video screens, suspended *passerelles* and stairs, a tensile glass elevator and two rooms floating in mid-air'. This 'allows for the *public mediatization*' of the otherwise specialised and obscure research that takes place in the centre.

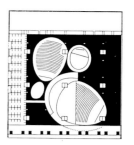
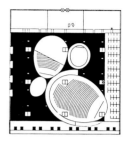
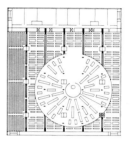
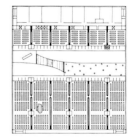
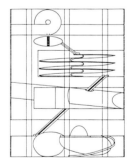
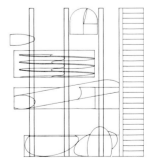

Office for Metropolitan Architecture, National Library of France proposal

Tschumi's proposal is significant because, unlike IM Pei's Media Lab at MIT, it reveals the processes and activities of a contemporary multimedia research centre by using advanced glazing technologies that also invite us to re-evaluate the nature of architectural enclosure.

Library as Void Carved from Information Blocks: OMA's National Library of France Proposal

OMA's 1989 design for the National Library of France was developed in consultation with systems analysts and electronic inventors. The library allows visitors to simultaneously access the book, music and film collections via 'magic tablets'.[18] The architectural premise recognises that the 'electronic revolution is dissolving everything solid' and that the role of the architect will be to create 'symbolic spaces that respond to the persistent desire for collectivity'.

To that end, Koolhaas envisioned creating a 'solid block of information' filled with stacks. Out of this block, he carved five primary public spaces whose shapes or 'absences of the built', use Euclidean and Boolean geometries. These seemingly suspended volumes are accessed through a system of regularly spaced elevators that sometimes pierce adjacent public rooms. The public spaces are based on programme elements such as the current events library, the study library, the catalogue room and the research library. The building's cubic volume is partially covered by semi-transparent glass facades. Cloud patterns, silk-screened onto the facades pointing toward the suburbs, contribute to the ambiguous reading of colliding interior volumes.

Though this proposal was not selected by the jury, it represents a prescient interpretation of the library's transition from the physical to the electronic realm, while creating symbolic public spaces.

Library as Research Centre: The MIT Media Lab

Designed by IM Pei in 1985, MIT's Media Lab provides few external clues that it is in the vortex of cutting-edge multimedia research. Its undistinguished exterior, like the boxy and modular designs of most computer CPUs (central processing units), reveals little of its interior workings. While the grand campus gateway immediately adjacent is heroically scaled, the interface between the campus' public realm and the Media Lab's interior is underplayed. Security access to the workspace is strictly enforced and the black exterior glass dims the luminous and vibrant colours of the Lab's computer monitors. The design, which contains a number of public communal spaces, raises important issues about public and private thresholds in the physical and virtual environment. Furthermore, it is one of the few examples of what might be considered a multimedia library.

The Media Lab is the brainchild of Jerome Weisner, former president of MIT, and Nicholas Negroponte. Its charter is to examine the implications of emerging technologies in three overlapping fields: the print/publishing world, the broadcast/motion picture industry and the computer industry.[19] Research is funded by a consortium of international technology companies and by MIT. Research projects include schools of the future, information appliances, interactive cinema, opera of the future and spatial imaging (holography). The building houses computer research labs, faculty and administration offices, the List Art Gallery, lecture halls and a 14.5-metre cube experimental theatre.

Much of the work (or 'hacking') takes place in the 'terminal garden', a large communal space inhabited by a multitude of students and computers. The computer terminals are arrayed in clustered configurations, providing each user with private and shared workspace. At the windows, a continuous, narrow band of dark glazing helps minimise computer-screen glare. The architecture manages to be animated not by the simple, container-like space, but by the ever-changing illumination coming from the computer screens.

In its chaotic and non-hierarchical organisation, 'terminal garden' defies conventional architectural notions of communal space. Yet this environment's ambience conveys a strong sense of community, attributed in part to the students' shared sense of purpose and lifestyle. They share meals (Chinese take-aways) and work nocturnal hours while exchanging ideas and formative experiences. The superimposition of virtual and physical domains enrich the sense of community that could not be replicated if students were working in isolation at home.

Designing environments to support a multimedia library can pose different technical and spatial challenges. The kind of lighting needed for conventional libraries conflicts with the lighting levels required by computer environments. Similarly, space in the multimedia library, unlike the clearly differentiated plan of a conventional library, needs to be flexible. The design of the Media Lab provides a banal and undifferentiated, albeit flexible, space. Space in the Media Lab is preconfigured for future computers by raising the floor two feet to provide access to electrical conduits. As Nicholas Negroponte notes in *Being Digital*, 'buildings of the future will be like the backplanes of computers: "smart ready". Smart ready is a combination of pre-wiring and ubiquitous connectors for the (future) signal sharing among appliances'.[20]

The Media Lab is an example of the technology-based resource centre providing access to information, software and hardware in a fully integrated architectural environment. It not only allows its participants (the elite cyber class) to access information and knowledge but to process and disseminate it. Its users not only become consumers of information, but with the aid of hardware and software, they are also their own editors and publishers.

While the Lab's 'virtual' web site is open and accessible, its physical environment is closed and forbidding. Paradoxically, its stolid architecture prevents sharing the Lab's interior sense of community with the rest of the campus. The challenge for future designers is to create environments that keep structures such as the Media Lab secure, while loosening up the demarcation between the Lab's internal and external worlds – to let the architecture express the openness of the virtual world.

Library as Cafe: Cybersmith Cafe

Cybersmith Cafe, located in Harvard Square in Cambridge, Massachusetts, is a commercial venture providing patrons access to the latest software, CD-ROMs and databases (as well as technical assistance and training) in a cafe setting.[21] Marshall Smith, Cybersmith's founder, chafes at labelling the venture an 'Internet Cafe'. Instead, he emphasises his commitment to providing 'access to technology' and to building 'community through technology'.[22] The cafe's design by Patti Seitz attempts to create a parallel yet overlapping sense of 'virtual and real community'.[23] She refers to the cafe as 'stage set for performance art' where 'people are watching people who are sometimes engaged in parallel but virtual worlds'.

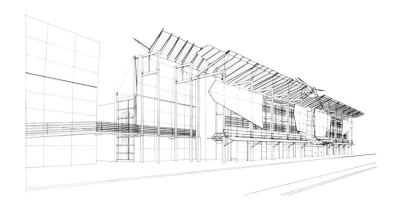

Located on the prominently visible second floor of a corner building, the Cybersmith Cafe features a dramatically illuminated entrance foyer that previews the visual delights to come. Windows wrap two sides of the dimly lit, main rectangular space. The nexus of the open plan is a bar and library featuring the latest technological literature. Circumscribing the cafe's outer perimeter are the regularly spaced 'cyber-booths' housing computer stations and on-line services. Computer accessories (including several virtual reality stations) inhabit the inner perimeter in a seemingly random arrangement.

The cyber-booths have been cleverly designed to reconfigure into multiple seating arrangements. Two crescent-shaped benches, seating up to four people each, face a table with two swivel-mounted terminals.

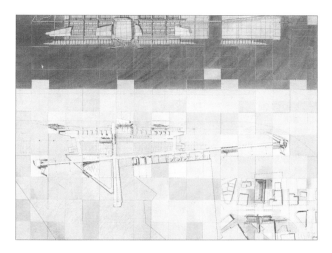

According to the architect, this flexible grouping of people and machines allows visitors to 'learn as a group'. Permutations of real and virtual communication are unlimited and allow for what Seitz refers to as 'serendipitous opportunities'. For instance, two groups of people can be simultaneously engaged in the same virtual world while still engaging in face-to-face conversation.

A preconfigured and prewired open plan provides the cafe with an 'intelligent shell' (whose design was co-ordinated with the demountable cyber-booths) that enables the space to support technologies with a half-life of up to two years. An 'open system of steel trays', suspended from the exposed wood-beamed ceiling, houses all the computer cables intertwined with dimly lit fibre optic cables, revealing the source and destination of the electronic network. Here, lighting and glare problems have been solved by placing the computer screens more or less perpendicular to the windows.

While the Cybersmith Cafe successfully fuses the virtual and real in one environment, the programme does raise serious issues. The public face of the building is open and inviting, yet its promise of access to the latest technologies is only available to those who can afford to pay the price of admission. Will this perpetuate the gap between the information haves and have-nots? The fact that there is a market for such services indicates a gap in the responsibilities typically assumed by our public institutions. Where does information/knowledge and entertainment begin and end, or are these boundaries forever blurred?

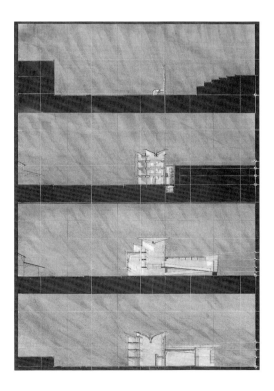

Library as Resource Centre: The Computer Clubhouse
Another private initiative, the Computer Clubhouse attempts to fill the gap between the information haves and have-nots.

Paul Lukez, The Intelligent Marketplace

Located on the edge of Boston Harbour and sandwiched between the Computer Museum and the Children's Museum (for which Frank Gehry is designing an addition), the Computer Clubhouse was started by MIT Professor Mitchell Resnick to give children from economically disadvantaged neighbourhoods access to computer technology. The centre is funded by a consortium of foundations and corporations. Its after-school programme allows children to pursue individual, self-directed projects, using advanced hardware and software and guided by mentors and staff members.

The Clubhouse, housed in a nineteenth-century warehouse facing the harbour boardwalk, is small (only eighty-four square metres), but its effect on participating students is noticeable. Sam Christie, associate director, describes the Clubhouse as part 'library, science lab, artist's studio, music studio, inventor's workshop and newsroom'.[24] Packed with machines, robots, mechanical devices and reference material, the interior space is utilitarian yet animated by the activities of the students and their mentors. Twenty computer stations, each with its own robots and technical accessories, are centred around a large communal space and table.

What distinguishes the Clubhouse from the usual school curriculum programmes is the one-to-one guidance provided by the volunteer mentors and the availability of professional-calibre software. Resnick contends that social status will not only be determined by access to information but also by the ability to digitally and intellectually process it. This powerful hardware and software empowers the children not only to develop significant learning and technical skills, but also to become publishers and producers of their own work. The clubhouse's web site, which is used to disseminate ongoing student projects, shatters the economic and social confinement that limits opportunities for advancement. In fact, it works so well that some of the students have been offered corporate sector jobs by virtue of the work done on the web site.

The Clubhouse is a successful prototype for a future library design that provides the hardware or software for access to on-line information. It also demonstrates that these resource centres can supply the training and skills required to process and disseminate information. Such initiatives can address the widening gap between the information haves and have-nots.

Library as Marketplace: The Intelligent Marketplace

In response to an effort by the University of Massachusetts to give communities just outside campus walls access to university resources, this project by Paul Lukez Architecture proposes a prototypical marketplace for information. Through this 'intelligent marketplace', nearby cities, plagued by social and economic problems, would gain access to the latest tools of empowerment: on-line information services and data bases.

A marketplace can be defined as a place for the exchange of goods and services. An intelligent marketplace is where the exchange of information and other services occurs. The intelligent marketplace, a prototypical community building type,

makes computer hardware and software and informational data bases available to lower income communities and gives form to a 'real world' public place celebrating an evolving electronic infrastructure. Networked with other databases in low- and middle-income communities around the country, this facility would give individuals access to information systems to develop creative work, conduct studies, network with others with similar interests and use electronic multimedia equipment. The intelligent marketplace provides the physical armature for celebrating information technologies and their abilities to enhance cross-cultural communication.

The intelligent marketplace typology is based on the Greek agora. Like the agora's bar-shaped stoa elements, the marketplace's building masses bound and shape its interior and exterior spaces. Object-like elements, stairs, theatres and central halls shape the public realm. A shoji-like electronic screen becomes an information wall that runs the entire length of the building and serves as the physical and informational armature of the intelligent marketplace. Electronic impulses in the form of images, text and video continually dance across this information wall. The silhouettes of the computer mainframe, the video disc storage and the associated electronic equipment and staff serving the marketplace are projected on the scrim of the information wall.

City as Library: Kawasaki

In 1987, an international competition calling for proposals to convert Kawasaki, Japan, into an information city was announced. Many of the resulting competition entries suggest that the physical and virtual architecture of the library of the future could be fully integrated into the fabric of the city. Peter Droege's winning scheme proposed 'informationising' the city so that 'every laboratory, office, or household could become a classroom wired into a city-wide, even international, network'.[25]

An international workshop on the 'Information City' held in 1988 in Kawasaki developed more concrete proposals (based in part on Droege's winning entry) for Kawasaki as an information city.[26] The urban plan calls for developing a network of neighbourhoods or 'homebases' where, within one square kilometre, 'parents with small children could find ample opportunity for work, commerce, day care and leisure: where people share access to information and opportunity for life-long education'. An 'information spine' would link the neighbourhood 'homebases' with a system of 'media cores', which include neighbourhood offices and Community Information Centres serving up to a thousand people with direct access to Kawasaki, Tokyo and beyond, thus reducing the amount of long-distance commuting. The information spine would also have smaller-scale outlets networked throughout the city in markets (*intelligent souks*), streets and plazas (*intelligent shojis*) and public spaces (*intelligent fountains and gardens*).

Embedded in the physical landscape, the city's information network enriches the community's quality of life. The library then becomes part of a larger urban electronic topology, where

As controversy raged between opinion groups, in 1991 the first call for tenders was launched. In 1992, as site work progressed, revisions were made in the allocation of book storage sites. The next year the concrete structure was completed and by the end of 1993 the first technical systems were in, the building was externally complete, and landscaping was in progress. In autumn of 1996 the building was open to readers and to the public at large. This year, 1997, will see the first complete year of full operation.

RELATIVE VALUES

It is at this juncture that it is all too easy to jump to certain conclusions. In the famous fable of the tortoise and the hare, it seemed that close to the end, the hare had won out through sheer speed. However in the end, owing to some unforeseen development, the tortoise was first. Likewise, the relative speed by which the Bibliothèque de France accelerated appears to outclass the British Library as, in a classic English syndrome, it bumbles along to a delayed, or incomplete, finish. The fact is that comparisons tell a very different tale, even though the British Library is only open in part this year, and is unlikely to be formally, royally opened before 1998.

It is vital to assess the relative progress and ultimate achievement of the two national libraries on a rather more detailed range of criteria. Perhaps one can first elucidate the political, social and cultural background which has conditioned the development of each project in characteristically differing ways.

Every nation creates its own institutions. National libraries are no exception. When the library of each nation also contains the historical record of a specific language group, the shelves upon shelves of books, silent volumes and containers of memory cells, are literally beyond any material value: such are the sacred tomes that contain the unique impressions from the first printing, both in original and accessible form.

There is a certain sanctity about the book, which any encroachment notably violates. When a parent or teacher destroys a child's accumulated scrapbooks, or when a nation decimates its own museums and collections of printed rarities, as is currently happening in Kabul, Afghanistan, something is irreparably lost in life. When Viipuri town library, a jewel of evolving Modernism designed by Alvar Aalto, was temporarily abandoned in the Russo–Finnish War (it was hit by only one shell, but desecrated more thoroughly by jealousy and political apathy) its contents were dispersed irretrievably; the heart of the city, dating from medieval times, was broken, psychologically if not physically torn apart. When the Stalinist regime permitted this to occur, it

FROM ABOVE: British Library, section model of vertical distribution; Viipuri Library, interior c1940; Viipuri Library, children's library, 1941

perpetrated a heresy no less heinous than Hitler's burning of Jewish libraries.

At a national level, both Britain and France approached the question of re-inventing the concept of the national library with not only the fullest awareness of the national significance of building a new library to house a country's complete collection, but also in full recognition of the absolute cultural significance where each nation was respectively the core cultural entity of a distinct world language group. It is less a coincidence than it might seem that on the threshold of the new electronic age, two of the core world languages (French can still, if with difficulty, sustain a global status) have embarked on new repositories for their books, for completion within the final decade of this century. Viewed from the Pacific Rim, for example, the two events certainly have considerably more in common than a purely Euro-centric view might realise.

These developments coincide with the decline in Europe's status in the world growth leagues, both in absolute and relative terms. They also concur in recognising the global explosion in electronic media. But whereas the British initiative is recognisably progressive and expansive, building upon the British Museum's long tradition as a global cultural repository, on closer examination the parallel – if more dramatic – French initiative is essentially an embattled, defensive expediency.

On the other hand, the resolution of the dilemma posed by a new library of France represents, in a way alien to the British, the vindication of the peculiarly French intellectual hegemony, and in a manner contrived both to enshrine liberal cultural values (in an age of popular culture) and preserve the concept of a globalised civilisation française. If the library's role can be consolidated, it is within this context.

NINE GATES TO HELL
In 1979, an important revisionist text was published in Paris by the author Régis Debray. Entitled, Le Pouvoir intellectuel en France,[1] it established new parameters for the definition of the domain of French intellectual groups and their prevalence and influence in the country. Debray chose to isolate three 'cycles' in France since the mid-nineteenth century: an 'academic' cycle he defined as lasting until 1930; a period of 'publishing' from 1920 to 1960; and a 'mediatic' phase that had begun appropriately in 1968 and continued in the ascendancy. The latter saw a new elite emerge, predominant in the new media, pyramidal in structure, and which subsumed the preceding successions. Debray identified a cultural restructuring of intellectual power groups that reflected 'Nine Gates to Hell', a seemingly unavoidable conclusion. First, complex technology would lead to ever-simpler and more assimilable ideologies. Second, the growth of an intelligentsia on a wide frame, via mass media, ensured the 'maximum socialisation of private stupidity'. Third, 'truth becomes more and more expensive' and 'bad information drives out good information'. Fourth, the abandonment of theoretical polemic in the written press, and multiplication of news flashes (sound bites) contributes to the loss of truth. Fifth, 'the more the "objective" world is "rationalised"' the more the irrational comes

to control the subjective. Sixth, demand for the 'irrational' reaches critical mass with the accelerated rationalisation of the social and material environment, with intellectual activity now controlled for the first time by laws of supply and demand. Seventh, technological progress inhibits and complicates authenticity, but media establish that communicating as a process becomes primary rather than the 'true' information process itself. Eighth, it is all done to music anyway, a process of minimal encoding with maximum reception. Finally, 'what is meaningless becomes what is most easily understood'.

Debray pauses to itemise curious events that occurred at that time (1978) both at the Elysée Palace (the Horizon 2000 Writers Lunch) and elsewhere; the press announced, 'the President seems pleased that in ideas and philosophy, France's trade balance is favourable'. An irrevocable shift in the balance of power had however occurred, where the new intellectual power group (entrenched in the media) had become a force to be reckoned with politically. The Malraux days were over. In the following ten years the creation of a new power symbol of French culture became both essential and inevitable. It was to be the Bibliothèque de France. Debray, ten years earlier, had established an accurate prognosis. Only President Mitterrand could prescribe a cure. Indeed, he would do more, in sovereign terms: he would select the design to be built. Future Systems did not have a chance in hell.

BRITISH PROGRESS
In London, the design and construction of a new national library was arrived at by a more relaxed protocol. Given that Sydney Smirke's archetypal circular Reading Room had generations of admirers and user-supporters in the world of English literature and the humanities, despite the accelerating accretion of titles, there was little momentum for change until the 1960s. Certainly there was little anxiety to promote the status of intellectual life, nor, despite the predictions of Richard Hoggart[2] and Raymond Williams,[3] any real sense of urgency about the abyss into which Western literary culture was about to sink, as viewed from across the English Channel. There were the great universities with their accumulations of knowledge, and the constant reassurance that home-grown talent from Britain was much in demand by American universities. Thus, from a political and parliamentary viewpoint, an attitude existed in the late sixties which has persisted through until 1996, that the British Library project probably has to happen, but is of no great priority. Indeed, the view passed from one generation of politicians to another, was that if any economies could be found by cutting back the budget, all to the good. There has been no inspiration, no dream, no public or corporate lobby, no academic appeal of any significance. Yet, the building complex that has emerged, duly savaged by economies, held up by technical incompetence and bureaucratic indecision (none of which is the architect's responsibility), is the sole British institutional programme at a national level to have been realised before the end of the twentieth century. It is also the product of an enlightened architectural 'revisionist' theory, of undoubted credibility, and of international importance as a work of architecture.

IF NOT . . . NOT

It is ironic that the great tapestry by RB Kitaj selected for the entrance hall has this title. A masterpiece by any standards, it describes an allegorical scene of particular dramatic content, derived from the text of TS Eliot's *The Waste Land*, originating as a painted image in 1975. The title might have been the phlegmatic motto of the architect Colin St John Wilson, as he battled through a generation of board and committee meetings. However, the building is now approaching completion, the criticisms of royal and political patrons have gradually subsided, and as the nineties broke, and the sweeping brick outline rose to a level with the adjoining architectural masterpiece of George Gilbert Scott to more or less grudging praise, reality has dawned.

Against all the odds, and through an amazingly virtuoso financial trapeze act, the British nation has acquired (or one might say stumbled into) a work of architecture of superlative quality, of great elegance inside and out. In 1997 (light years away from the seventies when it was conceived) it is of considerable importance, whether viewed within its period context, or in terms of what is currently under construction. The British Library is inevitably a work of the seventies, a generation ago, but it is one of the few buildings stemming from that period to contain the DNA imprint of earlier Modernist ideals, tempered with a post-revolutionary candour that indicates a progeny and a continuity. The complex now visible on Euston Road comprises many buildings, repeated codifications of earlier Modernisms, in a mosaic rich enough to hold emblematic resonances, yet clear enough in its formal coherence to dispel any semantic confusion. One might almost think that the design had been realised without a hitch, as one moves through the entrance lobby to the great spatial experience of the soaring ceiling structure: just as in Wells Cathedral, or Ely, one has to be told about the structural failures to realise that excellence is only achieved with tribulation. Here it has been flawless. The problems have been other.

The French experience has been very much more cinematic, as scenario of political and intellectual intrigue followed scenario, and the end result has been a work of architecture that owes as much in the public eye to Jean-Luc Godard's *Alphaville* as it does to its stated affiliation with the minimalism of Robert Morris. The period from April 1989 to autumn 1996 had been considerably shorter than that experienced for the British Library. Nonetheless it had accommodated some remarkable amendments to the original brief. Perhaps the most drastic in terms of effect was the decision, taken at a late stage, to accommodate not just the three to four million post-1944 volumes first envisaged, but all volumes, numbering some twelve million.

Dominique Perrault's design concept offered an open square of massive dimensions, below which lay two levels, focusing on a rectangular green 'oasis' at a depth of twenty-one metres. The upper level would house half a million volumes for the use of the general public, plus audiovisual facilities, a restaurant and cafe, and some bookshop retail space. The lower level accommodated, in a conceptual 'cloister', exclusive space for the scholarly researchers able to access the original Bibliothèque Nationale collections as now transferred. A twenty-

FROM ABOVE: If Not, Not, *tapestry by RB Kitaj; Bibliothèque Nationale under construction, view from garden level; British Library, large Humanities Reading Room*

storey glass tower stood at each of the four corners of the square, in the L-plan form later dubbed 'open-book'. The towers caused great antipathy in the intellectual community of France. They are now complete book ends, since they have been filled up with the revised quota of books. The metaphor of grain silos feeding grain (as books) is perhaps one that Perrault himself now regrets. It would seem that Debray's 'Nine Gates to Hell' was already a reality rather than a threat. The historian Patrice Higonnet attacked in a notable critique the 'monument to the evisceration of French socialism as it inscribes in steel and glass the institutional triumph and moral bankruptcy of French social democracy, a "high-tech" substitute for reflective humanism'. Dr David Looseley has elucidated the stages of a gradual acquiescence by President Mitterrand to accommodate revisions, in the face of unremitting intellectual pressure groups.[4] On the pronouncements of Mitterrand, two storeys were removed from the towers and the public and academic users were separately enshrined. Further concessions were sought of an ailing President: that storage of books in the towers be stopped; that suspect retrieval technology be downloaded; and that the garden could now be built upon, if necessary. In the end Mitterrand conceded that rare, precious books would not be stored in the towers (which removed their ultimate credibility).

As Looseley points out, a more fundamental basis underpinned the bitter polemical infighting: a suspicion that the very written word was at risk, central to French national identity. 'Une bibliothèque, ce lieu de mémoire par excellence, est un des elements constitutifs de la conscience nationale . . . c'est à dire un consensus fondé sur un histoire.'[5]

MEMORY TRACES
The common factor of both the Bibliothèque de France and the British Library is that both were born out of existing institutions. The paradox is that while, as mentioned above, Smirke's round Reading Room is notable, Henri Labrouste's Bibliothèque Nationale (1862-68) recognised the architectural genre demanded by the exponential increase in printed publications in the nineteenth century and transformed this into a space of great elegance, by means of structural innovation in cast-iron. Gridiron floors and banisters of cast-iron complemented succinctly the sixteen cast-iron columns of the reading room itself. Giedion astutely recognised the future significance of Labrouste's work: 'the wearisome struggle with the Academie in which he was involved after 1830' and 'the resistance he encountered that made a full realisation of his ideas impossible',[6] while Rowe has emphasised, as Giedion did not, the importance of the exterior versus the interior, of masonry exterior to cast-iron interior. 'Incredibly simple, inscrutably grand, the building is both intensely private and enormously public.'[7] In addition we are reminded, by Frampton, of the superlatively tectonic nature of the enterprise.[8]

For both the Bibliothèque de France and the British Library such memory traces within the genre evoke cultural ramifications of inescapable power. For Perrault, the Presidential edict to democratise the Bibliothèque Nationale had lined up his critics in alarm for a 'Beaubourg Syndrome', with Disneyesque ghouls.

The transference of institutional flagship from the benign classicism of Labrouste, to a Post-Modernist *entrepôt* was one thing. To compound this with the new electronic media tools would lead to the end of the book itself, in the lamentable grip of the 'book ends', as the critics saw it. For Wilson, in the more anaemic and less overt intellectual climate of Bloomsbury, there was the deep-rooted English suspicion of any 'grand project'. While the architectural precedents from the nineteenth century were less distinguished, there was a well-layered nostalgia over the inherent loss of the circular Reading Room. As Appleyard has pointed out, after the Falklands War, and with Margaret Thatcher safe in power, there persisted an extension of a twenty-year long antipathy in government circles, a populist New Right argument against Modern architecture.[9] The social purpose content of Modern architecture was disavowed. For Wilson, the precedent of Aalto committed him (and a whole generation) to precisely such intuitions of responsibility as the commentators such as Watkin and Scruton claimed to be irrelevant.

Perrault has created a monolith which is opaque, rather than transparent as once thought. From a distance the Paris skyline appears punctuated, in no unique manner, by yet another business complex of towers. Even the sound detailing cannot eliminate associations of the banal. The so-called garden lacks authenticity, even though a random *jardin anglais* idiom prevails. The scholars in their cloister seem to lurk in confinement. There is no evocation of *la civilisation française*, even metaphorically. The idea of an oasis is far-fetched – it is Labrouste's Bibliothèque Nationale that still holds the historic manuscripts. Even the bland profiles reflected in the Seine seem indeterminately ordinary. The problem is all the more pronounced since Perrault is now an architect of proven quality. The superstructures of bureaucracy and the greyness of institutionalism have prevailed.

For Wilson, the problem is quite different. The British Library can never resemble in the public mind a business complex. Here in Britain there has evolved, in the generation since the project was first considered, another shared image. The aesthetic of supermarkets has come into common usage, relying on relatively cheap brick cladding for finishes and duo- or mono-pitched roofing over wide-span spaces. What to an educated architectural-historical sensibility in twentieth-century design indicates English Free Style, a Chinese tradition, or the superlative public and academic architecture of Alvar Aalto, Ralph Erskine, or Louis Kahn – each of whom, like Wilson, have used brick with great skill – does not transmit likewise to the British consumer.

At the British Library ironically this insouciance may, however, ultimately work in its favour. The democratisation of culture has been sustained by this remarkable building, in ways not immediately apparent to the informed critic. Those who have criticised the building (something technically not yet wholly possible, since the building will not be complete until later in 1997) have not as yet conceded there to be any benefit from the use of brick in a wholly contemporary manner: perhaps today only Carrara marble or St Paul's Roach bed Portland Stone will satisfy materialist ambitions. In fact the high quality red Lincolnshire brick, Welsh slated roofs, and granite facings perfectly match the adjacent St Pancras.

Perhaps the triumph of this aspect is to have built a major institution for a consumer society that speaks in that society's chosen material: here is a rare monument that offers a benign yet absolute monumentality of its time. Alvar Aalto achieved this with the important Baker dormitory for MIT at Cambridge, Massachusetts (1947), as well as the massive National Pensions Institute building in Helsinki (1954-57), subtly breaking up the various functions among several interrelated volumes. Louis Kahn achieved the same high quality using brick in the library and dining hall for Phillips Exeter Academy, New Hampshire (1965-72). Wilson has used the same means to achieve significant meaning and institutional gravitas on the Euston Road, achieving the formal resolution of this highly complex building in a manner that adequately reflects the importance of the individual in society. Internally, he has followed Kahn's maxim, placing the individual reader's satisfaction as the highest priority. Kahn had been inspired by the medieval reading carrels provided for the monks at Durham. In France, he appreciated Etienne-Louis Boullée's Bibliothèque du Roi of 1784, which he said 'conveyed a feeling for what a library should be – you come into the chamber and there are the books'.[10] Wilson has contrived to create this condition on a major scale: the six-level high bookcase containing the rare leather bound books of the King's library rises dramatically from the lower level to dominate the epicentre of the entrance hall. (See p209.)

Fortunately there has been a considerable bonus for the location of the library, paying all due homage to the Scott masterwork of St Pancras Station Hotel, drawing back from the site frontage, creating a relaxed forecourt from which it will be fully evident. For the Station has now been re-invented as the new and principal point of arrival for the Channel Tunnel rail link. Not only is the library ideal for migrant scholars from Cambridge: it has been said in Paris that from 2002 the best investment a research fellow there can make is a season ticket to the Euro-terminus at St Pancras.

Notes

1 Régis Debray, *Le Pouvoir intellectuel en France* (Paris), 1979. English Trans, D Macey, *Teachers, Writers, Celebrities: The Intellectuals of Modern France*, Verso (London), 1981.
2 Richard Hoggart, *The Uses of Literacy*, Pelican (London), 1957.
3 Raymond Williams, *Culture and Society*, Pelican (London) 1960.
4 David Looseley, 'The Politics of Fun', *Cultural Policy and Debate in Contemporary France*, Berg Publishers (Oxford), 1995.
5 Translation: 'A library – a place of memory par excellence – is one of the constituent elements of a national conscience . . . it is a consensus founded in a history.' David Looseley, 'The Bibliothèque de France: Last of the Grands Projets', in *Modern and Contemporary France*, no 46, July 1991, p44.
6 Sigfried Giedion, *Space Time and Architecture*, Oxford University Press (Oxford), 1959, pp220-226.
7 Colin Rowe, *The Architecture of Good Intentions*, Academy Editions (London), 1994, p92.
8 Kenneth Frampton, *Studies in Tectonic Culture*, MIT Press (Cambridge, Mass), 1995, p48.
9 Bryan Appleyard, *The Pleasures of Peace*, Faber & Faber (London), 1989.
10 David B Brownlee and David De Long, *Louis I Kahn*, Rizzoli (New York), 1991, p391.

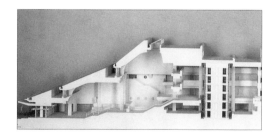

FROM ABOVE: Bibliothèque Nationale, Seine-side view; concept sketch of the visitor's first view of the British Library having arrived at St Pancras; British Library, section detail at entrance hall (to left) showing the six storeys of the King's Library (right)

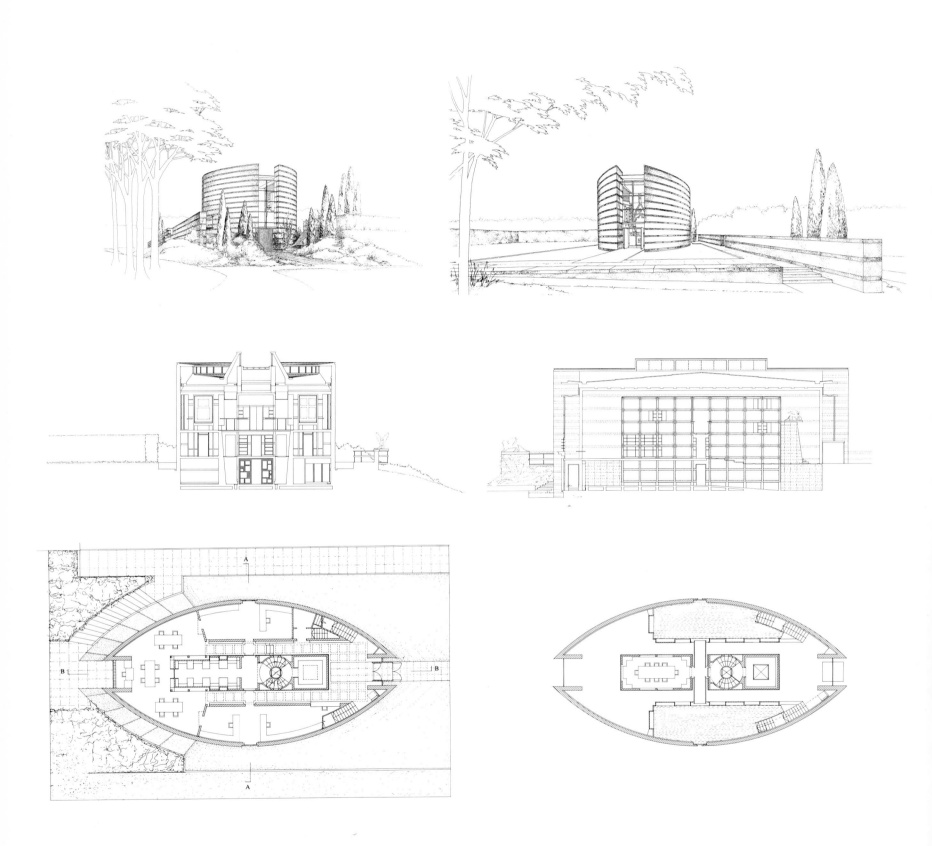

FROM ABOVE, LEFT TO RIGHT: Perspective to rear; perspective to entrance; cross-section; longitudinal section; ground level plan; gallery level plan

ARCHITECTURE, MEMORY AND METAPHOR: THE RUSKIN LIBRARY

Richard MacCormac

■ Designing the library to house Ruskin's work and his collection of books, paintings and photographs precipitates a question – a Ruskinian question – about architecture. Is there a relationship between the language of Modernism and the historical tradition represented in Ruskin's thought? On the one hand, Modernism has been seen as deliberately dislocated, an abstract technological language from which historical associations have been banished. On the other hand, the historical tradition is locked into a taxonomy of style isolated from other contemporary discourses about architectural theory, and is irrelevant to the typological, spatial and constructional characteristics of late twentieth-century architecture.

The question itself defines a familiar conflict and says something about the discontinuity in our culture; the past is preserved but not made a part of the future. Our purpose, as architects, must be to rediscover how our inheritance can become vivid and relevant to what we make now. The Ruskin Library project has allowed us to do this in a very special way.

The sixth chapter of Ruskin's *The Seven Lamps of Architecture* is 'The Lamp of Memory', in which he says 'we cannot remember without architecture'. The chapter resonates with such analogous words as monument, memory, history, story, each of which emphasise the idea of recall – and invite us to find the means of recall – without losing the authenticity of the architecture of the present.[1] This, in turn, stimulates the realisation that architecture, like literature and landscape, is part of our collective memory, which we must incorporate into our present experience.

Ruskin's concern with memory, with the memorial and monumental, was complex. He saw architecture as a text of cumulative history. He believed that architecture could convey information metaphorically, through its surface decoration and he thus likened buildings to books, referring to St Mark's as 'a vast illuminated missal'. Today, it is difficult to dissociate Ruskin's ideas from the stylistic legacy of pseudo-Gothic and, in particular, the pseudo-Venetian style which he himself recognised as 'an accursed Frankenstein monster of my own making'. This is an interesting admission as we perceive that, when Ruskin calls upon the architect 'to render the architecture of the day historical', he is addressing an issue more fundamental than style: the potential for architecture to say something through its antecedents rather than simply to describe its own structure and function.

This Ruskinian reminder is particularly important for the mainstream of late twentieth-century British architecture, which tends to subsume all aesthetic and symbolic issues within innovative structural and programmatic arguments. Given that there are reasons for this, but taking in a wider context of the visual arts, sculpture and painting, this is uncharacteristic of British Modernism which has synthesised metaphor and formal invention. This synthesis is evident, for example, in the work of such artists as Henry Moore, Barbara Hepworth and Paul Nash, and in the current work of artists contributing to what has been called the 'unpainted landscape': Andy Goldsworthy, Richard Long and Ian Hamilton Finlay.

In the works of Nash and Finlay, objects may be recognisable but their juxtapositions are surprising and, as in the fiction of Gabriel Garcia Marquez, it is as if a basis in practical reality is required to generate the metaphorical and the dreamlike. This is important for architecture because it has to be real. The potency of a metaphorical image lies in its ambiguity: not being one thing it can be many, it is neither literal nor abstract. In terms of architecture, this ambiguity is what distinguishes a metaphorical use of the past from the adoption of an historical style. It allows a creative relationship between present and past and an active, rather than passive, engagement with history. This is the possibility which the Ruskin project and its progenitors in our work have sought.

The two main antecedents to the Ruskin Library in our work, the unbuilt library for King's College, Cambridge, and the chapel for Fitzwilliam College, Cambridge,[2] both contribute to the development of a series of themes. All three projects use curved walls to evoke ideas of protection and each consists of 'buildings within buildings', with the inner buildings having an expressed architectural presence within the space.

The curved masonry outer wall of the King's Library was to consist of tiers of galleries displaying the College's collection of ancient books and manuscripts, a kind of memory bank of knowledge, monumental in the sense of being a 'reminder' (from the Latin *monere*, to remind or warn). In contrast, the undergraduate library, a freestanding wooden object, was to be a kind of grove of transient information standing in the internal space. The project explored dualities and ambiguities of inside and outside, under and over, which are reiterated in both the chapel and the Ruskin Library.

The Fitzwilliam Chapel combines the linear and circular origins of Christian church architecture, the basilica and the Pantheon. It does this with abstract forms which draw on the two typological traditions without stylistic recourse. In cross section, the building is also traditional, consisting of a crypt with the place of worship above. Here, however, it is the object within the space, defining the duality between what is above and what is below, which is the principal symbol of the building; it is a vessel, an ark, which floats over the dark underworld of the crypt and holds aloft the place of worship.

The image of a vessel was precipitated by visits to the Viking Ship Museum in Oslo, in which the concave interior surfaces of the space protect the sensuous elegant wooden ships; and the Vasa Ship Museum in Stockholm, where the wonderfully preserved seventeenth-century ship is like an enormous toy in its box. It was not until the design developed, however, that the power and universality of the ship metaphor became apparent. The vessel is the *nave della chiesa* where the congregation come together for a shared rite of passage. In medieval manuscripts images of Christ in a ship are metaphors for his transforming and redemptive journey. This idea of transformation is also behind the story of Noah's Ark, and the meaning of Viking and Egyptian burial ships and, in a special sense, Jonah and the Whale, where the transforming experience is that of Jung's 'night sea journey'.

THE RUSKIN LIBRARY

The Ruskin Library is the further development of an architecture combining seemingly abstract formal language with a series of narrative ideas. It is Ruskinian, not only because it alludes to Ruskin, but also because, by doing so, it fulfils Ruskin's expectation that architecture should be metaphorical.

The building avoids historical style but is 'rendered historical' in the Ruskinian sense. The true character of the concrete construction is exposed internally, in the giant portal frames which span longitudinally, but externally it is 'encrusted' – to use another Ruskinian term – with white masonry and dark grey/green courses, joined with stainless steel bosses. These bosses are similar to the visible fastenings used in the cladding of Italian buildings, which Ruskin called 'confessed rivets'. The construction of the archive cabinet, standing within, mimics this combination, but different materials – polished red plaster, oak frame and bronze fastenings – 'encrust' the concrete box.

The building's plan is a succinctly abstract idea – two arcs split apart to contain the rectangular archive. But the building is also symbolically and literally a 'keep', a refuge for Ruskin's bequest, appearing as a secure tower, and fulfilling the verb 'keep' by preserving the collection. It is also a monument celebrating the memory of the life of Ruskin, a life monumental in itself in the sense that Ruskin's life's work was continuously to remind.

Like Venice, the building is an island. As medieval Venice was Ruskin's moral refuge, so the building, as a symbol of Venice and separated from the University by a causeway which crosses a dry moat (Venice's lagoon), is also a place of refuge.

The causeway enters the building and again the metaphor of island and lagoon is replicated, as the archive itself emerges from an underlit transparent glass and slate floor to convey the perilous maritime condition of the city and to allude to Ruskin's dream of looking into its waters, and seeing the horses of St Mark's being harnessed.

The idea of the archive as a building within a building, or 'keep within a keep', recalls a visit to the cathedral of Albi in the South of France, a fortress-like cathedral within which the masonry choir formed an additional internal line of defence. This idea suggested an environmental proposition which uses the thermal stability of the two masonry 'keeps' and the large volume of air between them to protect the collection and create the first passively air-conditioned major archive in the UK.[3] In terms of the building's symbolic and visual intentions, the memory of Albi also precipitated a church-like plan in which the archive stands for the choir separating the public entrance, and the aisles on each side, from the sanctuary/reading room which is situated in the most secure location at the west end of the building.

The centrepiece of the building is, of course, the archive itself and, like the vessel in the Fitzwilliam Chapel, it is loaded with associations. In an abstract sense it is a large object which gains its presence from blocking the axis through the building. Richard Serra's *Weight and Measure* exhibited at the Tate Gallery in 1992 had a similar effect. It is the great treasure chest, in Venetian red plaster, the cathedral chest strapped together with oak and bronze. It is also a cabinet, like a giant piece of furniture by William Burgess which acquires the scale and character of architecture – a building inside a building. It is an ark or reliquary, a tabernacle, a bookcase or, by inference, a great book; 'a vast illuminated missal' and corpus of Ruskin's work. Shutters can be opened to hint at its interior. At the east end, facing the public entrance, these open to reveal a hugely amplified image of one of Ruskin's daguerreotypes of St Mark's – a Proustian fleeting, or as Ruskin would say, 'fugitive' image, a symbol of the fragility of memory and its capacity to recall the past.[4]

Notes

1 I owe this observation to Professor Michael Wheeler, Director of the Ruskin Project at Lancaster University. Michael Wheeler and Nigel Whiteley (eds), *The Lamp of Memory: Ruskin, Tradition and Architecture*, Manchester University Press (Manchester), 1992.

2 Exhibited in the 1992 Venice Biennale, 'Architettura e spazia sacro nella modernita'.

3 Institute for the Conservation of Historical and Artistic Works, *The Ruskin Library: Architecture and Environment for the Storage, Display and Study of a Collection*, pre-print, Ottawa Conference, 12-16 September 1994.

4 Proust's *A la recherche du temps perdu* is arguably the literary monument to Ruskin's concern with memory.

LIBRARY AND ARCHITECTURAL CHARACTER: THE CHARACTER OF THE LIBRARY

Merrill Elam

■ In the winter of 1993, the *Georgia Librarian*, the official journal of the Georgia Library Association, asked several architects to contribute short commentaries on the process of realising libraries or on their attitudes concerning the library as architecture. My contribution, only slightly edited, is as follows:

Public libraries may be the only truly public buildings in America today, and their librarians the quintessential optimists. In a society of increasing privatisation of public spaces and services, and increasing pessimism, depersonalisation and distrust, the public library and librarian are, more than any other institution, the stewards of open thought and potential. Given this unique position in our culture, and the architect's continuing dilemma of making civic architecture in the American landscape, the programme for the public library is perhaps the richest and most challenging of our era. Given the need to be hospitable and friendly and simultaneously dignified and orderly, the character of the public library is often elusive. There is the impulse for the library to identify with the wealth of historical precedents. Yet, there is also the equally compelling impulse for the library to ground itself in its own community, condition and time. It is all of these conflicting energies and aspects of the public library that have most fascinated and befuddled us in the search for architecture that celebrates and nurtures a society sorely in need of both.

Rereading this short piece in 1996 I realised that the crux of the article or 'the issue at stake' is *character*.

It is hard to explain, without braggadocio or seeming overzealous, the importance of the character(s) to the US Southern psyche. It is a long-standing regional, cultural trait or habit to nurture and love the character, even to the point of absurdity (or, maybe the point is, or approaches, absurdity). This in both the actual flesh and blood sense as well as the literary sense. I need only to refer to the amazing personalities that develop with astounding depth and clarity in the work of William Faulkner and Eudora Welty. Their characters' idiosyncrasies, visions, fears – in short, their humanity – are flawlessly, carefully conceived and structured so that we enter emotionally, intellectually and willingly into the territory of the characters and find enormous satisfaction. Often it is a satisfaction born of disturbance: the revelation of a quirky, unusual personality bringing forth into full view some binding human condition, one that we thought was carefully tucked away forever in the attic trunks of our own characters. We come to find that these powerful, difficult or delightful characters of the great writers (or of our own communities) put life back into perspective for us.

So it is with architecture. It is not the overly smooth, euphemised buildings that enthral, delight or terrify us and hold in our memories. Rather, it is the buildings where character has been coaxed out and developed: character resistant to oversimplification, immersed in its own specificity: complex and rich. Complexity clarified but not diminished by its development; a structuring of character through the very manipulation of the medium: brick, steel, or glass, replacing or doubling for words. So character emerges and elicits a response because it touches us in ways that confirm our humanity and the continuity of human endeavour and thought.

With this proposition in mind, I offer two character comparisons; in each case, an architectural figure with a literary figure.

In the opening lines of William Faulkner's *The Sound and the Fury*, we are in the experience of the wondrous world of Benjy before we realise it:

Through the fence, between the curling flower spaces, I could see them hitting. They were coming toward where the flag was and I went along the fence. Luster was hunting in the grass by the flower tree. They took the flag out, and they were hitting. Then they put the flag back and they went to the table, and he hit and the other hit. Then they went on, and I went along the fence. Luster came away from the flower tree and we went along the fence and they stopped and we stopped and I looked through the fence while Luster was hunting in the grass.

'Here, caddie.' He hit. They went away across the pasture. I held to the fence and watched them going away.

'Listen at you, now.' Luster said. 'Aint you something, thirty three years old, going on that way. After I done went all the way to town to buy you that cake. Hush up that moaning. Aint you going to help me find that quarter so I can go to the show tonight.'

They were hitting little, across the pasture. I went back along the fence to where the flag was. It flapped on the bright grass and the trees.

'Come on.' Luster said. 'We done looked there. They aint no more coming right now. Les go down to the branch and find that quarter [...]'

It was red, flapping on the pasture. Then there was a bird slanting and tilting on it. Luster threw. The flag flapped on the bright grass and the trees. I held to the fence.

'Shut up that moaning.' Luster said. 'I cant make them come if they aint coming, can I. If you dont hush up, mummy aint going to have no birthday for you. If you dont hush, you know what I going to do. I going to eat that cake all up. Eat them candles, too. Eat all them thirty three candles. Come on, les go down to the branch. I got to find my quarter. Maybe we can find one of they balls. Here. Here they is. Way over yonder. Wee.' He came to the fence and pointed his arm. 'See them. They aint coming back here no more. Come on.' We went along the fence and came to the garden fence, where our shadows were. My shadow was higher than Luster's on the fence. We came to the broken place and went through it.

'Wait a minute.' Luster said. 'You snagged on that nail again. Cant you never crawl through here without snagging on that nail.'

Caddy uncaught me and we crawled through. Uncle Maury said to not let anybody see us, so we better stoop over, Caddy said. Stoop over, Benjy. Like this see. We stooped over and crossed the garden, where the flowers rasped and rattled against us. The ground was hard. We climbed the fence, where the pigs were grunting and snuffling. I expect they're sorry because one of them got killed today, Caddy said. The ground was hard, churned and knotted. Keep you hands in your pockets, Caddy said. Or they'll get froze. You dont want you hands froze on Christmas, do you.[1]

Benjy denies us the luxury of an easy explanation or formal terms or definitions, keeping us somewhat perplexed by the events he observes, their sequence in time, even the extent of the territory observed. The territory we do enter, that of 'curling flower spaces', 'hit ... hit', 'caddie ... caddie', 'Luster was hunting in the grass', 'My shadow was higher than Luster's on the fence', conjures up the shifts and juxtapositions of a surreal landscape or garden: an intriguingly disproportionate and fascinating world.

Our own route of entry has not been clear. Even though the figures across the pasture are crystalline, physical images – 'It flapped on the bright grass and the trees' – all else is enigmatic and magnetic. From the first sentence, Faulkner challenges your entry and perception through the skilful treatment of the Benjy character.

I find an amazing comparison, maybe only a personal observation, with Louis Kahn's Phillips Exeter Library. There is a Benjy-like phenomenon about the building. It rises, clear and large on its meadow, but there is an uncertainty about it; a disjuncture. Entry is rendered enigmatic, not easy. The formal aspect or definition of the door is eschewed and one must fumble a little, work to unravel the question of entry.

'We came to the broken place and went through it' but not without 'snagging on that nail', is suggested by the Exeter Library's lower level and the required ascension through it to find the unexpected 'meadow' let into the building – the meadow where the books should be. The books are now the next thick fence through which to achieve the literal meadow again. The meadow is seen again through the fence of the facade. We find zones of individuality . . . 'I looked through the fence while Luster was hunting in the grass.' Facade/fence functioning as a boundary and simultaneously as an optical sieve. Similarly the presentation on the exterior of the building of the individual spaces just behind the facade, requires and offers a shift in scale through the thin section of the wall, simultaneously grand, oversized on the exterior with the entirely touchable study carrel on the interior. The surreal garden is rendered material through the section (a zone that carries the capacity for magic, in my opinion). It seems that both authors knew instinctively that too much clarity numbs: too little clarity confuses. Skilfully manipulated clarity intrigues and demands.

There is, for me, an aspect of the Bibliothèque Ste-Geneviève in Paris, that lends enormously to its character: the text carefully etched into its exterior surface: the generosity of its interior projected to the exterior, prefacing and announcing the richness and wealth inside. A proclamation of humanity's collective intellectual and artistic generosity to itself. Both a serious and a joyous celebratory presentation, offering greater quantities than any one of us has time or mental capacity to absorb, but leaving us feeling good about the company we find ourselves in. We are left somewhat uncertain about how to handle such generosity.

All of this brings me to another literary character: Uncle Daniel Ponder in Eudora Welty's *The Ponder Heart*. Edna Earle, Uncle Daniel's niece explains:

My Uncle Daniel's just like your uncle, if you've got one – only he has one weakness. He loves society and he gets carried away. If he hears our voices, he'll come right down those stairs, supper ready or no. When he sees you sitting in the lobby of the Beulah, he'll take the other end of the

Henri Labrouste, Bibliothequè Ste-Geneviève

sofa and then move closer up to see what you've got to say for yourself; and then he's liable to give you a little hug and start trying to give you something. Don't do you any good to be bashful. He won't let you refuse. All he might do is forget tomorrow what he gave you today, and give it to you all over again. Sweetest disposition in the world. That's his big gray Stetson hanging on the rack right over your head – see what a large head size he wears?

Things I could think of without being asked that he's given away would be – a string of hams, a fine suit of clothes, a white face heifer calf, two trips to Memphis, pair of fantail pigeons, fine Shetland pony (loves children), brooder and incubator, good nanny goat, bad billy, cypress cistern, field of white Dutch clover, two iron wheels and some laying pullets (they were together), cow pasture during drouth (he has everlasting springs), innumerable fresh eggs, a pick-up truck – even his own cemetery lot, but they wouldn't accept it. And I'm not counting this week. He's been a general favorite all these years.

And later:

You'd know it was Uncle Daniel the minute you saw him. He's unmistakable. He's big and well known. He has the Ponder head – large, of course, and well set, with short white hair over it thick and curly, growing down his forehead round like a little bib. He has Grandma's complexion. And big, forget-me-not blue eyes like mine, and puts on a sweet red bow tie every morning, and carries a large-size Stetson in his hand – always just swept it off to somebody. He dresses fit to kill, you know, in a snow-white suit. But do you know he's up in his fifties now? Don't believe it if you don't want to. And still the sweetest, most unspoiled thing in the world. He has the nicest, politest manners – he's good as gold. And it's not just because he's kin to me I say it. I don't run the Beulah Hotel for nothing: I size people up: I'm sizing you up right now. People come here, pass through this book, in and out, over the years – and in the whole shooting match, I don't care from where or how far they've come, not one can hold a candle to Uncle Daniel for the looks or manners. If he ever did a thing to be sorry for, it's more than he ever intended.[2]

Like the Bibliothèque Ste-Geneviève, Uncle Daniel's fortune

is exceeded by his ability to give it away. All of his outward qualities, actions and image, conspire to divulge the interior condition. Like the inscriptions on the exterior walls of Ste-Geneviève seem to penetrate and permeate the interior, Uncle Daniel's exterior physical presence is a declaration of his disposition and interiority. In both cases the delineation between the two zones is a mental and physical act. Memory, movement, the passage of time and mental registrations are all at work. As with Uncle Daniel, character is built, simply at first, but finally demanding participation and validation by the reader and the other characters in the community of the book. It is interesting to note that the Bibliothèque Ste-Geneviève and its architect Henri Labrouste, were summarily shunned at the time of the library's conception: considered unusual and out of order. Uncle Daniel leads a fictional life similarly considered.

So what does all this issue of character mean to the practising architect? The strong and the enduring characters are born of anything and everything other than svelteness or easy facility. Character penetrates, demanding substance. The search for character exceeds monetary achievement. Secondly, it means that not all architects are equally capable of engaging the great characters. Like writers we operate at varying degrees of skill, satisfying various degrees of expectations. It also means that some moments of architectural achievement endure, continuing to enthral and titillate just as the characters of greater literary works endure and endure. It is my observation that architects, for the most part and regardless of varying talents, enjoy the search and make works that embrace the collective wisdom of an era, continuing the process of cumulative understanding. This is no small endeavour. Yet, to expand the cumulative understanding of an era through the complex exercise of building is another achievement.

These achievements validate the capacity of architecture as character: engaging, illuminating and finally becoming the experience. Skilfully woven in all its various aspects, the great architectural character can transcend the materials of its making.

Notes

1 William Faulkner, *The Sound and the Fury*, David Minter, W W Norton & Co (New York), 1987, pp3-4.
2 Eudora Welty, *The Ponder Heart*, Harcourt Brace & Company (New York), 1982, pp7-8, 11.

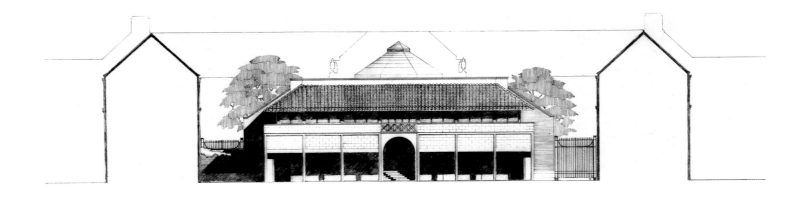

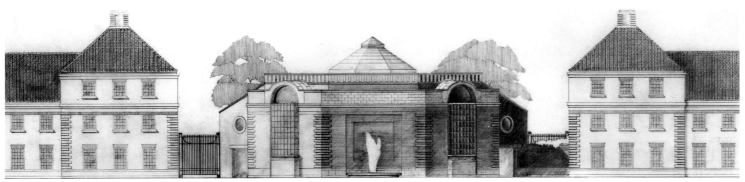

ARUP ASSOCIATES
FORBES MELLON LIBRARY

Clare College, Cambridge, UK

This library is one of several college libraries which have been built recently in Cambridge, a city with a rich architectural legacy of historic educational buildings. In evaluation, many of the existing faculty libraries have been seen to be lacking in space and facilities and many new buildings have been commissioned.

In 1979 Clare College concluded that its most pressing needs were for a new undergraduate library, facilities for musicians and support for the research students whose numbers were growing as a result of Clare's tripos success. Therefore in the autumn of 1983 the college launched the Thirkill-Ashby Appeal with the object of raising £1.25 million to enlarge Forbes Library, and to provide a

recital room and music practice rooms.

The brief was to design the library and music facilities on the Memorial Court site, preferably within a single building which was to be as modern in style and function as consistency with the existing architecture of Memorial and Thirkill courts would allow. The governing body accepted the design and, due to the success of fundraising, was able to seek tenders for the building early in 1984.

On a small site the architects have managed to include not only the library and properly insulated music facilities, but also a common room, a photocopying room and a computer room. The building stands in the centre of Giles Gilbert Scott's original court, but respects the surrounding

architecture such that it seems not to intrude on Scott's design, but to complete it. The Octagon at the centre of the building is reminiscent of the beautiful eighteenth-century octagonal antechapel in Old Court and, as in the Old Fellow's Library, the books in the new library are ranged back against the outside walls, leaving a spacious and well-lit working area at the centre.

The building marks a new development in the life of the college. Two of the main criticisms of Scott's design have been removed: the domestic scale and function of Memorial Court no longer serves merely as a triumphal approach to the University Library, and Memorial Court and Thirkill Courts are no longer seen as dormitory suburbs of Old Court.

OPPOSITE, ABOVE: West elevation; OPPOSITE, BELOW: East elevation

DE BLACAM AND MEAGHER
REGIONAL TECHNICAL COLLEGE LIBRARY
Cork, Ireland

This library, the first phase of work at the RTC campus, is designed to function alone until the second phase, an information technology centre and lecture theatres, completes the dramatic brick facade that arcs around a central open space at the arrival point of the campus. With the building of phase two, the curved enclosing wall will form an almost symmetrical facade with a centralised entrance hall. This entrance lobby will be the first access to an internal clerestoried street running east–west through both buildings.

The main reading hall is a triple-height space that fans out from the entrance to the south of the east–west axis. Periodicals line the first floor gallery on the interior of the curved wall. The book stacks, in the manner of the North Library of the British Museum and the Long Room of Trinity College, Dublin, are arranged in three-storey-tall vertical galleries, running at right angles to the main axis, with reading areas beside large vertical windows facing north.

Like Louis Kahn at Phillips Exeter Academy, the architects placed considerable importance on the provision of natural light and the quality of the space for readers. By providing wiring to all study carrels, computers can be input to most locations, if necessary. Each area for study has a unique quality; some seats have window views or views across the reading area, others are entirely enclosed and private.

The red brick of the exterior continues in the major internal structural details and influences of Kahn's library at Phillips Exeter, on which Shane De Blacam worked at the time of its completion, are apparent in the interior spaces, surfaces and details.

The furniture, including the stairways, galleries and bookcases, has been designed by the architects, using beech wood for the furniture and natural fibre-board for the bookshelves. Natural light is let into the heart of the building by the clerestory lights of the spine; uplighters project artificial light from columns and perimeter walls, book stacks are lit by strip lights and individual lights are provided at each reading position. Natural ventilation would have been fully workable in the volume due to its massing and circulation, but was rejected on the grounds of security, to restrict the illegal movement of books through opening windows. Grilles to the outside secure locally-operated air vent openings.

The rest of the campus is designed in the standard uninspired manner of many sixties colleges and universities – fully functional and modularised – but the college has added a building which, with its architectural form and qualities, can fulfil a higher aspiration for the future development of the campus.

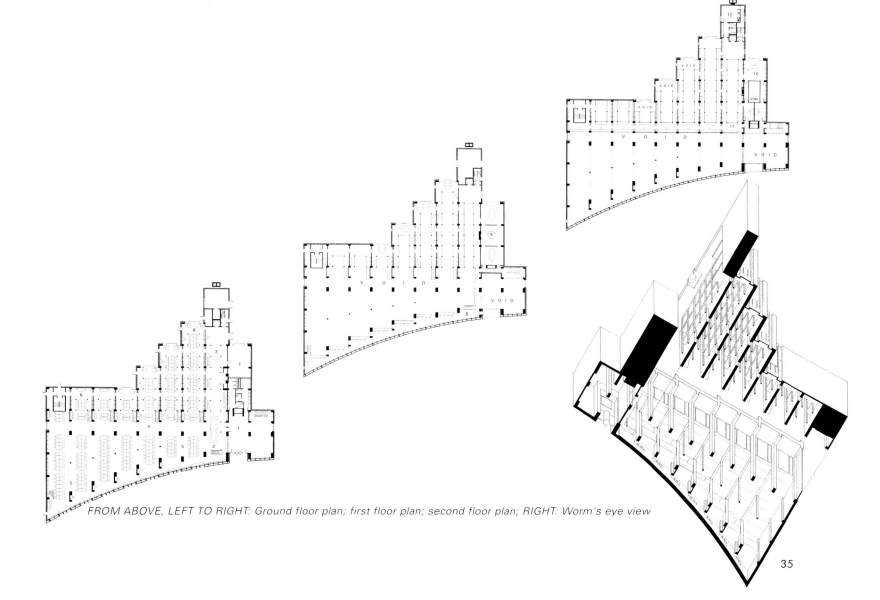

FROM ABOVE, LEFT TO RIGHT: Ground floor plan; first floor plan; second floor plan; RIGHT: Worm's eye view

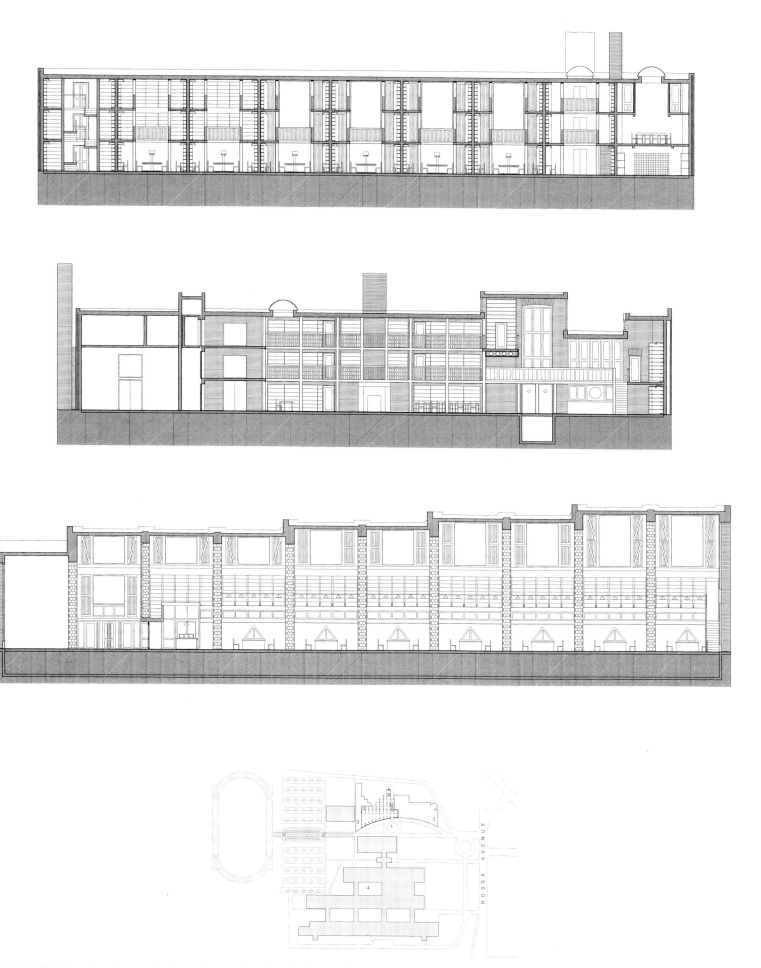

FROM ABOVE: Section through book stacks; section through librarian's hall; section through long passage; site plan

ARCHITEKTURBÜRO BOLLES-WILSON + PARTNER
MÜNSTER CITY LIBRARY
Münster, Germany

One of the most dramatic and colourful libraries of the last few years, Münster City Library's jewel-like qualities are a delightful expression of form and materials. It occupies a site in the centre of the fortified historic city, where the majority of the buildings are post-war reconstructions of Gothic, Baroque, eighteenth- and nineteenth-century buildings which follow a medieval street pattern. The 1956 theatre is one of the few successful examples of Modern architecture in evidence. Other more pervasive modern interventions have created voids in the street fabric, and it is within one of these voids that the new library has been built.

The library's two divergent wings enclose a pedestrian street, Büchereigasse, which is on a direct axis with the Lamberti Church. The rear 'slab' forms a closure to a triangular residential block, and the second

wing, a ship-like wedge, sits on the perimeter of the city block. The division also splits function and programme, according to the three functional zones of the library: the 'Far Zone' for long-term storage and no public access; the 'Middle Zone', the lending library, a quiet, book-lined circular segment; and the 'Near' or active zone which encompasses all of the immediate information activities, including a cafe, exhibition space and reading salon towards the entrance. This latter zone, described by the architects as a 'super-market of information', is on the ground floor and first floor balcony of the slab and connects to the Middle Zone by the first floor bridge over the Büchereigasse. In the basement the children's library and sound library occupy the only space where the two buildings merge into one.

Sloping seamed copper cladding covers

the interior walls to the Büchereigasse and folds over the internal circulation of both the slab and the ship. Internally, light washes down the inside of these to the ground where glass strips expose the ground floor to the view of the passer-by. External features serve to exaggerate the motifs of the slab as 'information building' and the ship as 'book building': large windows to areas where reading takes place; small book-like windows to the enclosed stack areas; and the expression of the 'toy' towers of the children's library projecting into the protected internal courtyard.

Increasing technology has minimised the presence of information, and this library has addressed the issue of creating form for a new mode of access to the information point.

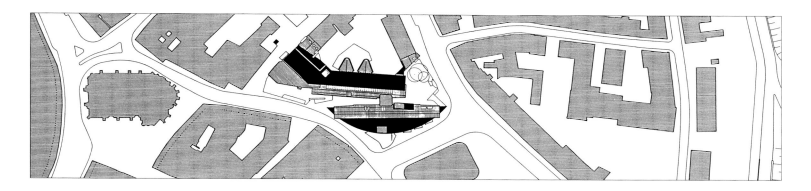

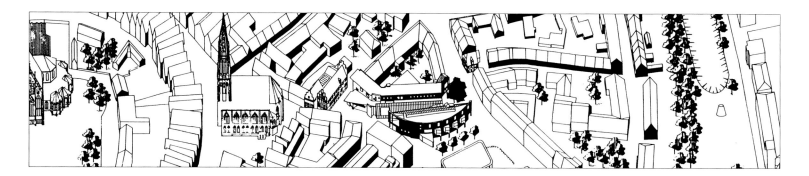

FROM ABOVE: Site plan; axonometric showing site context

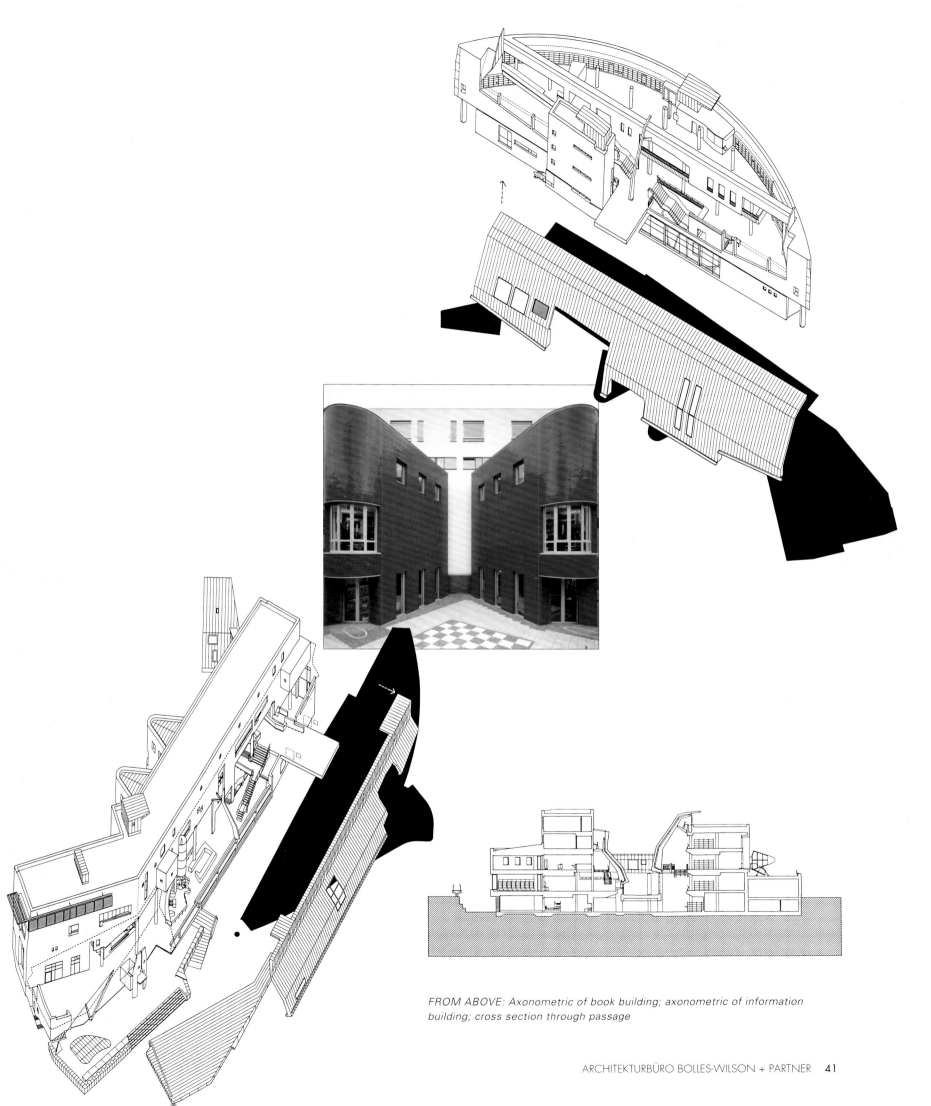

FROM ABOVE: Axonometric of book building; axonometric of information
building; cross section through passage

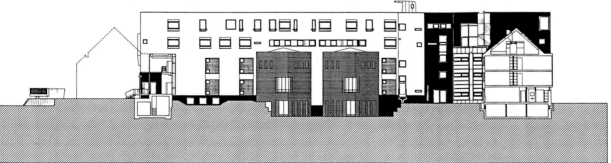

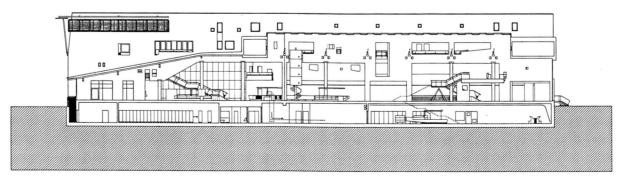

INFORMATION BUILDING; FROM ABOVE: North elevation; longitudinal section

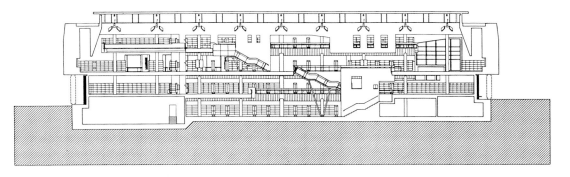

BOOK BUILDING; FROM ABOVE: South elevation; longitudinal section

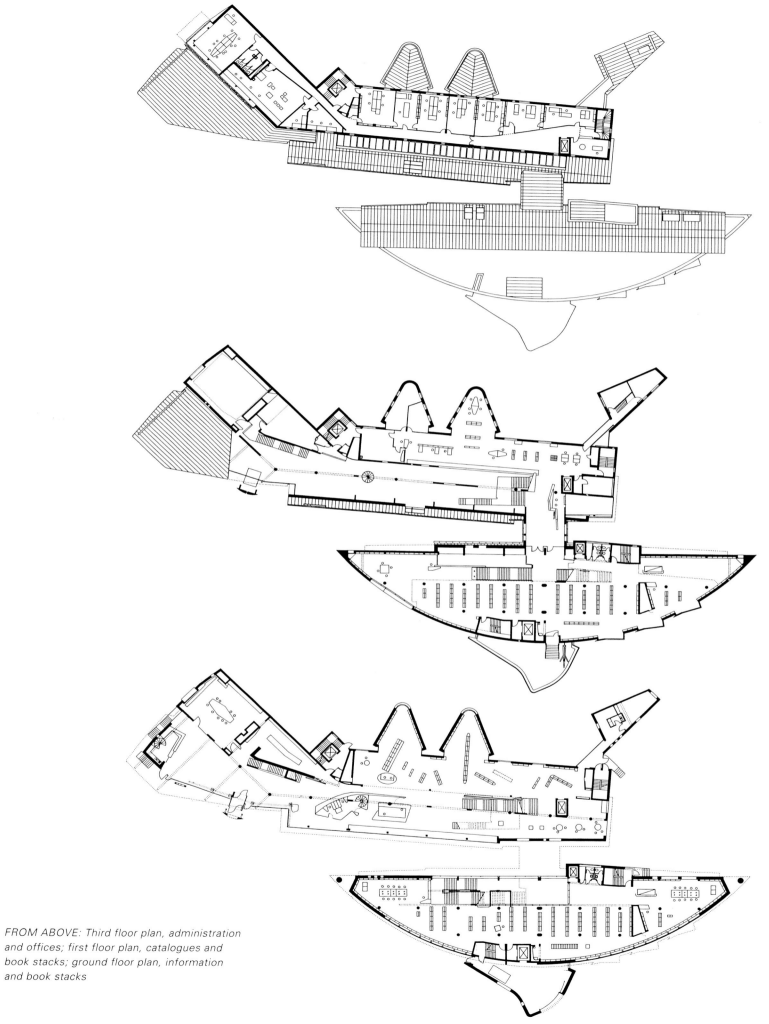

FROM ABOVE: Third floor plan, administration
and offices; first floor plan, catalogues and
book stacks; ground floor plan, information
and book stacks

THE NATIONAL LIBRARY OF SRI LANKA

Colombo, Sri Lanka

National libraries are simultaneously national monuments and great warehouses of information. The information has also to be made available to a wide public and the libraries therefore need to be accessible, easy to use and to provide the appropriate environment in which the public are able to consult a variety of sources.

These functional aspects have immediate and significant architectural implications. Not all of them are at first sight compatible with each other. On the one hand, the library presents itself as important and impressive, on the other, it welcomes, promoting an openness and an ease of approach. Similarly, the need for large areas of book storage, closed and undifferentiated, contrasts with the equal demand for individual spaces or collective spaces to break down the volume of the building into areas where small numbers of people can

feel comfortable when sitting alone.

In Colombo the problem is compounded by a climate unkind to books and one in which readers need shade and circulation of air. The National Library has one great roof under which the floors are shaded and sheltered by large overhangs. At the outermost edge of the building, a large gutter projects beyond the edge of the uppermost floor. From the roof downwards each floor steps inwards so that it is protected by the one immediately above.

The organisation and environmental control of the building is revealed by the section. In the middle of the building, an enclosed air-conditioned core, the warehouse part of the library, contains the stacks; this volume is entirely shielded from the sun, and thus requires minimal air-conditioning. Moreover, this arrangement leaves the perimeter of the building free for

readers to enjoy natural daylight, views and air movement.

This subdivision of the total volume of the library into a central enclosed zone and an open perimeter also ensures that the reading areas are not within a large impersonal space. The perimeter zone is also further subdivided by large rectangular hollow concrete columns which create recognisable bays on the inside and provide a rhythmic external subdivision of the long elevation. Within the rhythm, however, no two bays on Independence Avenue are the same.

The use of the varied rhythms, large roof structure and weighty supports echo elements of the traditional architecture of Sri Lanka, without resorting to copying a particular precedent. From the very early stages of the design, it has been imperative to preserve these crucial elements throughout a difficult building process.

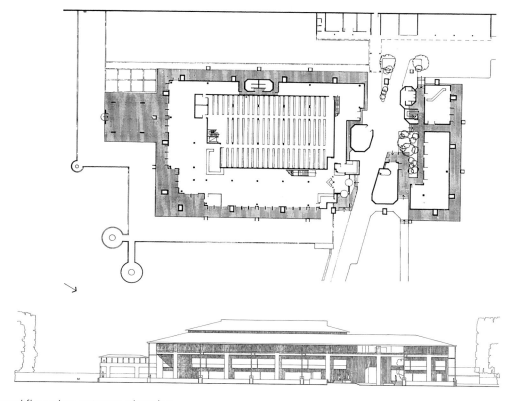

FROM ABOVE: Ground floor plan; entrance elevation

BRUDER DWL ARCHITECTS
PHOENIX CENTRAL LIBRARY
Phoenix, Arizona, USA

Phoenix Central Library is to serve as the city's public library until 2040 and beyond. The library rises above its site on Central Avenue as a poetic metaphor of Arizona's unique natural beauty; a majestic mesa transplanted from the landscape of Arizona's Monument Valley. Functionally, it incorporates both a programme of logical library planning, and the concept that a library must have a vision which acknowledges future change.

The building's five floors, in a simple rectangular configuration, provide 26,000 square metres of flexible space. A simple orthogonal grid comprised of square ten-metre bays (based on library stack modules) creates the matrix of the building. The fixed services, including fire stairs, service elevators, mechanical, electrical, plumbing and lateral structural systems, are contained in two service walls flanking the east

and west, thus completely freeing up the central floor area for library-related use. The library's internal public spaces are simply organised around a futuristic 'crystal canyon' atrium. Set in a stainless-steel rotunda above the atrium, nine computer-controlled, tracking skylights animate the space from dawn to dusk. Three glazed elevators and a grand sculptural staircase rise from a black, reflecting pool at the foot of the light well.

The fifth floor is a great public reading room, in the spirit of the past, which houses the entire nonfiction collection. Natural daylight is carefully orchestrated internally by the steel roof structure which maintains the building's primary structural grid.

The prevalent external materials of the library are concrete, copper, stainless steel and glass. The east and west elevations are dominated by the heavy corrugated

and flat panelled copper skin of the service walls. This skin will patina to the colour of an old penny, with flashes of purple and gold. Reflecting the changing colours of the sky, stainless-steel panels set into the east and west elevations accent the points of entry. To the north and south the building's transparent glazing showcases the books and the library users inside, emphasising the building's operation in the community. The entirely glazed south elevation uses automated solar tracking devices to minimise heat gain and glare. A system of 'fabric sails' on the north elevation eliminates the harsh glare of the summer sun while optimising views.

The design of the new Central Library has created an urban environment in the starkly dramatic desert setting, offering its occupants the illusion, not imitation, of buildings from the past.

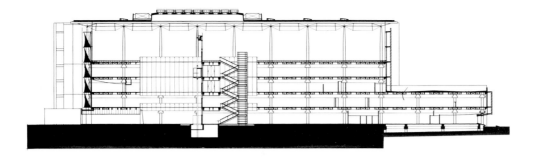

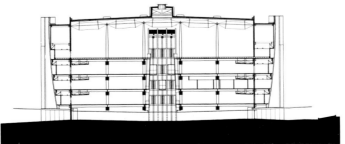

FROM ABOVE: North-south section through atrium; east-west section through entrance

Site plan

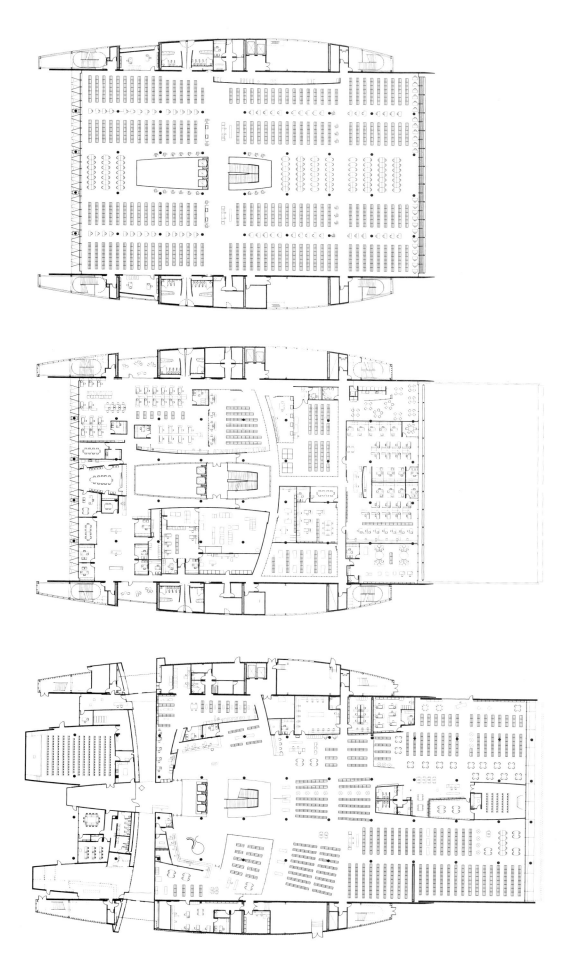

FROM ABOVE: Fourth floor plan; second floor plan; ground floor plan

AJ DIAMOND/DONALD SCHMIDT AND COMPANY
RICHMOND HILL CENTRAL LIBRARY
Toronto, Ontario, Canada

The Richmond Hill Central Library is the hub of the town library system, and also the first component of the Richmond Hill Civic Centre to be built. The building is adjacent to the historic town centre, and stands on the hill after which the town is named. Oriented towards the south, the building has its primary entrance on a green that will be the central public space of the civic centre.

The library houses one hundred and seventy thousand volumes in 7,000 square metres of space. The building is conceived of as a loft structure, with a regular structural bay that is either filled with shelving to provide book storage, or left open to provide reading rooms. The building is comprised of two double-height volumes stacked one above the other, each with an intermediate mezzanine. Activities requiring ground-level access, such as the children's area, multi-purpose rooms and staff work areas are housed in the lower volume. The main public rooms, including an airy, nine-bay reference room facing north, and an open, light-filled reading room facing south, are housed in the upper volume. A stair and elevator hall provide physical links, as well as visual connection, between the various volumes of the building.

A notable aspect of the design is the high level of integration between structural, mechanical and electrical systems, and the manner in which the structure has been used as an element of the architecture. Conically capped columns support grids of deep double beams at the third and roof levels. These beams form both deep coffers which determine the regular bay of the building, and a mechanical plenum which houses air handling units, sprinklers and power/communication conduits.

While natural light is harmful to print material, it is also an essential ingredient in the achievement of satisfying, humane buildings. Thus, light has been admitted, filtered, screened or blocked as appropriate to each of the library functions and spaces. Glazed canopies on the arcade provide protection from the elements while admitting the warmth and light of the sun. Brise-soleils and suspended cones above the reading rooms filter or reflect light for the indirect illumination of the collection. Vertical fins on the north windows block the low north-west light that would otherwise penetrate in the summer months.

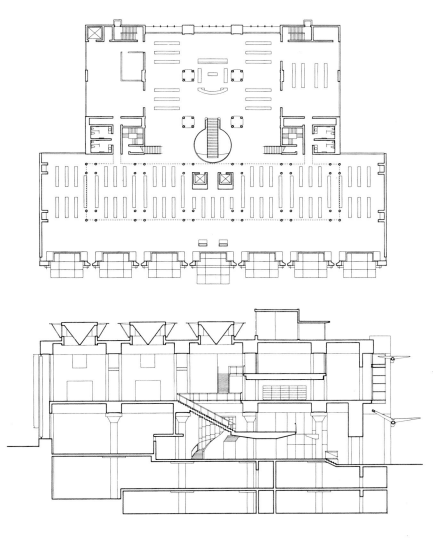

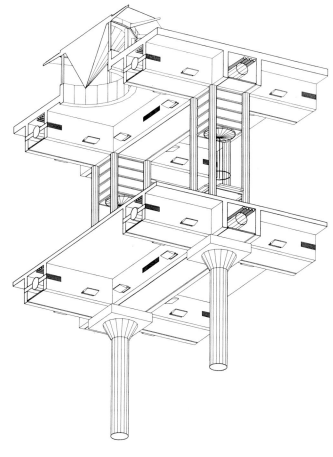

LEFT FROM ABOVE: Third floor plan; north-south section; RIGHT: Axonometric of typical structural bay

JEREMY DIXON.EDWARD JONES

DARWIN COLLEGE STUDY CENTRE

Cambridge, UK

The purpose of this building is to provide facilities for postgraduate students to study in a good working atmosphere. The building is designed to offer a choice of study environments: overlooking the River Cam, sitting outside on the balcony or steps, looking towards Silver Street, sitting around a large table, choosing to be isolated under the lantern, relaxing on a sofa, or working with computers in the computer rooms.

The site, a long narrow rectangle, lies between the curve of Silver Street and the Cam mill pool. The College itself is linear in plan. Over time the existing buildings were joined together by new buildings. The site is therefore the linear end of a linear plan.

On the street side the building is low and appears to emerge from the existing curved boundary wall. On the river side there are two storeys of accommodation and within this section computer rooms are placed at ground floor level along the river front. The main reading room, overlooking the water, is a space that extends from ground floor to first floor. A variety of study spaces are thus provided.

The interior of the building is like one large piece of furniture. Structure, cladding, windows, floors, bookcases and furniture are all made of oak. The timber has different characteristics varying from the dramatic texture of shakes and splits in the structural elements to the refinement of veneers in the furniture.

The dominant aspect of the interior space comes from the geometry of the roof. The straight line in plan generated by the waterside and echoed by the clerestory is set against the curved wall to Silver Street. The inside of the curved wall is lined with books and the rafters forming the roof reconcile the straight line to the curve and generate a gentle three-dimensional curved plane when seen in perspective.

The building is constructed of brickwork and English oak. Soft lime mortar is used to avoid movement joints. The oak structure uses large sections, of a size that was only available 'green' or unseasoned. The timber was cut and dried for the project but moisture contents remain high and the structure will continue to dry for several years. Stainless-steel mechanical fixings allow the joints in the timber to be tightened as it dries. The oak rafters which form the surface act compositely with a double skin of plywood deck and provide lateral stability. The ground floor is natural stone and the roofs are natural slate and lead.

To the head of the plan are located a seminar room, a small flat and a timber lantern. To avoid opening windows on the street side, the lantern automatically opens and closes, providing cross ventilation to the reading areas.

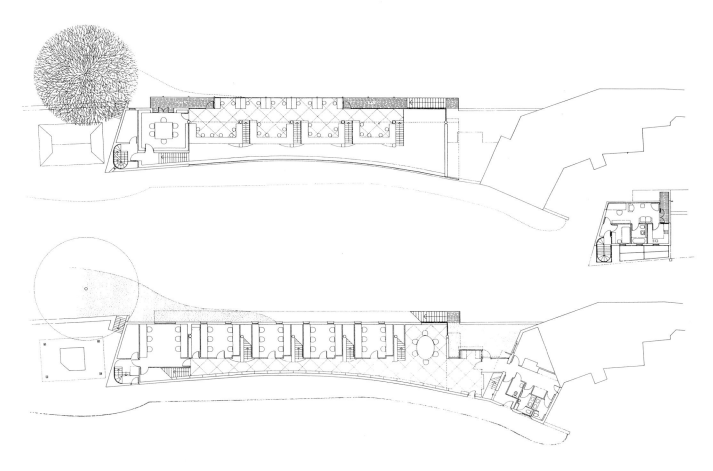

FROM ABOVE: First level plan; second level plan; ground level plan

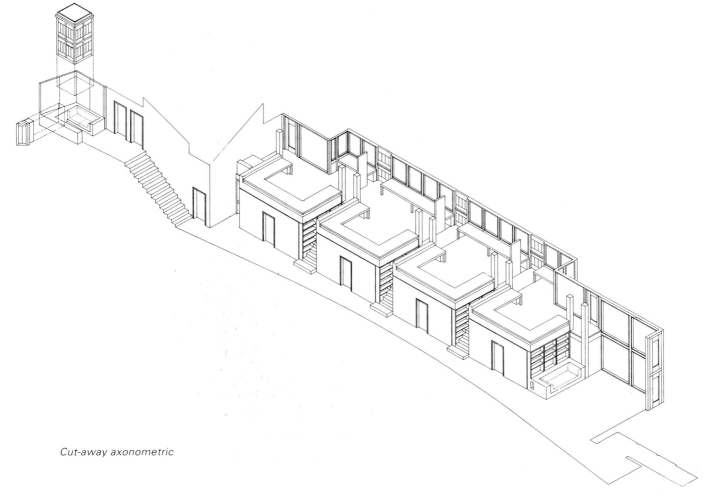

Cut-away axonometric

EVANS + SHALEV
QUINCENTENARY LIBRARY

Jesus College, Cambridge, UK

The Masters and Fellows of Jesus College set out to build a new court to the south of the Chapel Court between Morley Horder's residential building and Jesus Lane. The designated land was partially derelict (formerly the nunnery's vegetable garden) and is partially used as a car park.

New Court, which was subject to an architectural competition in late 1991, was to be formed by the existing Morley Horder building, a new college library to replace the War Memorial Library, sixty new rooms for students and Fellows, and a music suite around a two-hundred-seat auditorium.

To design a collegiate court for the twenty-first century which is in harmony with over five hundred years of architecture and to design a court which incorporates two new common spaces – the library and the auditorium – side by side with residential rooms, was a difficult challenge, but one which the architects have achieved.

Using devices from the existing architecture – skyline, ground line, fenestration, scale, colour and texture – and materials (brick, stone, wood and glass), detailed to suit contemporary building technology, and adhering to the collegiate spatial hierarchy

has resulted in a warm new addition to Jesus College.

The library is the first building to be completed as part of the new court, to replace the existing War Memorial and Law Libraries and to combine a new computer centre. It was designed to be in harmony with the historic setting of the college and to create a calm environment for reading and study.

The building is approached from Chapel Court through an old gate, through a small antespace created by the library and the thirteenth-century chapel, and entered from New Court.

The library is essentially a single toplit volume overlooking both New Court to the east and the Master's garden to the west. The space is designed to permit at once oversight and good orientation and a variety of private reading places.

It is open twenty-four hours a day, can house forty thousand books and caters for one hundred and twenty-five readers. All furniture and fittings, including shelving, worktops and loose furniture is purpose-designed as an organic part of the architecture. From the double-height rotunda

entrance a gentle staircase cuts through the middle of the plan within the space and leads up to the main reading room comprising seven book-lined alcoves and six carrels. A gallery surrounds the space and its vaulted ceiling allows natural light to permeate down to the middle of the plan. Large windows puncture the external walls and their fan-shaped heads permit deep light into the vaulted reading alcoves, thus obviating excessive use of artificial lighting. Translucent blinds filter sunlight.

The main reading room is supplemented by a variety of smaller rooms: the Law Library, the computer centre, closed stack room and the librarian's office on the ground floor, a meeting/reading room and a lecture/reading room on the first floor, and the reading gallery within the roof space.

As in all good traditional collegiate architecture the answer was to create comfortable, well-lit and well-equipped spaces with an atmosphere conducive to study, and with plain elevations that honestly reflect the interior. Lofty space, soft light, warm materials and silent surfaces combine to create an intimate workplace.

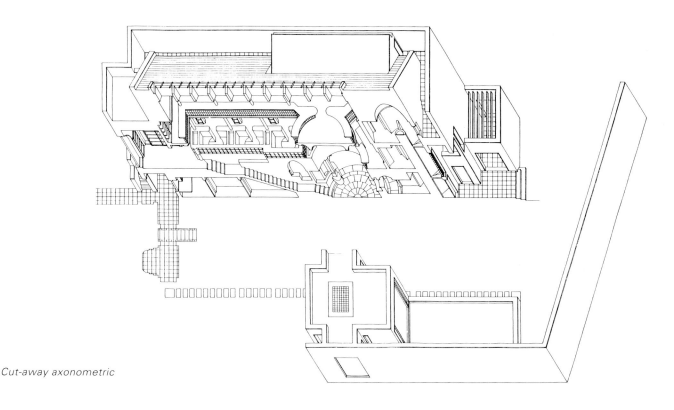

Cut-away axonometric

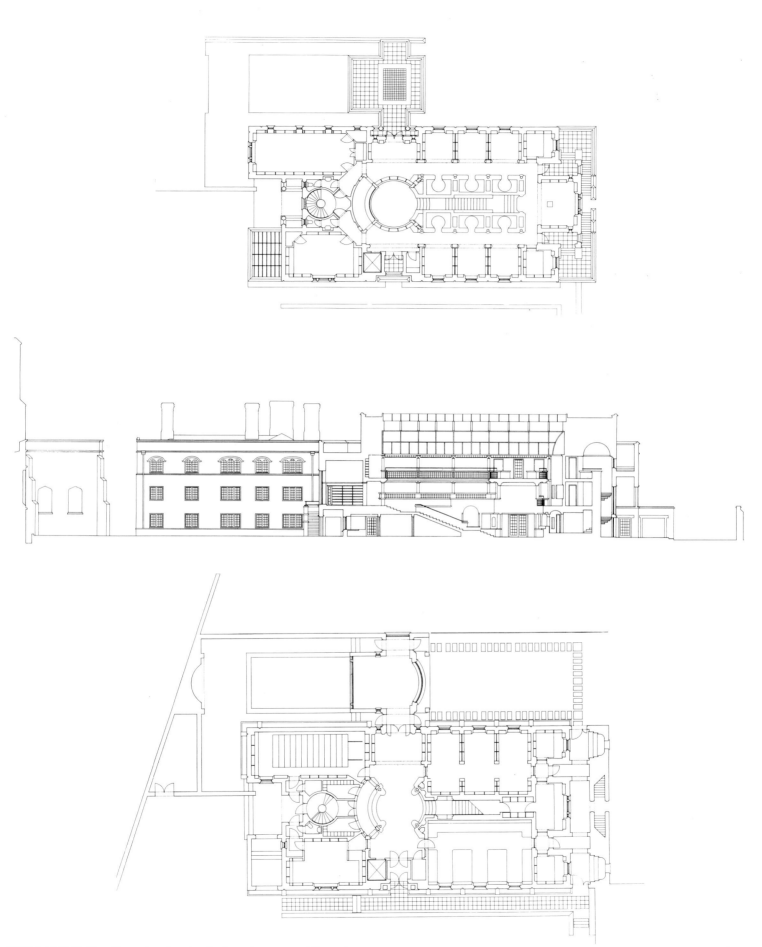

FROM ABOVE: First floor plan; longitudinal section; ground floor plan

SIR NORMAN FOSTER AND PARTNERS
CRANFIELD LIBRARY
University of Cranfield, Bedfordshire, UK

Cranfield Institute of Technology was founded in 1946 as an elite school for the education of aeronautical engineers, and now offers a wide range of postgraduate studies, with facilities spread over three campuses. The courses are heavily sponsored by the private sector, and range from rural land use to defence technology. The new library brings together the resources of the Science and Technical school and the School of Management Studies, two 'cultures' (technologists and managers) previously housed in separate, adapted buildings. This integration is implied by the building's symbolic placement at the focal point of the Cranfield campus. The structure and streamlined appearance of the building underlines the aeronautical engineering origins of the institute.

The Cranfield library consists of four steel-framed vaulted roof forms covering a square plan library building. The overhanging roof provides sheltered walkways along the side of the building.

The front of the building is covered by a complete roof bay which creates an entrance canopy. This canopy becomes a popular meeting place, similar to Foster's Carré d'Art in Nimes. The entrance vault's roof light brings natural light to the upper floor area and into the atrium. A central circulation space extends up through the building, providing a social focus, while quieter reading and study places are provided with muted light and shaded views from the edge of the library.

The external walls of the library are a clear glass curtain which allow views into the library study areas. Sunshading is provided by an external screen of silver anodised aluminium louvres.

The furniture system installed in the information areas, reading rooms and classrooms has been designed by Norman and Sabiha Foster.

The building, built to a very tight budget and completed within the scheduled time, is used for lectures, conferences and library storage. It has been designed to adapt easily in the future to the information technology advances which are essential to a technology institute, within 'a framework of an architecture which encourages easy access and social interaction'.

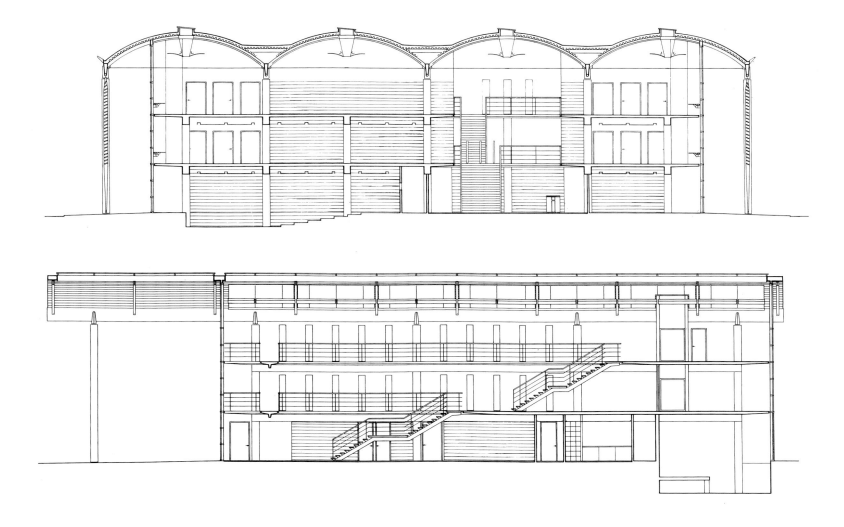

FROM ABOVE: Cross section; longitudinal section

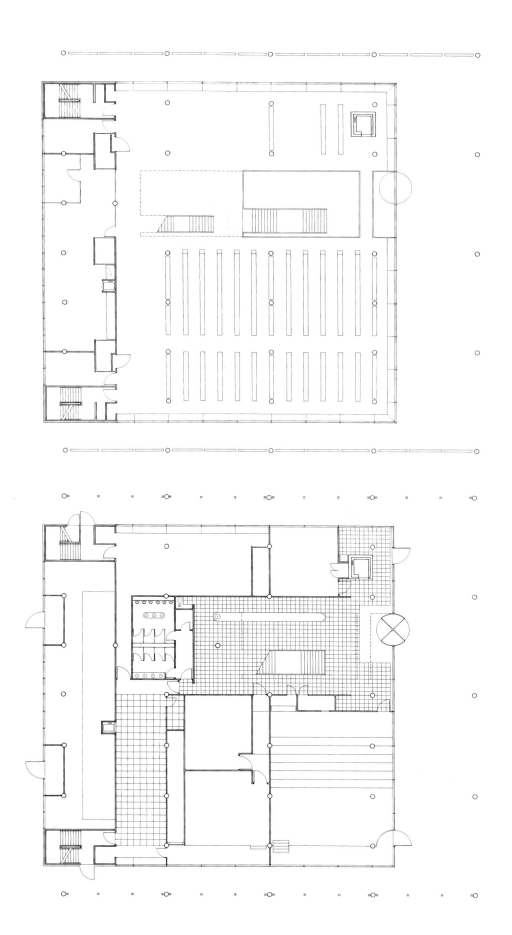

FROM ABOVE: First floor plan; ground floor plan

SIR NORMAN FOSTER AND PARTNERS
SQUIRE LAW LIBRARY

University of Cambridge, Cambridge, UK

Law has been taught and studied at Cambridge for seven centuries, and the university now has the largest unitary law school in the country, with over eight hundred undergraduates and approximately two hundred postgraduate students. The faculty includes specialists in almost every aspect of English law and its history, international law, legal philosophy and criminology. There are three specialist research centres within the faculty: the Wolfson Institute of Criminology, the Research Centre for International Law, and the Centre for European Legal Studies.

The faculty had outgrown its previous scattered accommodation, and in 1990, a limited architectural competition was held by the university for the new Law Faculty and Institute of Criminology. Built in two phases, the building was to provide up-to-date facilities for teaching and research. The site, with its lawns and mature trees, is at the centre of the Sidgwick site, the arts campus for the university. A considerable amount of space, 10,000 square metres in total, was required, although the site is relatively small.

Foster's winning scheme was for two pavilions sitting in the landscape, with the majority of the Law Faculty in one and the Institute of Criminology in the other.

Following the competition, it became apparent that the whole of the Law Faculty could be accommodated within a single pavilion, using a slightly enlarged footprint, which in turn allowed quite a different design to be pursued for the Institute of Criminology.

The 9,000-square-metre faculty building houses the Squire Law Library, five auditoria, seminar rooms, senior and junior common rooms and the faculty administration. Four storeys high, with a further two floors below ground, the building does not intrude on the established skyline. The eaves height on the southern elevation is level with Casson and Conder's original Raised Faculty building and the roofline is lower than Stirling's History Faculty to the west.

The ground floor contains the staff common room, teaching areas and administrative offices. The lower ground floors are taken up by auditoria, book stores and the student common room, which is lit naturally by means of a full-height atrium – the focus of the main entrance. This atrium creates a lofty spaciousness within the tightly formed configuration of the building.

Natural light is used to dramatic effect, especially in the library. Here the feeling of spaciousness is developed further with terraced floors following the line of the curved facade. This creates a single, grand volume, linking all the naturally lit reading areas of the three-storey library. Study areas are designed to have views out over the gardens to the north, benefiting from the fully glazed, north-facing elevation. Book stacks are located in the centre of the plan with staff carrels on the south elevation.

The *in situ* concrete structure is raked at an angle to reflect the terracing of the floors. The concrete floors are enclosed on the north facade and roof by a triangulated steel vierendeel structure, cylindrical in section, to which the cladding systems and glazing units are fixed. The triangular format allows for repetition of panel sizes and has been engineered to maximise structural efficiency. The modular steelwork units are factory-fabricated and then bolted together on site to form a 39-metre-diameter vault rising 19 metres above ground level. The outer vierendeel booms are set out on 3.9 metre centres to give depth to the structural section.

Externally, the curved north facade's structural glazing becomes a stainless-steel roof above. The glazed west facade and part of the east facade are carefully designed to address solar heat gain and glare. The west wall forms a sinusoidal curve in plan, resolving the 45 degree cut of the cylindrical form with the triangular geometry of the north elevation. The vertical south facade is clad partly in reconstituted Portland stone and partly translucent glazing with clear horizontal vision strips. These are shaded from the sun and incorporate opening windows for natural ventilation. Internally, the structure provides considerable flexibility, with generous column-free spaces. The visible surfaces of the columns and beams have a high-quality finish, achieved by sandblasting the concrete to expose its Scottish granite aggregate.

The client required the building to be energy efficient. Externally, various devices are used to shade the enclosing envelope and internally, use is made of the thermal mass of the concrete structure. This enables the building to be naturally and mechanically ventilated throughout, the auditoria being the only spaces to be cooled. Energy consumption is minimised through lighting management and reclaimed heat from extracted air.

The new Law Faculty uses natural light and spaciousness to create a modern building, which responds positively to its surroundings.

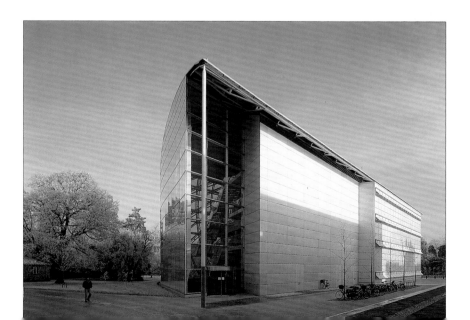

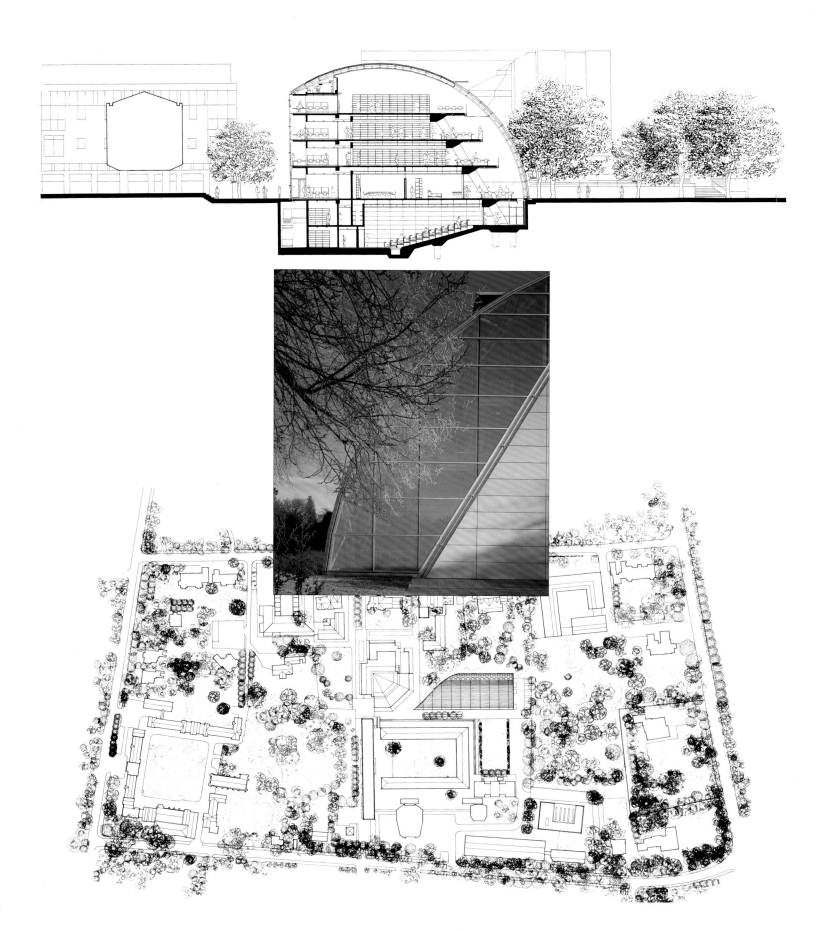

ABOVE: Cross section; BELOW: Site plan

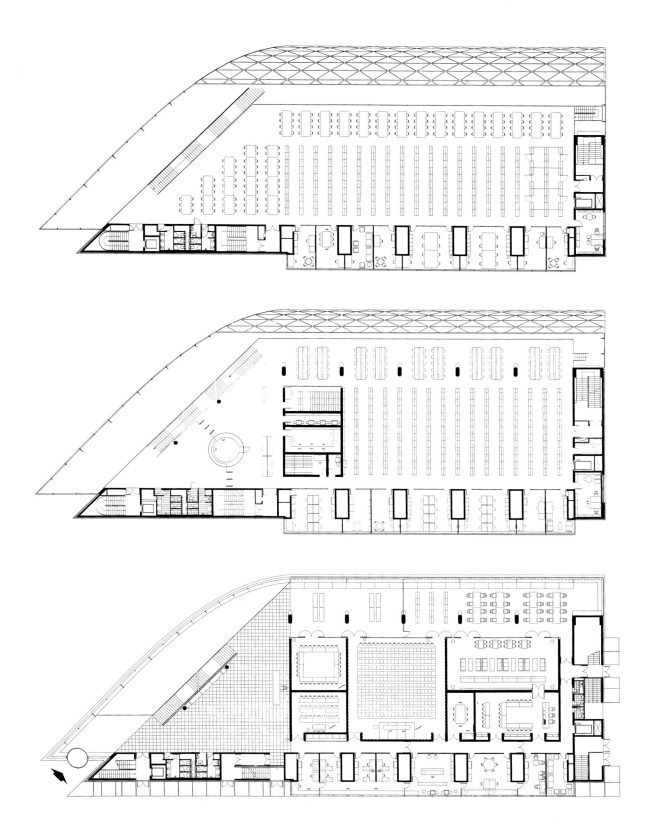

FROM ABOVE: Third floor plan; first floor plan; ground floor plan

GAPP ARCHITECTS
SANDTON LIBRARY
Sandton, Gauteng, South Africa

Sandton, a satellite of Johannesburg – the industrial and economic centre of South Africa – is a thriving and rapidly growing town. It is the preferred location of the head offices of many of South Africa's most important businesses and its suburbs are populated generally by people of a higher income bracket. Nearby Alexandra, also part of Sandton, is a very low-income suburb with very small houses, and few community facilities.

The library, on one edge of Sandton's new town centre known as Sandton Square, is intended to serve both of these communities. Sandton Square, although built concurrently with the library, is a neo-Renaissance retail development, reminiscent of Italian squares of the fifteenth century, which comprises three of the sides of the square. The library forms the fourth side and forms a link between Sandton Square and the Civic Forum, which is another square planned for the other side of the library but not yet completed. The wedge-shaped library takes up the angle between the axes of the two squares, as defined by the original urban design guidelines prepared by the architects.

The library, as a cultural centre, thus holds a suitably commanding presence over both Sandton Square and the Civic Forum. Going to the library is part of the experience of shopping in Sandton Square or of visiting the town's civic centre on the edge of the Forum.

The three wings of the library enclose a triangular full-height atrium topped by a rooflight. The two longer rectangular floors are where the bookshelves and public reading spaces are located, and the third shorter curved side contains administration. At each of the three corners the floor steps up by one-third of a level so that it is possible to walk upwards in a clockwise spiral around the building. This device allows for flexibility in the allocation of departments or sections of book collections as they change over the years.

The atrium contains a tubular lift shaft and a spectacular spiral metal ramp hung from the roof which serves all floors. This ramp is intended for wheelchair-users and book trolleys, but is used by almost everyone.

The top floor houses the mayor's offices and committee rooms of the council. Pride of place is given to the town's Council Chamber where the newly-elected councillors meet. This level connects, by a short bridge, to the adjacent civic centre.

Also part of the library complex is Sandton's art gallery which surrounds a green and tree-lined sculpture courtyard. This gallery has heightened the community's awareness of art and plays host to musical events which regularly take place in one of the wings of the gallery.

The building is built of brick, with internal concrete slabs and columns expressed as raw concrete but painted white for lightness. Semi-circular or low, segmental arches are of orthodox brick construction. The tall brick arcade on Sandton Square is symmetrical and essentially classical in expression, with, at the apex, a large triangular central window to the mayor's office. The arcade completes the walkway that was intended to surround the Square. A playful walkway in steel along the side of the art gallery courtyard connects Sandton Square with the Forum.

The Civic Forum facade is more sedate and three-dimensional, expressing more directly the library function within. The central entrance is flanked by two soaring towers of brick. One contains a lift shaft for the mayor, the other an escape stair with small circular windows.

The architects' search here is for an architecture that is both of Africa and out of Africa, without reference to the architectural antecedents of Europe or tribal Africa. In its use of materials – brick, concrete and steel – to express their respective poetries, without reference to any particular architectural style, the library is trying to develop an architecture for today's new South Africa.

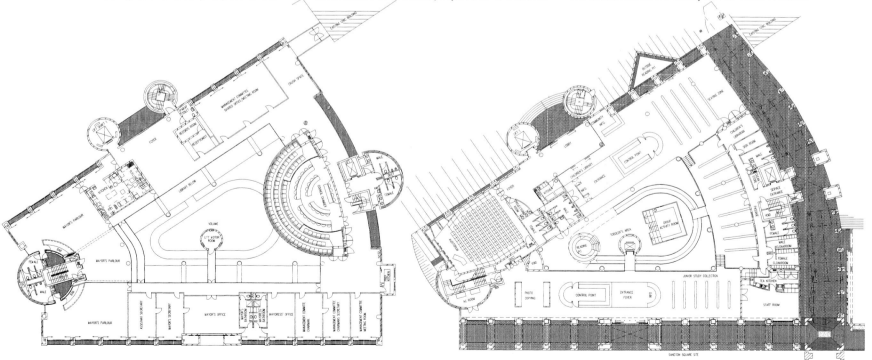

LEFT TO RIGHT: Fourth floor plan; ground floor plan

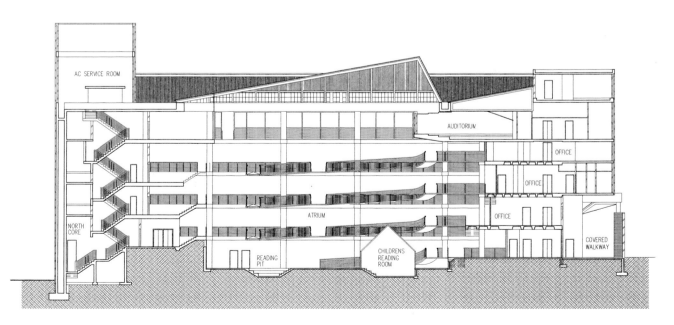

Longitudinal section through atrium

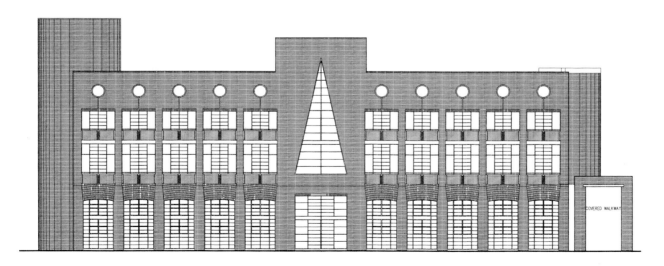

West elevation

PROF GERBER & PARTNER
NATIONAL AND UNIVERSITY LIBRARY
Göttingen, Germany

With a collection numbering over three-and-a-half million volumes and covering more than twenty specialist areas of interest, the National and University Library of Göttingen (SUB) is one of the five largest libraries in Germany. The new SUB building is situated north of the city centre, near the Humanities Centre of the Georg-August University. The campus is cut off from the centre by an expressway network – this problem was to be solved by the new library building, as required by the brief for the national competition.

With its location to the south of the Humanities Centre, the SUB forms the interface between the university campus and the city centre. It sits between the buildings of the surrounding Humanities Centre, which mostly date back to the sixties and seventies, and the open spaces of the adjacent green embankment to the south. The existing structures are arranged in a consistent orthogonal u-shaped layout with regular open spaces in between. The new building forms the southern boundary to the forum of buildings and provides it with a communications and information centre. The structural extension of the building (a hand with 'palm' and 'fingers') fulfils both urban planning needs and internal purpose-oriented requirements,

based on related functions and processes.

The whole building is divided into four distinct functional areas: a public/reader zone; an administrative zone; storage and technical services; and underground parking and building services. The public and administrative zones are housed in a compact four-storey form, while the storage, underground parking and technical services are located on the lower floors.

The building consists of a steel-framed reinforced concrete structure, with special emphasis placed on the choice of visible materials. The resulting interior design is restrained and simple in both material and colour. Structural support elements such as pillars, joists and ceilings retain their exposed concrete surface. The suspended ceilings are white, steel components such as supports and rails are metallic colours. Light grey flooring matches the natural stone used externally.

The choice of such materials as steel, glass, metal and natural stone allows users to identify the internal structure of the building even from outside. The roof of the new library can be seen from several neighbouring buildings and was therefore designed like a fifth facade.

A light-filled, glazed four-storey rotunda, visible from all around, marks the entrance

to the SUB, and clearly links the entrance hall with all the upper storeys. The transparency and scale of the rotunda helps to communicate the orientation of the library, providing access to all areas. The 'visitor-intensive' zones – areas of brief but concentrated use – such as the lending library and the textbook collection, are located directly adjacent to the entrance hall.

Administration is arranged uniformly on the four storeys and encircles the public zone on three sides. A service zone which spans all four storeys provides access to all installation and building services, the book conveying system, as well as lavatories and technical facilities. It constitutes the main technical thoroughfare and is an interface between the administration and public area. The offices, arranged to form the 'back of the hand' surrounding the building on the east, north and west, are illuminated by natural daylight.

Whilst these areas are oriented towards the north, users will find quiet, bright, working and studying areas in the 'fingers', where large windows face south towards the green open spaces. Readers can select titles from the four hundred and fifty volumes and sit or study at one of the six hundred brightly-lit workplaces or closed working booths.

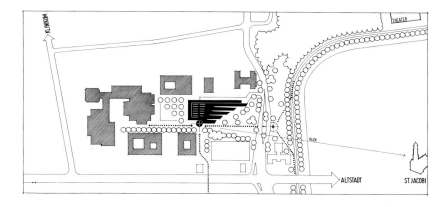

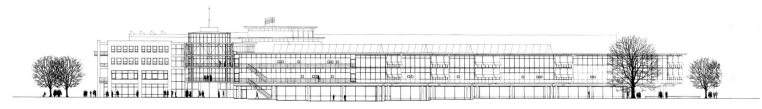

FROM ABOVE: Site plan; west elevation

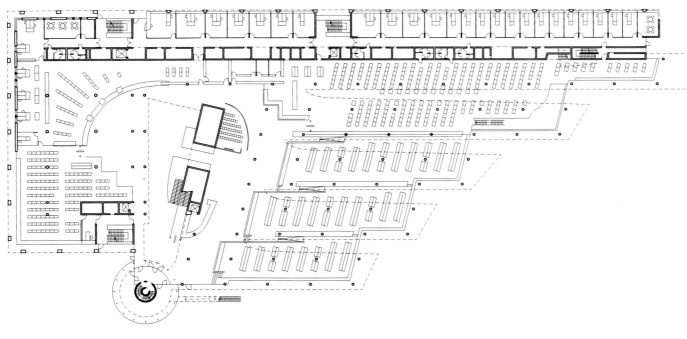

Ground floor plan

Third floor plan

HELIN & SIITONEN
JOENSUU LIBRARY

Joensuu, Finland

The layout of the centre of Joensuu, a commercial town in southern Finland, stems from plans drawn up by CW Gyldén and F Ohman in 1848 and 1867, respectively. Gyldén's town plan already featured two main axes intersecting at a right angle: the axis of Kirkkokatu, with a church at both ends, and the axis of Koskikatu and Siltakatu, along which the public buildings and squares of the town have been assembled.

The design of the library developed from the entry that won first prize in a competition organised in 1981, and has evolved over a long design period.

The site of the library on Koskikatu was originally designated as a typical residential block in Ohman's town plan. Because such plots were fairly substantial, there were usually not enough buildings to fill up all sides of a block; instead, gaps were filled in with fences, thus completing the image of a solid block.

Later construction has eliminated some of the enclosed street spaces typical of the older urban structure. However, Koskikatu has been reasonably well preserved as the delimiter of the park zone. Therefore, the library was also sited flush with the street.

The library facilities were designed on a 'library-town' principle. They are organised into four blocks by interior 'streets'. Near the entrance, at an intersection of streets, is the public cafe and newspaper reading room. Access to the other reading rooms is also from this intersection.

The staircase to the lending hall rises from the main 'street' that traverses the building. The rectangular volume of the lending hall has been geometrically and structurally sub-divided with fittings into open squares and low shelving blocks. One of the two squares contains the lending office, while the other displays artworks around a pool.

The squares are skylit and the sloping ceilings over the shelving blocks act as reflectors. Part of the light for the reading rooms comes through the opal glass ceiling.

Bridges over the main 'street' lead from the lending hall to the children's department and to the music department on the second floor. The administrative premises are located along Koskikatu; they are also connected to the lending hall by bridges.

The building contains a multi-purpose hall for meetings and exhibitions and, in the children's department, a room for story-telling and puppet theatre.

Apart from works by local artists, the library will house Martti Aiha's work *Jälkitalvimaisema* (Post-Winter Landscape).

The interior designer has developed a shelving system which is in tune with the general atmosphere of the building. The shelves are open at floor level and supported on legs, giving a light overall impression and making cleaning easier. The undersides of the shelves are covered with wool fabric to dampen sound. Sheet metal shelves proved to be more rigid and considerably cheaper than wooden shelves, as well as being safer in terms of fire risk.

The frame of the building is concrete cast in situ. The facades are rendered and partly faced with local soapstone, which is also used as a surface material in the foyers. Sunlight entering through windows on the south side of the building is diffused by slatted metal grids.

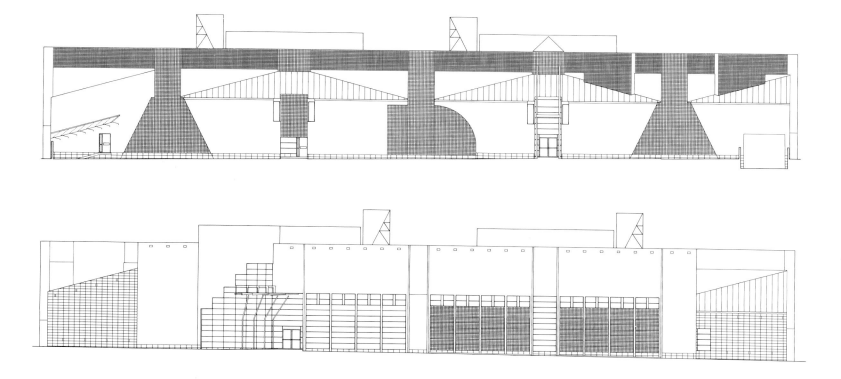

FROM ABOVE: South elevation; north elevation

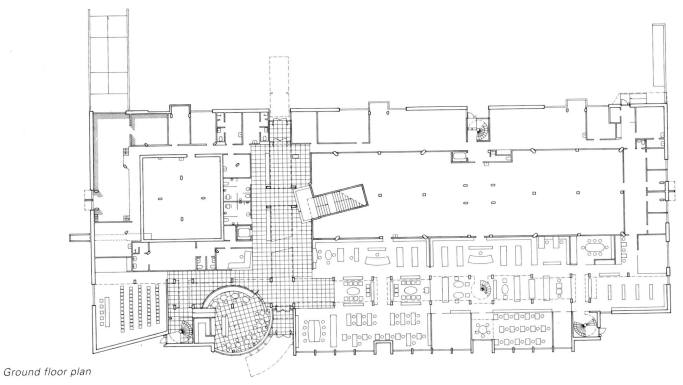

Ground floor plan

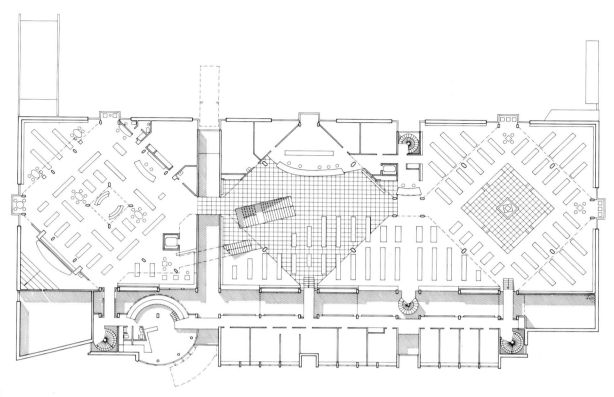

First floor plan

VAN HEYNINGEN AND HAWARD
KATHARINE STEPHEN RARE BOOKS ROOM

Newnham College, Cambridge, UK

The Katharine Stephen Rare Books Room, a smaller example of a Cambridge library, follows the traditions of many Oxbridge additions of projecting on to the street or college grounds, such as, for example, James Gibbs' Senate House in Cambridge, Wren's Sheldonian Theatre or Hawksmoor's Radcliffe Camera in Oxford.

The library was commissioned when it became apparent to the board of Newnham College that many items of their rare books collection were not being stored in ideal conditions; housed on the open shelves, in cardboard boxes, in glass-fronted cabinets or locked up in bedrooms. The College asked the architects to look at their library as a whole, with particular attention to expansion and to providing a safe environment for the collection.

This review elicited a programme of refurbishment, rearrangement and new building work. Other locations for housing the rare books were examined, but all had problems: meeting fire, security and environmental standards at a reasonable cost, impeding the future expansion of the existing library, or colonisation of spaces that could be better used for something else. Finally, it was decided that the rare books should be housed in a new free-standing building.

A small piece of land existed next to Sidgwick Avenue. The new building immediately introduced fire and noise separation, security and the ability to add environmental controls. In possessing a dedicated repository for rare books, the College also increased the likelihood of attracting future bequests.

Basil Champneys (1842-1920), laid out the College and designed most of the buildings between 1872-1910. An over-pretty quality is rescued by Champneys' underlying interest in symmetry (evident, even if discreet, on the outside) and his ability to raise the scale here and there using traditional seventeenth-century forms to produce two- or three-storey set pieces: oriels on the dining hall, bay windows on the residential blocks. Together these are at their most convincing in the view from the dining hall to the Pfeiffer Building.

Once started, the notion of doing something slightly subversive on Sidgwick Avenue continued. The windows are a similar pattern to those in the rest of the College but in this case made of metal and painted blue. Banded brickwork refers to nineteenth-century architecture (Butterfield rather than Champneys) and was accepted by the planners and the Victorian Society to whom the scheme was referred.

The Rare Books Room's immediate neighbour is Elizabeth Scott's Fawcett Building (1938), vertically banded in grey and pink, but stylistically, the library's antecedents include the Tuscan models of Siena cathedral, Verona and the chapel at Badio.

The library is for a collection of rare things; what it houses is unique and valuable to the College. What is contained is more valuable than the container. Consequently, the building was intended to look serious, with a formality resulting from the choice of simple architectonic form, symmetrical planning and hard-edged detailing.

At the same time the inflection on plan to the street and the banding introduce a note of informality and playfulness. (The banding could be read as a metaphor for the shelves of books inside.) This playful, rather provocative quality is extended by the siting of the building on the street, which reverses the convention of housing things of value as far away as possible from the public eye, again taking reference from Italian buildings and streets.

The proportions of the library are taken from the section of the original 1896 Yates-Thompson library: the height; the diameter of the vault; the white plaster, and the idea of the gallery. This was partly to suggest a continuity with the main library. Other external details take their references from existing buildings on the campus: the use of natural light; the curved lead-dressed cornice and lead roof; the low window; the window seat and the blue cushions, among other small details, like the lead rain-water hopper with over-flow spout.

Internally, the library is accessed from a top-lit oval vestibule which rotates the direction of the route into the new building. A subdued cool atmosphere was sought, with low light levels. The metal shelves and gallery are as if slid in one piece into the masonry sleeve of the building: the price-less hand-made leather sits on factory-made metal shelves. With such old and valuable books the monitoring of moisture and dust is made simpler by the introduction of spaces behind and below the shelves allowing air to circulate freely, and the heavily insulated structure evens out temperature and humidity peaks.

Usually empty, the building is a reposi-tory, not a user library. This contributes to idea of the library as a chapel. It is a space chiefly concerned with preserving something old, unconcerned with change or progress.

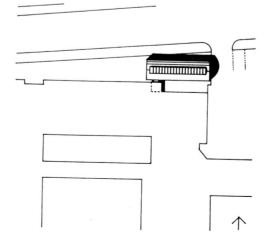

Site plan

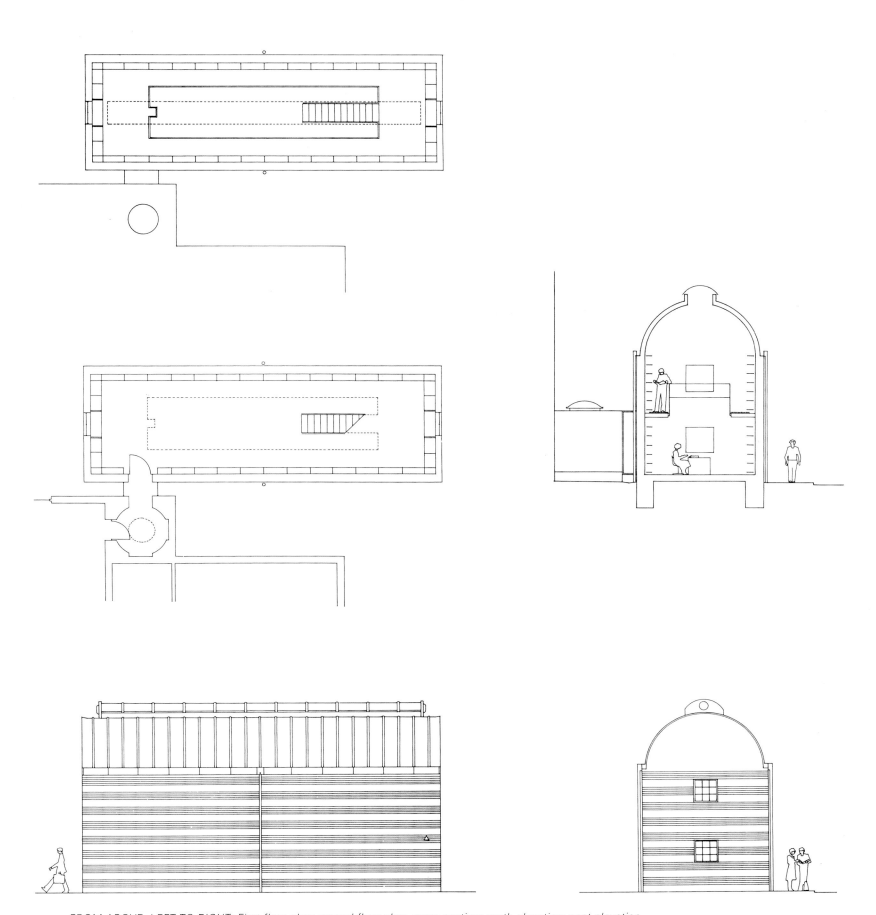

FROM ABOVE, LEFT TO RIGHT: First floor plan; ground floor plan; cross section; north elevation; east elevation

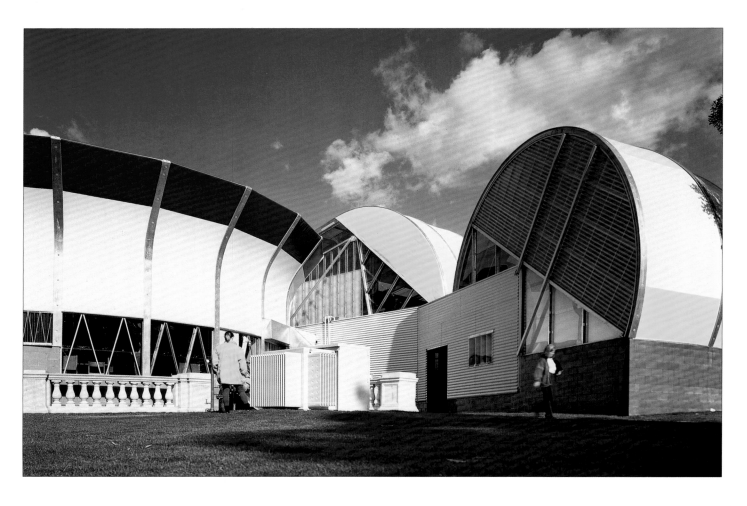

HODGETTS + FUNG DESIGN ASSOCIATES
TOWELL LIBRARY
University of California, Los Angeles, California, USA

This brightly coloured complex of temporary buildings is designed to house the collections of the Powell Library at UCLA for a three- to five-year period while the original library undergoes seismic renovation. The Temporary Powell, or Towell as it is now known, needed to appear unequivocally temporary, yet maintain the identity of a functioning library, as well as provide opportunities for multiple uses in the future. In addition, the firm was challenged to devise a building programme that would address the confines of a compact site and the loss of a primary hub of campus circulation, a place of prominence that had architectural and sentimental significance. Therefore, the grouping was arranged to receive an extension of the original campus axis and redirect it towards the active student centre to the south.

The Towell Library, with its playful colours, use of unconventional geometric forms and dramatic siting, was deliberately designed to contrast with the architectural sensibility of its surrounding ivy-covered neighbours. The complex consists of four linked tented landforms juxtaposed to form a varied and interesting profile. The focus of the assembly is the main library hall, a 10-metre-high, asymmetrically shaped 'hangar' that encloses a mezzanine on which the library's stacks are housed.

There are two reading rooms at opposite ends of the library, one circular and one semi-circular, which flank a cylindrical tube containing the library's administrative offices.

Severe time and budget constraints prompted the development of a reusable aluminium and fabric roofing system capable of rapid construction for the major enclosures, while an intentionally varied ensemble of disposable wood, masonry and plastic structures provide articulation to the sites of former landmarks. The yellow fabric superstructure (a school colour) and its ribbed supports are anchored to low-height brick-coloured concrete masonry walls, and are 'tacked' together with glazed, overlapping sheets of corrugated or clear fibreglass. The fabric covering is a brightly coloured industrial standard polyester substrate that features a separate layer inside to enhance insulation. End walls and non-loadbearing structures linking the primary spaces are framed with metal studs. Offices, framed in wood and clad in corrugated metal, open out of the concrete walls.

Since the building is, in essence, only 3 millimetres thick, structural materials and details of assembly were employed for decorative emphasis. The placement of fasteners, cables, exposed and off-the-shelf elements create a functional aesthetic.

Steel columns feature industrial uplights, exposed sprinkler pipes and fluorescent downlights. A braced steel substructure not only supports the main structure and stabilises the roof ribs at mid-span, but also undulates during an earthquake.

Due to the inherently transient qualities of the tensile fabric structure, special attention has been devoted to achieving 'library quality' acoustical ambience, lighting and environmental comfort levels. Spotlighting bounced from the acoustical lining of the fabric shell provides soft illumination of the general reading areas, while stacks are brightened with linear fluorescents, utilised for both their practical efficiency and geometric impact on the space.

Though most of the floors are concrete slab, part of the west reading room, which sits within the curve of an existing balustrade, is framed – for easy removal – by short columns aligned with the paving pattern of the existing plaza. Much of the rest of the building can be reused as well, including the fabric, the metal ribs, and the water-source heat pumps tied to the central university plant.

With a five-year minimum life span, the building was to be only a 'temporary invader' on the predominantly red brick campus. However, it has already become iconic, and has taken on an unforeseen permanence of spirit and identity.

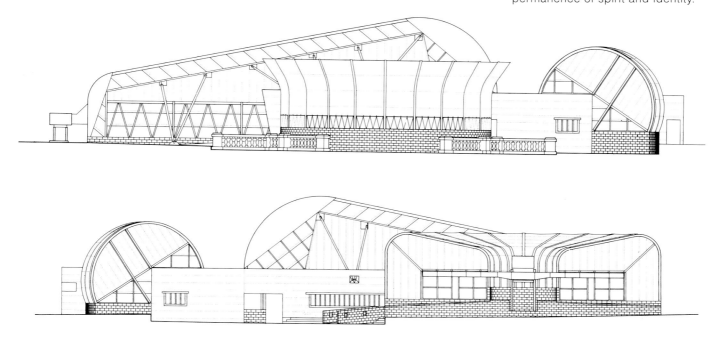

FROM ABOVE: West elevation; east elevation

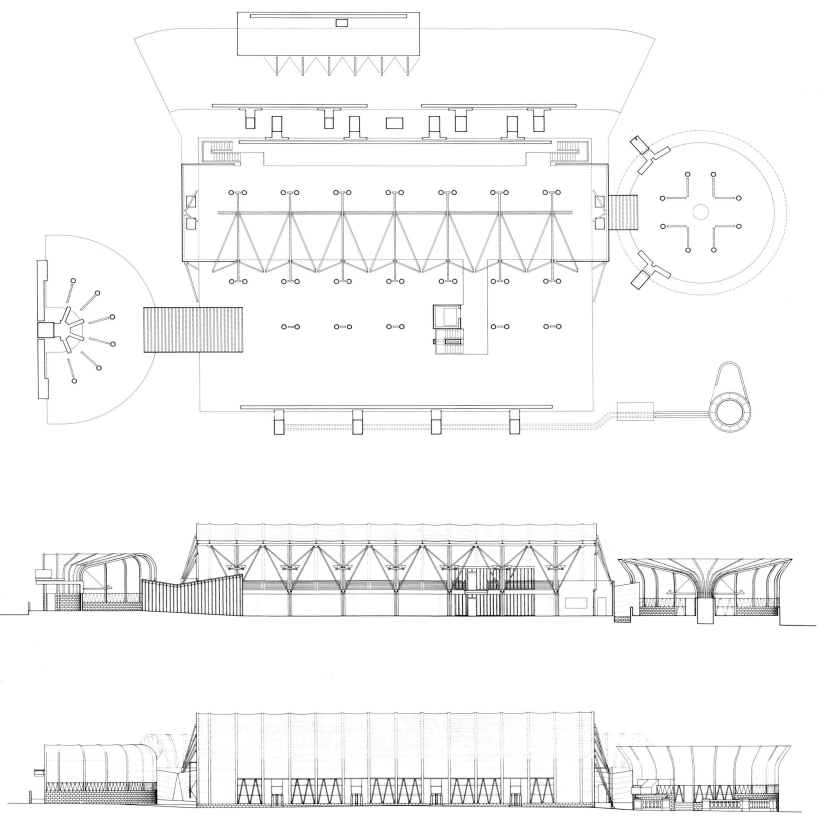

FROM ABOVE: Plan; section looking south; north elevation

AZUSA KITO
KANSAI UNIVERSITY CENTRAL LIBRARY
Osaka, Japan

This is one of the first early examples in Japan of the challenge to exceed the supposed upper limit of a library's open stack area, and it stands among the largest of all the university libraries in the country.

The six faculties of this university, with a total of about nineteen thousand students, had traditionally not separated the libraries for each faculty, but concentrated all the material in one building. This new central library integrates both the student library and the research library for the whole university. The two functions are each given an independent zone: the upper two floors for the students and the subterranean floors for the researchers.

The distribution of the huge amount of periodicals and reference materials on the main floor enables both the researchers and the postgraduate students to utilise the facilities and encourages the interaction of the faculties. The library's capacity amounts to over two million books with two hundred thousand in open stacks, and seats one thousand, six hundred and twenty-eight readers. The area of the building, and each individual floor area, therefore became immense, totalling 19,100 square metres; including the adjacent Data Processing Centre, the total area is 21,750 square metres.

In a library of this vast volume, and similar to the problems faced in the British Library, users must be able to orient themselves and locate their choice of material easily. A clarity and simplicity in the zoning of each floor plan was realised by having two wings to either side of the central zone, with a very large void space extending from the ground to the two upper floors through the central zone, providing a vertical and horizontal link through the whole building.

The challenge to overcome the limit in size subsequently involves a struggle to maintain a humanity in the architecture. While the vast flat floors promise a flexibility in the future disposition of materials, the furniture had to be carefully designed in order to retain a human scale, necessary for the researchers' and students' comfort and to increase their joy of encountering the treasure of knowledge.

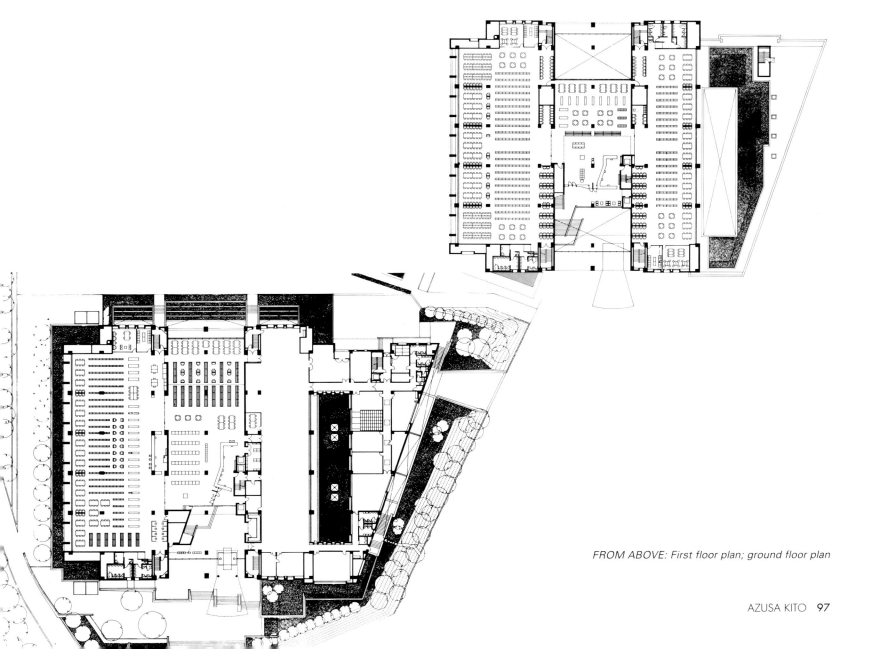

FROM ABOVE: First floor plan; ground floor plan

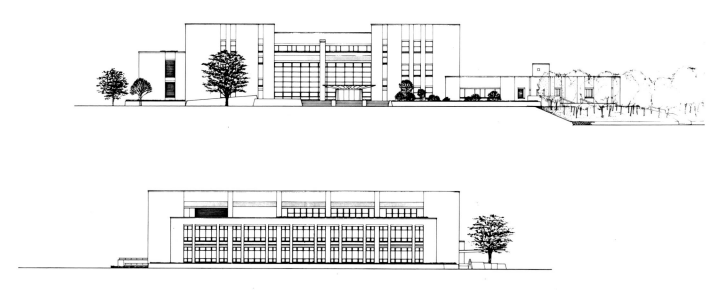

FROM ABOVE: Front elevation; side elevation

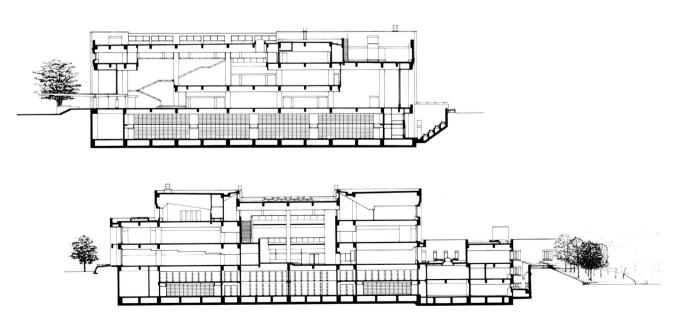

FROM ABOVE: Cross section; longitudinal section

KOETTER, KIM & ASSOCIATES
HARVEY S FIRESTONE LIBRARY

Princeton University, Princeton, New Jersey, USA

This 5,100 square metre addition to the Firestone Library is essentially an extension of the building's two vast subterranean book stack levels. While the notion of an underground 'book vault' does not, in itself, imply a rich and interesting architectural problem, the circumstances of the Firestone's situation produced many more opportunities – and challenges – than was initially apparent.

For instance, as the building site moves from west to east – towards the intersection of Nassau Street and Washington Road – the terrain drops so as to produce not a purely underground building condition but a tantalisingly ambiguous situation of 'semi-building', with construction projecting partially out of the ground. Thus this half-building, half-landscape/partial garden wall and partial terrace situation was bound to produce somewhat unorthodox and complex results with respect to the building's identity and image. This was coupled with the fact that this relatively thin double wafer of building had only one major surface exposed to the air – namely its roof.

As the existing library's truly subterra-nean and seemingly endless stack spaces produced a very dense, gloomy and somewhat disorienting environment, the building was conceived as a kind of perforated plateau or, in other terms, a rather extended block of Swiss cheese – with its upper roof membrane punctured by a variety of openings to flood the dark interior spaces with natural light. This system of natural illumination focuses upon a number of double-height reading spaces that occupy important points of convergence within the building, thus giving clarity and orientation to these spaces, while, at the same time, transforming an underground world into a bright, airy environment and a celebration of light.

Externally, the building's perimeter wall, built to the maximum site extremity allowed by zoning, defines a pair of new public spaces: a linear park dimensioned by the required zoning setback along Nassau Street and a small plaza at the corner of Nassau and Washington Road. These created spaces recognise the importance of the Nassau Street 'seam' between campus and town and provide shared public spaces – serving as common amenities for both the University and its larger Princeton setting. The importance of this place in the community is further marked through the placement of a small truncated tower at the Nassau/Washington corner plaza; a gesture that simultaneously houses a large toplit stairwell and meeting place within the building, legibly and dramatically connecting the building's two floors at its outermost perimeter.

At Firestone, light was used as a primary design 'material', in a building that is not quite a building and one which explores unexpected ways that building, landscape and the public city might interact.

The building utilises poured-in-place concrete frame and slab construction. Echoing the existing building, exterior walls are clad in hand-hewn ashlar granite and smooth-sawn Indiana limestone with polished black granite trim and Chelmsford granite base course.

Windows are factory finished aluminium. Roof terraces are composed of stone paviours and assorted plant materials over an inverted membrane roof.

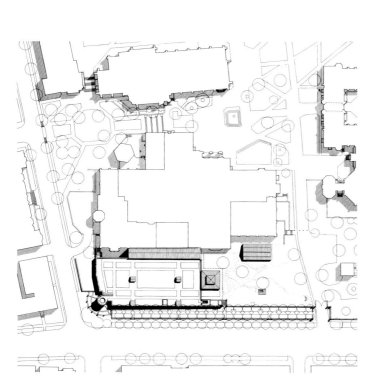

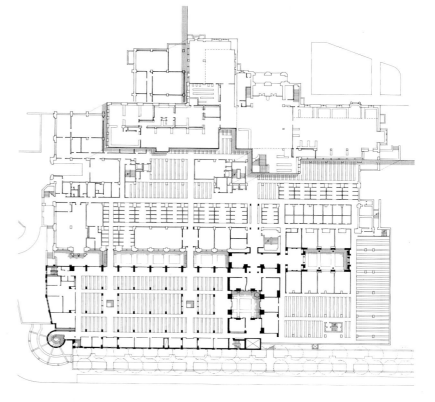

LEFT TO RIGHT: Site plan, subterranean library floor plan

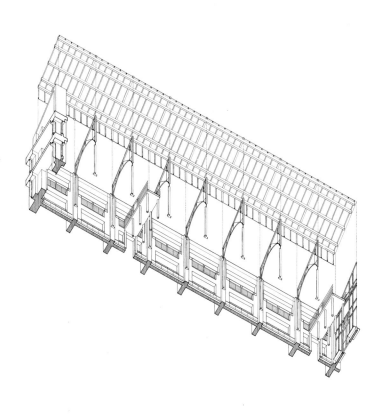

FROM ABOVE: Axonometric of common reading room;
axonometric of central reading room

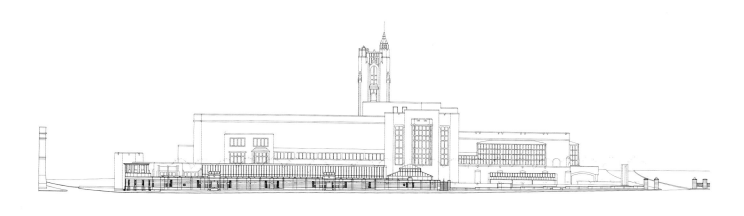

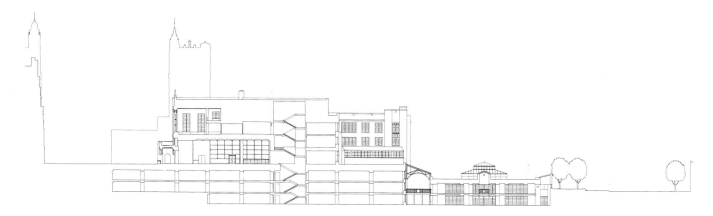

ABOVE: South elevation to Nassau Street; BELOW: Section through Firestone Library and addition

HENNING LARSENS TEGENESTUE
GENTOFTE PUBLIC LIBRARY
Copenhagen, Denmark

In Gentofte, a leafy suburb on the outskirts of Copenhagen, the municipality held a competition in 1974 for the design of its new public library. Henning Larsen won the competition and the library was completed in 1985.

The main activities of the library, located on the large and almost undivided ground floor – the book lending area, the children's library, the newspaper reading area, exhibition area, and the counter area – are daylit from circular skylights above and open glazed facades to the park alongside. An interior promenade runs through the building, from the main entrance to the park. Large parts of the first floor are cut away to allow light to filter from above, and the interior has a bright, airy atmosphere. The open arrangement of the library has also avoided traditional library barriers.

A relaxed predominantly white surrounding with highlights of pale and vibrant electric blue, has been created among the open book stacks, clean simple lines, fluid spaces and internal planning that allows unobstructed views through the building out to the park.

The services for the building, including the administration and staff areas, and the periodical stacks and individual study areas are located on the first floor around the atrium space.

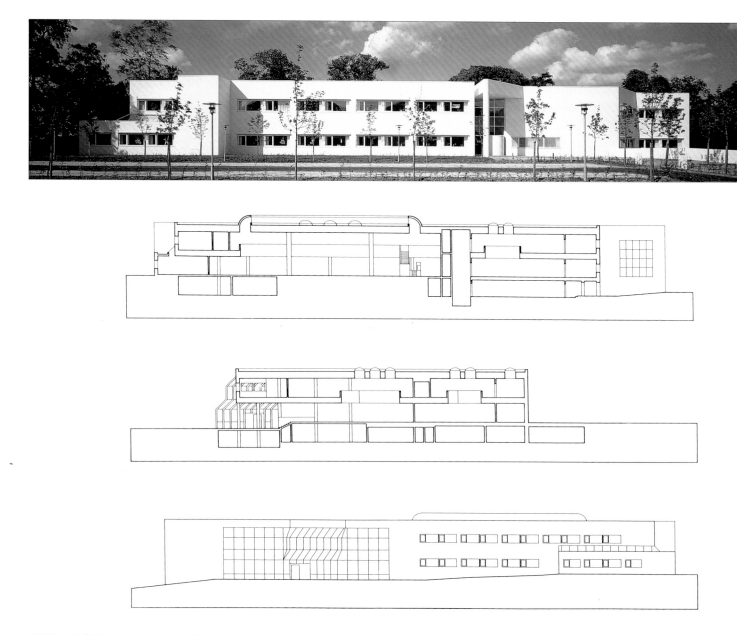

FROM ABOVE: North-south section; east-west section; north elevation

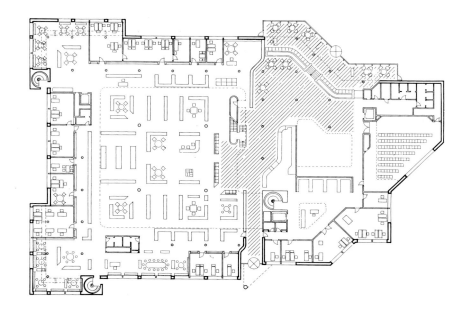

Ground floor plan

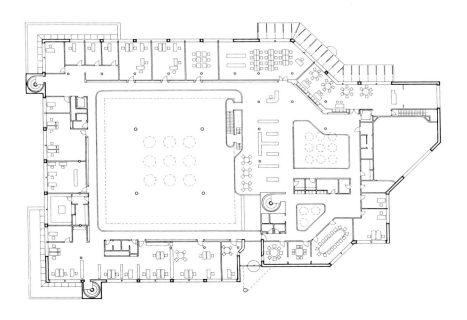

First floor plan

JOSÉ IGNACIO LINAZASORO
UNED LIBRARY
Madrid, Spain

This library, due to its location and its architectural character, stands like a gate-house to the campus of Spain's Universidad Nacional de Educació a Distancia – the equivalent of the Open University – on the banks of the Manzanares river in Madrid. It has an imposing exposed brick masonry facade which wraps around the volume, opening up only to the east, where the large windows to the research rooms and the entrance are cut out of the solid, and opening up to the skies where dramatic splayed soffits filter light from sixteen rooflights. The effect is to make an inviting and warm interior space which suits the introverted nature of the building's function.

Entering the building through a hypostyle hall, with a grid of columns, the control desk, catalogues and reading area are on the ground floor beyond a glass screen. The actual library space, on the next level, is grouped around an internal 'cone of light' formed by the gently tapering form of the circular voids, increasing in diameter as the building rises, towards the pine-panelled soffits of the rooflights. The rooflights are designed in order that no direct sunlight can reach the centre of the library and all rays are diffused by the panelling, generating a warm hued light. Parapets around the voids have been used to create reading desks which allow the users to look out over the space. Natural wood surfaces and fittings, shelves, screens and caissons add to the depth of colour and warmth of detail in the interior. Circulation through the library is easily achieved using one of two small staircases or the lifts to either side, and the contents are arranged on the different floors according to subject.

Slit clerestories appear on the facade and internally these bring light in over the heavy dark beech book stacks, arranged in parallel rows around the circular voids.

The library demonstrates the architect's expression of light as an element capable of informing the nature of the space in the most powerful way, while the elision of the two geometries of circle and square between floors – with the circular conical void lessening the dominance of the orthogonal grid – has been skilfully executed.

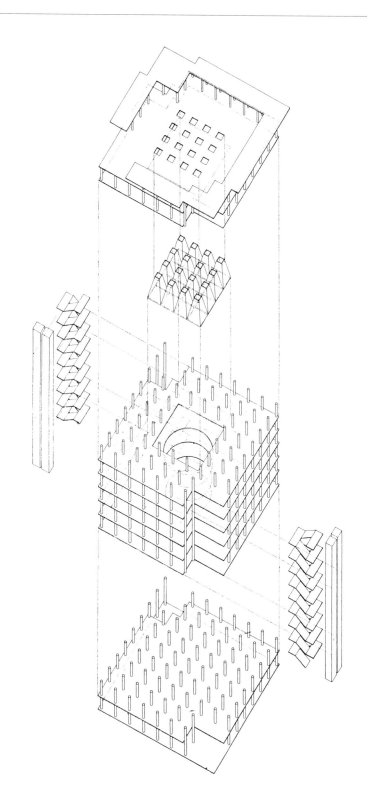

Exploded axonometric

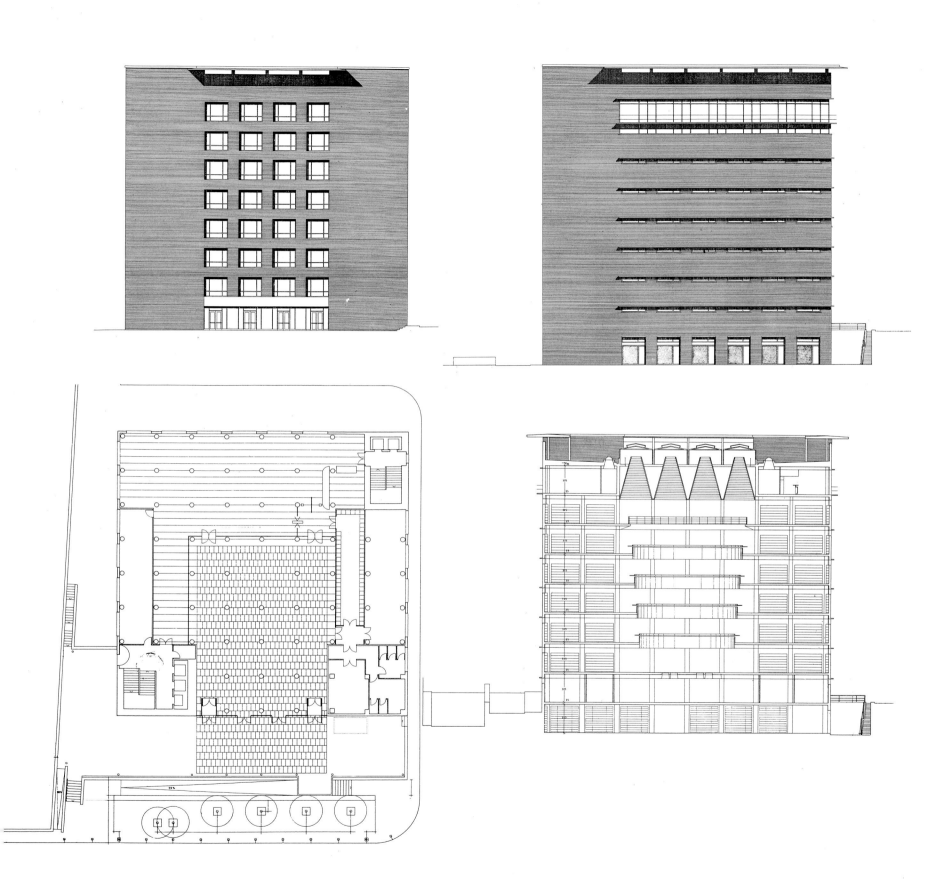

FROM ABOVE, LEFT TO RIGHT: East entrance elevation; south elevation; ground floor plan; cross section

VICTOR LÓPEZ COTELO
'THE HOUSE OF SHELLS' LIBRARY

Salamanca, Spain

The Casa de Las Conchas, the House of Shells, is a fifteenth-century building which, over the course of history and for various reasons, has undergone successive transformations. The original structure was a Gothic house with a central courtyard, and small doors and openings in the facade. Dated approximately 1492 it was built by Rodrigo Maldonado de Talavera, a professor of the University of Salamanca and a member of the Royal Council of the Catholic Kings. The building played a key role in the introduction of the Renaissance in Salamanca. On the death of the owner in 1517, his son proceeded to reform the decoration, uniting his heraldic symbols with those of his wife's family.

By the start of the eighteenth century, the facade on the Calle de la Rua was rebuilt, and in 1772 the height of the tower was reduced by twenty-three stone courses to lighten the load on the weak foundations.

In 1984, the Salamanca Town Council handed over ownership of the building to the State, who then designated it for use as a public library. It was in an extreme state of disrepair, which some partial renovation had tried to remedy. The most serious problems included the dilapidated state of the stone in many places, the subsidence and crumbling of the courtyard and the cloister, the poor condition of the walls, the deficient foundations (in many cases, actually non-existent) and the deterioration of the coffered suspended ceiling, roof structure and roof coverings. Above all, the inferior quality of many of the alterations had degraded the building to such a degree that it was unused for over twenty years.

The aim of the renovation was to eliminate all of the inherent structural problems, as well as construction elements and materials that are 'foreign' to the building. In developing the building for a public use that will enable the most important parts of the building to be visited, the library has been integrated organically within the existing typological limitations. Communication in the building has been improved with the insertion of additional circulation.

The design process focused on the identification, definition and construction of the minimum number of new elements necessary for the life of the building, elements which would co-exist with the original structures, and share the essence of the historic spirit of the building. Furniture and interior detailing is elegantly proportioned, incorporating different forms of storage and display of the library volumes. These elements have been integrated authentically by a sensitive approach to the rebuilding process.

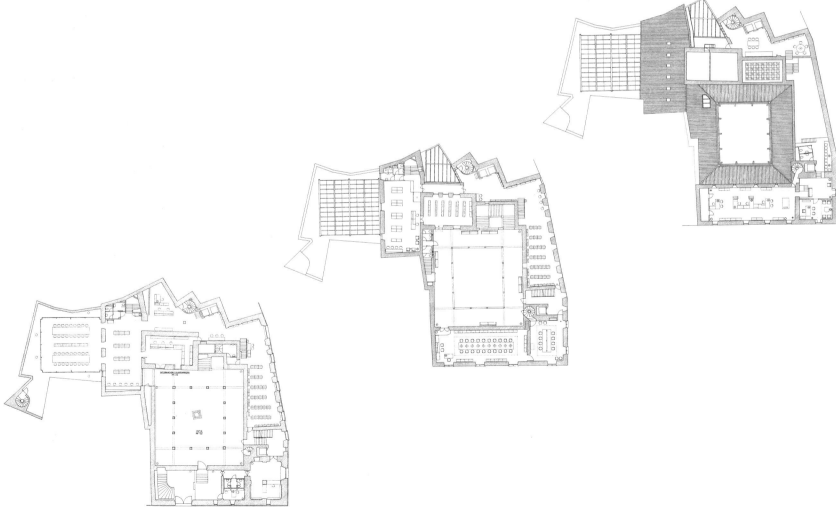

LEFT TO RIGHT: Entrance level plan; gallery level plan; third level plan

FROM ABOVE: Section through reference and audiovisual room; cross section through patio; longitudinal section through patio

LUNDE & LØVSETH
TØNSBERG PUBLIC LIBRARY

Tønsberg, Norway

For many years the Tønsberg Public Library occupied a rather old building at Haugar, in the centre of the city. A national architectural competition was held in 1988 for a new library building to service the city and surrounding communities. The inclusion of the main library of Vestfold Fylke, which covered the neighbouring cities and communities, consequently increased the project's financial viability and enhanced the administration of the library.

Under kunnskapens trær (under trees of knowledge), was the title of the winning scheme, which, after a series of political and economic difficulties, commenced development early in 1990. To a large degree this was due to the constant efforts of Erik Carlson, Tønsberg's mayor. The estate developers established and administer a limited company, which acts as the landlord of the building.

The new library is constructed directly on the ruins of the St Olav Monastery, founded in 1180. The ruins of buildings and ship graves from the Viking age were uncovered during a comprehensive archaeological excavation between 1987 and 1991. The history and the design of the original monastery was a main source of inspiration in the design of the new building, explained in the following competition description:

The new library should express modern times and evoke images of the monastery and the Middle Ages in Tønsberg. Interacting with the library square, the ruins and the circular St Olav Church, the new library must act as a key building in the city, and as a gate to the city centre. To underline the historical context, a new 'monastery' wall will be constructed on the probable position of the original wall. This new wall will form a fragment of a circle, with its centre in the ruins of St Olav Church. In this way a new geometrical framework will be created as a basis for the new library.

The new wall will divide the library into two departments with different functions and design. One part, containing the staff areas and the quiet public zones will be given a heavy and closed expression. The other, facing north, the main street Storgata, the library square and the St Olav Church, will contain the main public spaces, and be light and transparent.

The original monastery gardens have inspired a light, airy roof structure covering the public spaces, formed as a number of large vaults in steel and glass. These vaults will resemble the original Roman vaults of the monastery. The construction materials of the original monastery – stone and brick, timber roof structure, and courtyards covered with stone tiles and occasional bricks – have determined the choice of materials.

Light steel vaults cover the main spaces. These consist of vaulted main beams and straight secondary beams, resting on steel 'tree trunks'. In contrast, the other, quieter department is constructed of concrete floor slabs and walls, with exterior brick facades.

The main public space is dominated by the brick-covered 'monastery' wall, stone tile flooring on the ground floor and light wooden boards on the galleries. The columns are made distinct by their dark grey paint, the colour used for all the load-bearing steelwork in the building.

The corrugated aluminium roofing sheets and the alloyed steel ceiling sheets create a very light expression, in contrast to the heavy brick wall. The minimally detailed curtain wall uses a non-profile system, loads being transferred through glass fins from top to bottom, at right angles to the glazing panels. The interior walls of the staff department are painted stucco, or simply painted. Most offices have interior glass walls towards the common areas.

A local history exhibition displaying archaeological artefacts and poster boards occupies the north-west corner of the main public space. A brass model, sunk into the floor, shows the ruins and a reconstruction of the original monastery. The ship graves are marked in the ground floor at their point of discovery. Original writings, signs and objects appear in the masonry of the new 'monastery' wall, and the end of the wall is crowned by a masonry head of St Olav.

Lunde & Løvseth have designed the historical exhibition and model, in co-operation with the Norwegian National Preservation Fund of Tønsberg, as well as the reception and information desks on each floor. The remaining furniture was designed by a local interior architect.

The entrance to the library is on the square, where a surface of concrete and stone tiles, a continuation of the ground floor of the library, is designed to incorporate chess and other games from the Middle Ages. Trees are planted in the square on the axis of the structural steel columns.

The design of the library and the organisation of its services anticipates more than a thousand visitors a day. The staff of the library have installed modern equipment, including a specially-designed automatic book-handling machine. In addition to a collection of approximately three hundred thousand books, the library will gradually develop a separate music department, a collection of local literature and other topics of special interest.

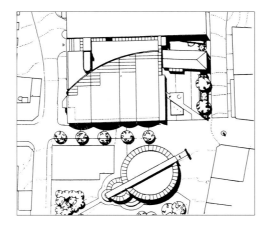

Site plan

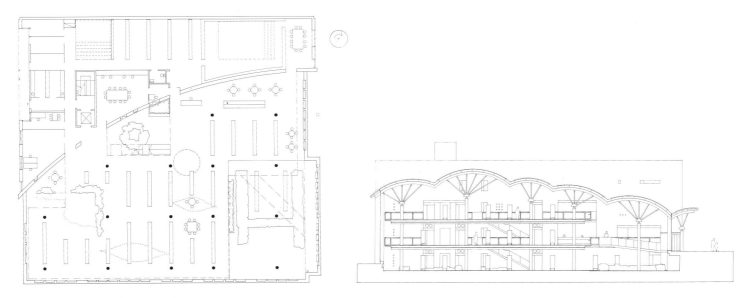

FROM LEFT TO RIGHT: Basement level plan; section

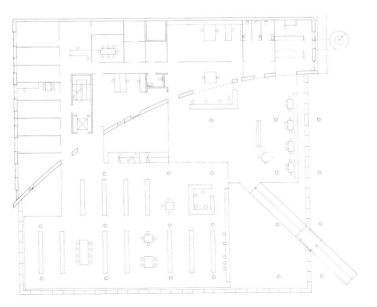
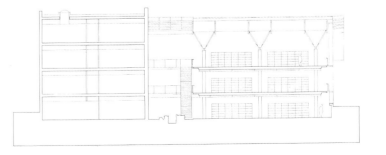

FROM LEFT TO RIGHT: Entrance floor plan; section

MECANOO
ALMELO PUBLIC LIBRARY

Almelo, The Netherlands

The site chosen by the municipality of Almelo for the new public library is opposite the town hall, a Modernist building which was the last work by the De Stijl architect, JJP Oud. The close proximity of this building, along with the complex urban context and the diverse requirements of the project's brief – which included the provision of space for a local radio station – presented a formidable challenge.

In designing a public library, the architect must address contradictory requirements: on the one hand the building must appeal to the public by being open and inviting, while on the other it must provide a secure and controlled environment for the books stored within. At Almelo the resolution of these divergent factors became the leitmotiv of the design. Three conceptual layers (the important features of the location, the specific features of the programme, and the required elements of the brief) informed the building's development.

Each of the individual elements in the programme – an information centre, a reading cafe, a studio for the radio station, reading corners and book storage (spaces which differ greatly in function and character) – have been given their own spatial articulation, which in turn has led to the different material surfaces and textural qualities.

The building's two volumes are also differentiated through their forms and various materials. In section, with levels vertically staggered at half-levels on the east–west axis of the building, they are separated by a relatively narrow light well. This open space is crossed by stairs which, although appearing temporary, like a ship's gangplank, join the different levels and make it possible to experience the dynamic space between them.

The elongated curved volume, like a ship projecting from the Haven Noordzijde along Het Baken to the Stadhuisplein, has a slightly receding, sawtoothed, transparent facade on the ground floor allowing passers-by to view the activities inside. The ground floor is the public zone, where the large free-flowing space incorporates the information centre, the lending counters and a reading area. This open area contrasts with the closed character of the copper-clad storeys above, where, on the first and second floors are located the book stacks and, to the south end of the plan, the spaces for the activities and reception area of the local radio station. The canteen, meeting room, offices and technical service areas are housed in the roof structure. Three enclosed, smaller volumes end in broad glass fronts over the full height of the ground storey. A spine 'wall' of dark grey brick running north–south between the two volumes contains services, stairs and offices.

By maintaining the line of the street, the appearance of the library is mainly determined by the slightly curved, copper-clad east facade. The zinc roof structure facing the town hall is designed as a separate volume. The ultramarine of the south and north elevations and the oxidising copper of the east facade enter into a modest modern dialogue with Oud's town hall.

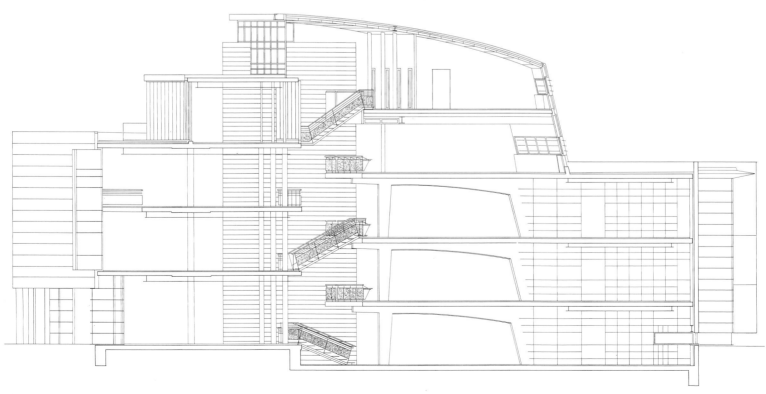

Section

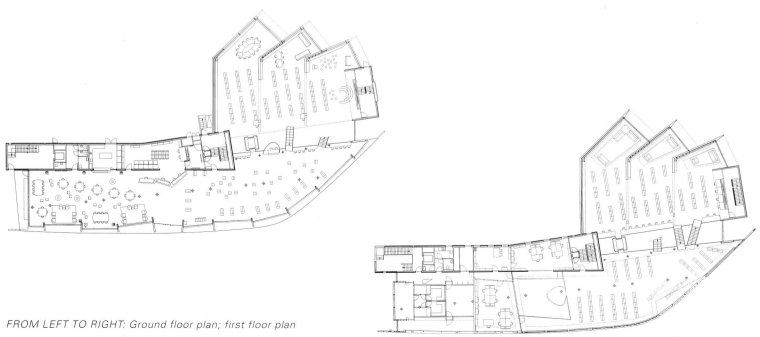

FROM LEFT TO RIGHT: Ground floor plan; first floor plan

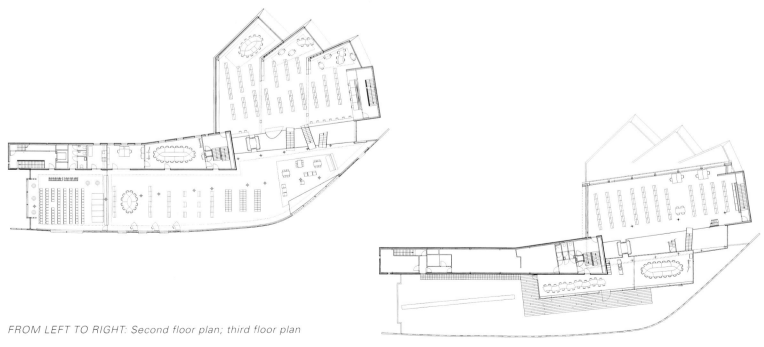

FROM LEFT TO RIGHT: Second floor plan; third floor plan

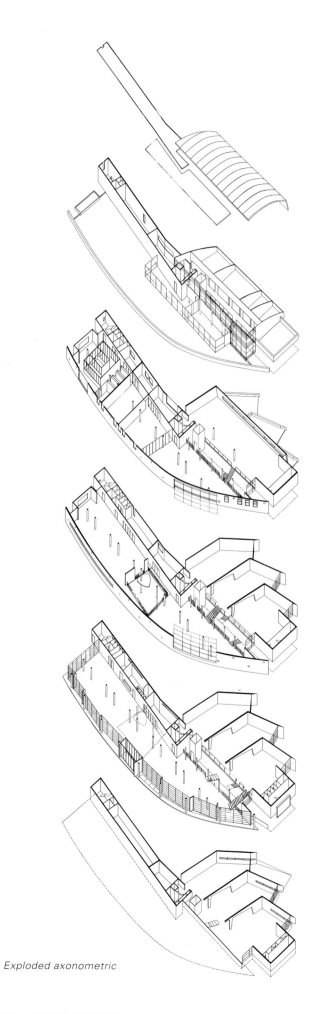

Exploded axonometric

RICHARD MEIER & PARTNERS
THE HAGUE CITY LIBRARY

The Hague, The Netherlands

Richard Meier & Partners won the competition for the City Hall complex in The Hague, with this scheme where the complex is organised around two grids that are derived from the outline of the available wedge-shaped site, situated between Kalvermarkt and Turfmarkt. The surrounding urban fabric is structured according to the same divergent, but orthogonal geometry.

This continuous structure, measuring approximately 240 metres by 75 metres and an overall area of 104,500 square metres, includes a council chamber, civic wedding room, central public library and a large number of local government offices. The library is located on the corner of the Spui and the Kalvermarkt, and the city offices in two wings on the Kalvermarkt and the Turfmarkt. These civic elements are combined with a semi-independent rental office building at its north-eastern end, on the Muzenplein, and an extensive shopping frontage on the ground floor. The main twelve- and ten-storey horizontal office slabs, which diverge from each other at an angle of 10.5 degrees, flank a large internal atrium that forms the new *res publica* of the city known as the Citizen's Hall.

The main library, with its concentric semi-circular plan, is located at the extreme north-western corner of the site, where its dynamic form imparts a strong character to the principal plaza that it also encloses and defines. Another element on the plaza at this point is the Hulshoff home furnishing store on the Spui that will be rebuilt and expanded beneath the library. The plaza extends into the library, into a reception and orientation area and a cafe. Free-standing escalators provide circulation between floors and, as in the City Hall, this sequence progresses from the more public at ground level to more private, administrative services on the upper levels.

The glass roof of the atrium is supported by free-beams. The aerial bridges spanning the atrium, together with the elevator cores, are of white painted steel, the lightness and elegance of which is intended to give the impression of a light screen subtly subdividing the large volume. The prefabricated and poured-in-place concrete structure is clad externally with white porcelain enamel aluminum panels.

The library provides a much-needed replacement for the old overcrowded central library on the Bilderdijkstraat. On the ground floor of the library are the lending desk, newspapers and magazines, exhibition space and a lively reading cafe. The information department is on the first floor and the children's department and general fiction on the second floor. The third, fourth and fifth floors house, respectively, linguistics, literature, geography, history and the Antillian collection; music, art and video; and technology and natural sciences, religion, social sciences, law and economics. Offices and administration are on the sixth and seventh floors. Throughout the library, computer terminals can access the library's catalogue, and six hundred individual study places are distributed on each of the floors. Twenty-four enclosed carrels for quiet study are on the third, fourth and fifth floors.

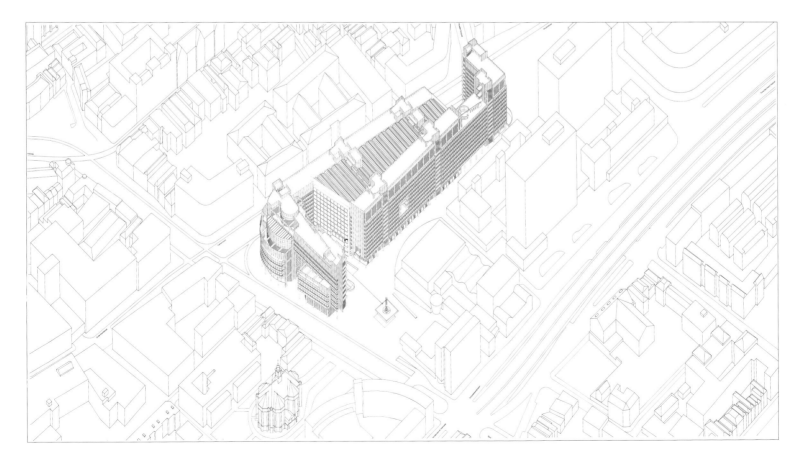

Site axonometric

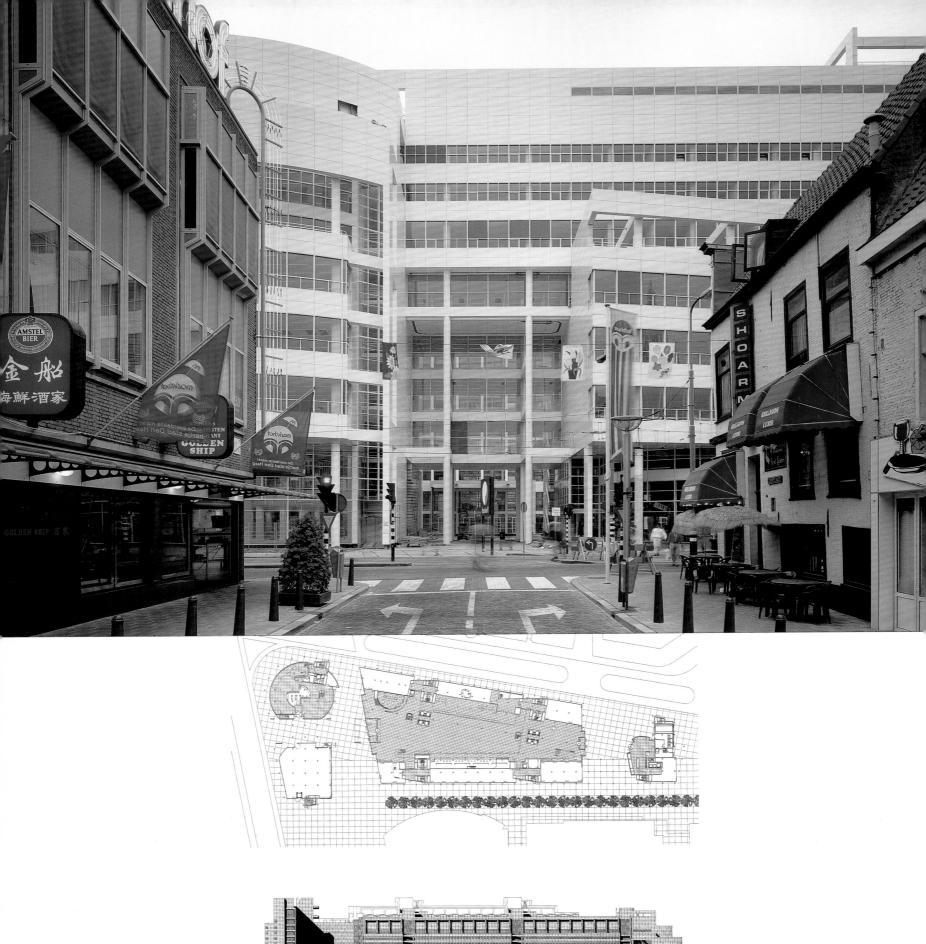

FROM ABOVE: Ground floor plan; north-west elevation on Kalvermarkt

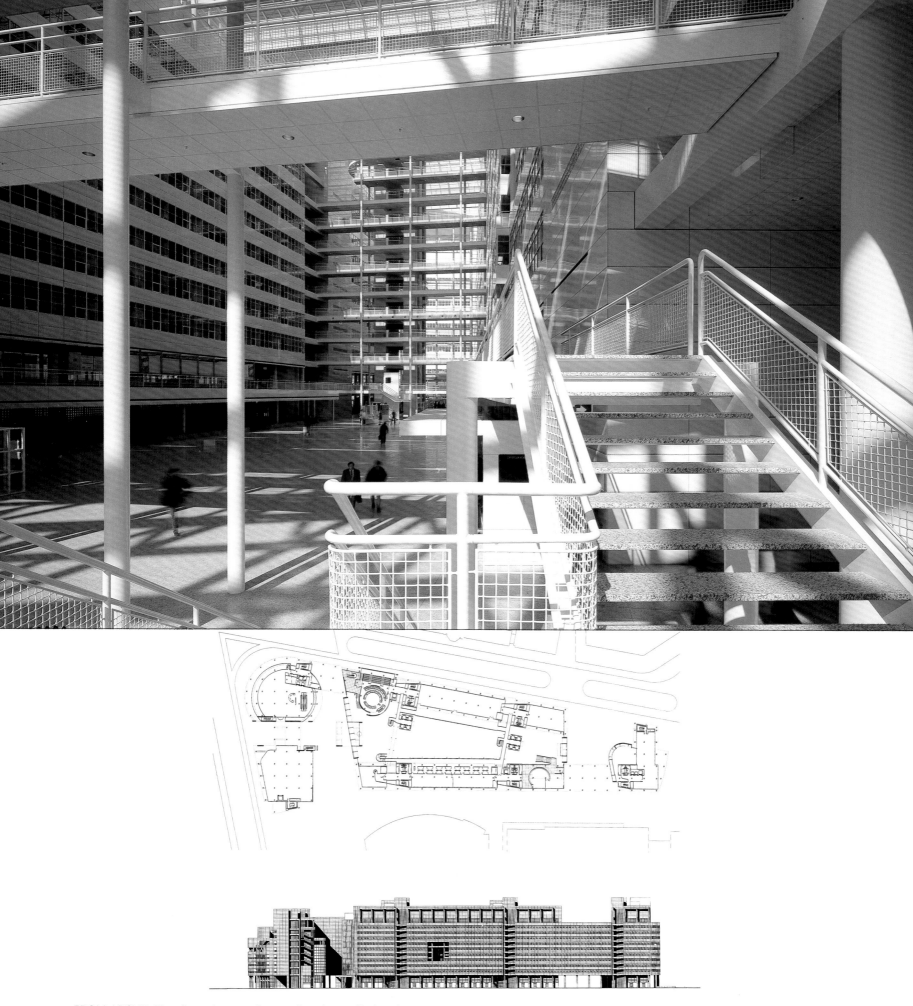

FROM ABOVE: First floor plan; south-east elevation on Turfmarkt

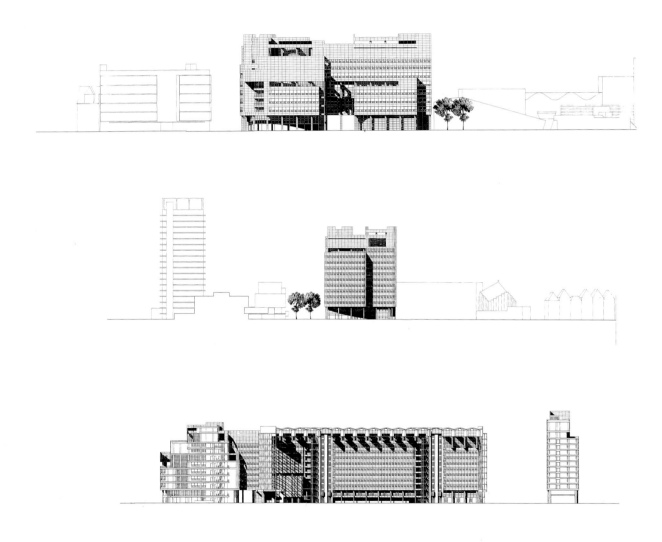

FROM ABOVE: South-west elevation; north-east elevation; east-west section

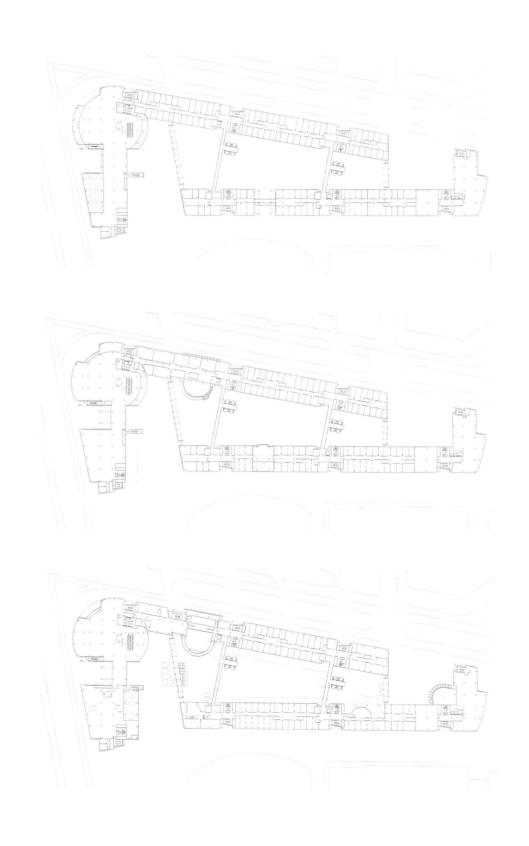

FROM ABOVE: Sixth floor plan; fourth floor plan; second floor plan

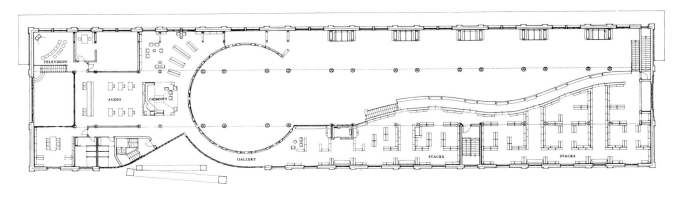

FROM ABOVE: North elevation; south
elevation; second floor plan; ground floor plan

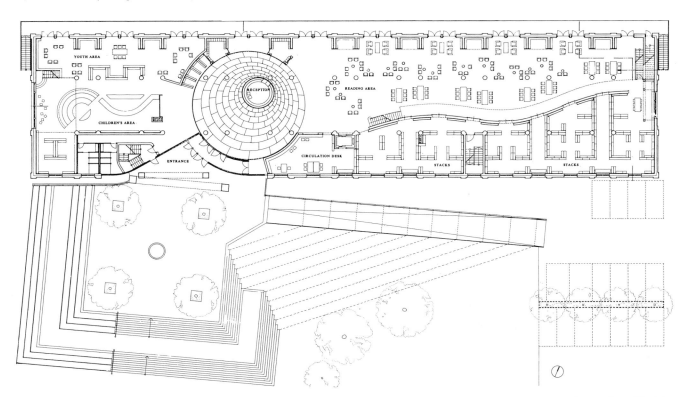

MOORE RUBLE YUDELL
HUMBOLDT LIBRARY
Tegel Harbour, Berlin, Germany

This branch library forms the first phase of the Cultural Centre for the Tegel Harbour Master Plan. Its construction, started in 1986, coincided with the creation of a large water area adjacent to the harbour, plus a waterfront promenade and three hundred and fifty units of housing.

The library forms one edge of the Cultural Centre, its long hall continuing the axis of the harbour, along the north boundary of the site. The view from the main reading room offers a forested landscape. Elsewhere, the presence of industrial structures contrasts with well-preserved buildings in a range of nineteenth-century styles.

The carefully proportioned industrial loft became the prototype for the library. Its classical facade is broken with a glass entrance bay, framed by a pair of free-standing portals. This leads to a central rotunda encircled by an arcaded balcony on the second floor. From the rotunda, a grand wall of books meanders along one side of the main reading room, and gives access to the open stacks and smaller reading alcoves beyond. Passing continuously above the various areas of the loft is a double-layer, vaulted ceiling lit by a clerestory window, which throws light around and through the lower vault. On the north side, the light is balanced by a series of bay windows and doors that alternate with niches for books.

The steel and concrete frame is exposed on the interior, and this industrial toughness is elaborated into a playful, almost baroque set of details for arches and ceiling. The book wall itself is composed of painted and natural hardwood. Exterior materials – metal sash, stucco and the standing seam zinc roof – combine with the classical elements of precast concrete.

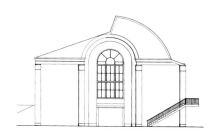 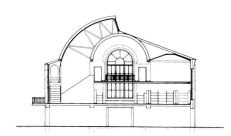 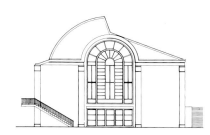

FROM ABOVE, LEFT TO RIGHT: East elevation; cross section; west elevation; cut-away axonometric

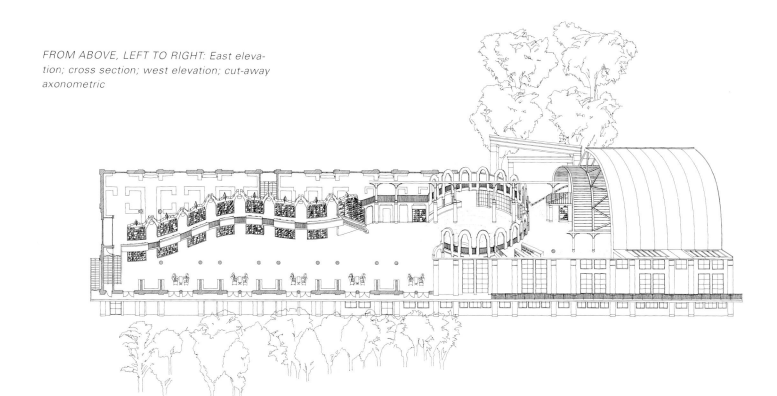

JUAN NAVARRO BALDEWEG
PUERTA DE TOLEDO LIBRARY
Glorieta Puerta de Toledo, Madrid, Spain

In order to fully understand the nature of this project it is essential to take into account the comprehensive redesign of the area around the Puerta de Toledo.

Firstly, the ground levels were redefined, which was most noticable at the rear of the Glorieta (a small square), and where the highest part meets Toledo Street. The levels of the square in front of the Iglesia Virgen de la Paloma (Virgin of the Dove church) have been mostly retained, following the ground's natural slope until it reaches the Glorieta, which can then be reached by a ramp. A supporting wall and the ramp are mirrored in the library's plinth on the other side of Toledo Street.

The library building has a deliberate scale and presence in the Glorieta of the Puerta de Toledo. Over-scaled buildings around the edge of the square would have obscured the Puerta de López Aguado and destroyed the visual links with the Parque de Bomberos (fireman's park), which had to be preserved. The openness of the high square on the opposite side of Toledo Street will complement the fullness of the Library's drum-shaped dome. The simultaneous opposition of concave and convex spaces introduces a tension which is essential to the spatial experience of the square.

In the library project it can be appreciated how three important elements were exploited. Firstly, the effect of the floor plan on the programme, secondly, the identification of the external form as an archetypal domed drum and finally, the internal layout and programmed requirements as a result of the form. The library as a civic building stands out in the square, its profile clearly marked. The drum's volume, by the generality of its form, adheres to the very varied requirements of the surrounding urban space.

The building has four floors into which the functions of the library's general programme have been divided.

On the ground floor and basement, with an independent side entrance, is a children's library. Some eighty reading seats, thirteen thousand four hundred books for loan and a reading room are fitted together and there are tables and an activity area for twenty children. The children's library can also be reached from the floor above, which allows flexibility, should one desire a centralised control by the main entrance at street level, or an independent control. This lower floor also has a general book storage which is about 160 square metres, and a machine and air-conditioning room accessed from the side street.

The floor above, at street level, contains a lending room with a capacity for forty-four thousand books in book shelves placed in a circle for easy access and control. Also on this floor can be found the meeting room, with a capacity for seventy people. From here visitors can reach the next floor either by stairs or lifts. The reading room also has an independent entrance by stair ramp from the Glorieta of the Puerta de Toledo. The room has a split level area where bookshelves are placed in a series of steps. It houses a hundred and fifty-six reading seats and can take up to ten thousand books on its shelves. An audio-visual area with room for fourteen audio posts and eighteen video seats complete the layout of the second floor. A magazine area with about twenty seats has also been planned.

The structural design and the effects of natural light inside the drum dome have created a special effect in the project.

The exterior faces of the plinth are grey granite and the upper part of the library is natural white stone. In the design of these facades, the quartering of the stone, the composition of the hollows and the treatment of the cladding, as well as their relationship to buildings on the other side of Toledo Street have been fully considered.

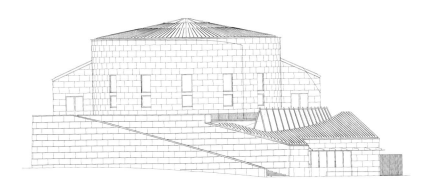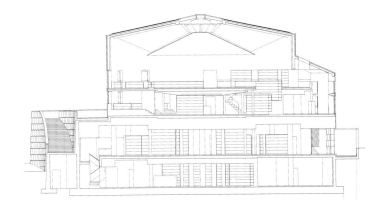

LEFT TO RIGHT: Entrance elevation; cross section

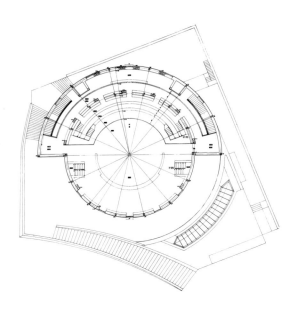

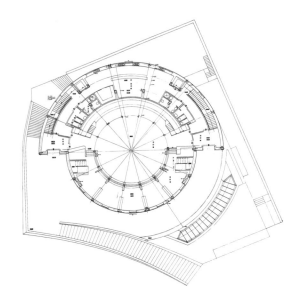

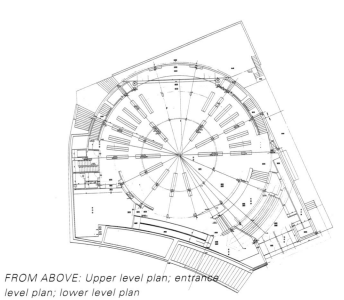

FROM ABOVE: Upper level plan; entrance level plan; lower level plan

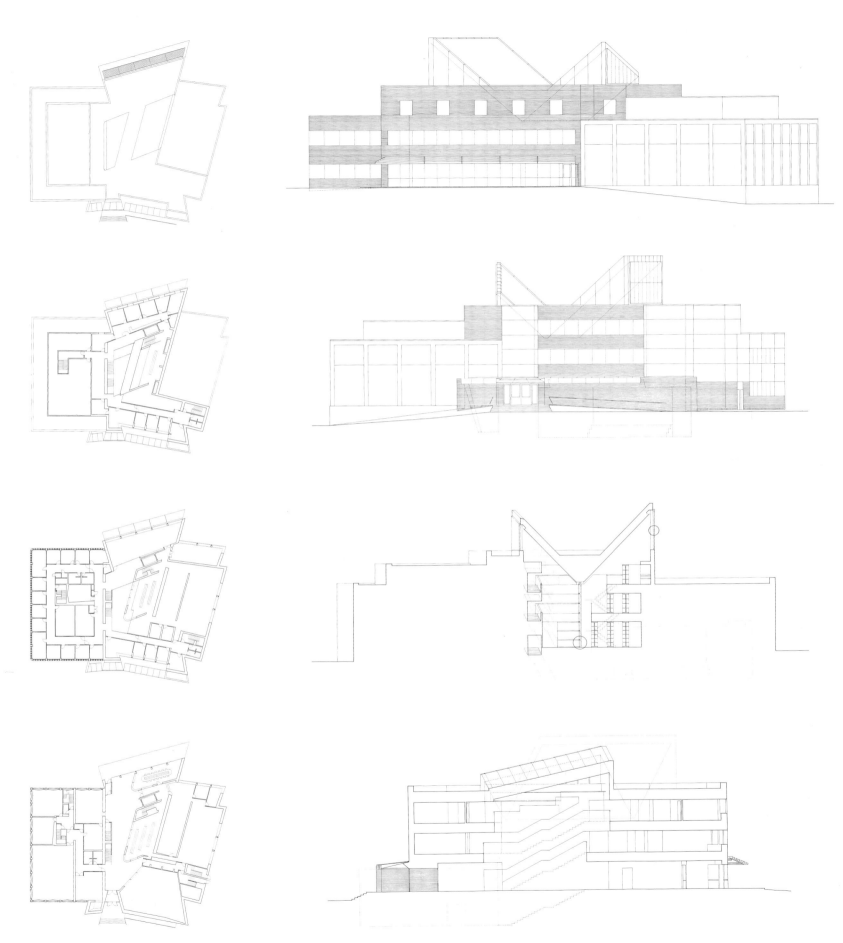

LEFT, FROM ABOVE: Roof level plan; second floor plan; first floor plan; ground floor plan; RIGHT, FROM ABOVE: West elevation; east elevation; cross section through central circulation space; longitudinal section

JUAN NAVARRO BALDEWEG
WOOLWORTH CENTER LIBRARY

Princeton, New Jersey, USA

Within the formal structure of the Princeton campus, it is possible to distinguish the characteristic patterns created by the superimposition of buildings, open spaces, streets and walkways. These existing patterns helped to inform the preliminary designs for the new addition to the Woolworth Center of Music.

The Woolworth building sits between two very distinct open spaces. The 1879 Green, located between 1879 Hall, Palmer Lab, the School of Architecture and McCosh Hall, is a beautiful open space that is crossed by pedestrian walkways. It is like a plaza or street, enlivened by students travelling to classes. To the west, the garden of Prospect House has a more tranquil character, on a domestic scale.

The new addition to Woolworth houses the library, a new rehearsal room, additional faculty offices and a new administrative suite for the Music Department. It is entered on the existing entrance axis and the proposed atrium lobby fans out to welcome the visitor to the building, taking on the contextual characteristics of a street, covered walkway, route and plaza. It is also a connection between the green and the garden of Prospect House.

The lobby divides the building in half. On one side is the teaching wing with classrooms, offices and practice rooms, and on the other, the entrance to the new rehearsal hall and the library. On entering the lobby,

it is possible to glimpse through a window, down into the double-height rehearsal hall, as well as, through a glass wall, the symbolic terraced stacks of the library.

The building layout attempts to relate the functions of the building and their needs for proximity and independence. A staircase situated in the lobby will be the main access to the Center's activities. Primary access to the basement-level rehearsal room is by an internal staircase located within the hall. Also at basement level, there are storage areas, for students' instruments, musical scores and other needs of the rehearsal room, as well as the new practice rooms.

The library is entered from the lobby on the main floor and it is possible to proceed from here to the other levels by an internal staircase or lift. The lift, in addition to providing access for physically impaired users, also facilitates the transport of books and documents between floors.

The functions of the library have been divided to allow activities requiring supervision and assistance to be located on the first floor, less intensive activities on the second floor and finally the quiet, independent study activities at the top. Thus, the circulation desk, offices, workroom, record library, closed stacks, some open stacks and the listening room are located at ground level. Above this are the open stacks, microfilm stations and reading

area, as well as the graduate seminar room. Finally, on the upper level are the graduate carrels and a small number of stacks.

The quieter activities, including the listening room and the main reading room of the library, are behind the permeable and transparent west facade which looks out to the sheltered garden of Prospect House. The direct light is diffused by three-dimensional sunscreens.

Natural light has been carefully considered as a fundamental aspect of the design. Light entering the building emphasises the bilateralism of the addition: north light flows indirectly towards the terracing floors of the library from the main skylight and warm southern light illuminates the large vertical lobby space. Although the light in the library is cool, the use of wood for flooring and furniture gives warmth and increases comfort.

The new building has a revealed structural framework which can be thought of, abstractly, as bones and flesh: stone is the shell or covering and brick the flesh which is revealed when the shell is cut away.

The materials proposed both on the exterior and interior are selective (brick, stone, wood, glass and opaque white walls). However, the careful use of these materials highlights their intrinsic qualities and allows the organic nature of the architecture to be clearly expressed.

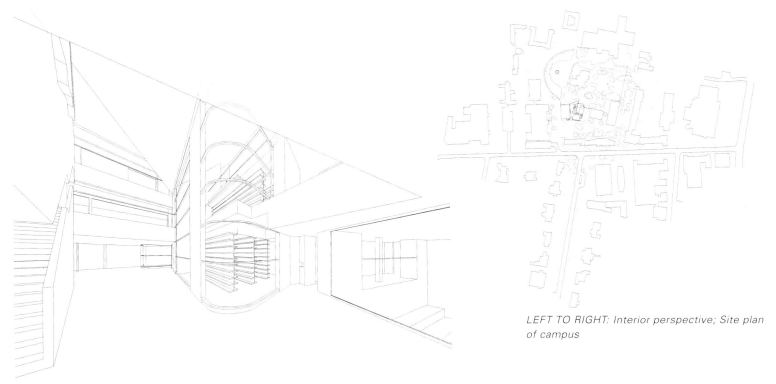

LEFT TO RIGHT: Interior perspective; Site plan of campus

NURMELA – RAIMORANTA – TASA
KUHMO LIBRARY
Kuhmo, Finland

Kuhmo Library was built on the basis of a competition entry, 'Atalante', which won the open design competition in 1984. In form, it looks for an abstract expression which is in line with the Modern tradition yet enhances certain subjective qualities, such as a sense of locality, an element of surprise and openness to interpretation. The desire for a comprehensive design meant that nearly all of the furnishings and light fittings were also designed by the architects.

Externally the building presents different faces to the surroundings. A colonnade of blue concrete columns regulates the facade to the lake and the entrance portico extends through the building as a circulation route intersecting several parts of the library. Rendered and painted clay bricks form the outer skin and a patterned concrete plinth is highlighted in dark blue

ceramic tiles to distinguish specific areas.

The interiors have used light, colours and high internal spaces to achieve airiness and freshness. The large windows of the library hall look out over the lake to the north, a clerestory allows light in from the south on to the sloping ceiling and dramatic conical skylights provide channelled light.

The main library functions – reading room, children's activity area, children's books and lending hall – are located on one level, on the circulation route which runs alongside the core wall that starts from the entrance. Star and sky motifs are a recurrent image throughout: a playful stair enclosure has cut out lozenges in the glossy blue surface, and the constellations twinkle in the ceiling over the children's section, an oval glass box which stands apart from the main construction, both

internally and externally.

A section for children to listen to music is housed in a 'giant's hat', with the technical equipment concealed in the crown. This section is opposite a cafe which is floored with parquet and fitted with red beech furnishings. An upper gallery above the children's section, reached by the blue stair tower, offers a view over the library hall and has seating arranged in groups.

Ceiling and roof structures change throughout the different areas, lending to the distinction of each zone. Timber and cable trusses support the roof over the circulation route and timber trees reach into the starry sky in the oval children's area. The sloped ceiling in the main hall has been faced with painted horizontal wooden panelling; elsewhere, painted plasterboard or concrete is used.

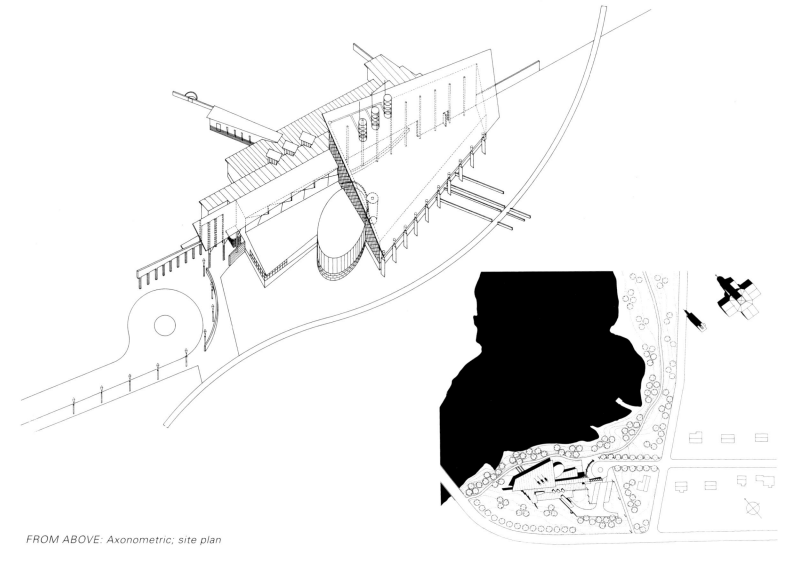

FROM ABOVE: Axonometric; site plan

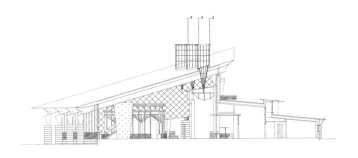

FROM ABOVE: Cross section through main reading room; cross section through children's library and entry space

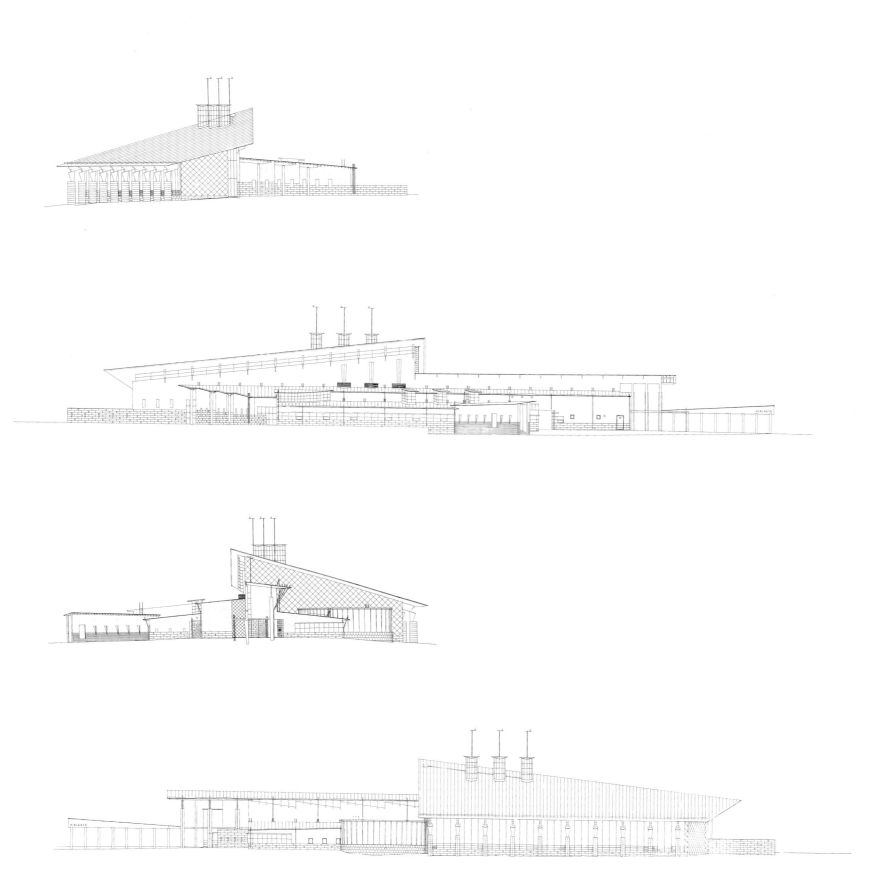

FROM ABOVE: West elevation; south entrance elevation; east elevation; north elevation

PATKAU ARCHITECTS
NEWTON PUBLIC LIBRARY
Newton, Surrey, British Columbia, Canada

The library's six-acre site (also shared with a senior citizen's recreation facility) is adjacent to a neighbourhood retail centre and surrounded by existing and proposed, low-density residential neighbourhoods. Prior to development the site was largely covered by a scrub deciduous forest of alders with intermittent patches of evergreen rain forest of cedar, hemlock and fir, characteristic to the region.

Special attention was paid to retaining the original evergreens by careful location of the library, recreation facility and associated parking. New deciduous trees were planted in a regular grid in the parking areas to create a clear juxtaposition between the apparently random nature of the original forest and the simple geometric order of buildings and parking areas.

The library was located along the south edge of the site. In order to give it the presence appropriate to a public institution adrift in the sea of 'strip malls' and residential suburbs, as well as to give some definition to the street, the height of the single-storey perimeter walls to the north and south were exaggerated. Not only does this give the building greater presence on the street, it also allows large amounts of natural light to enter the building in controlled ways. The south side is layered and shaped to modify the sometimes harsh south sun while the north glass 'curtain wall' allows soft north light to fill the interior with a quiet luminosity. The resultant 'sidedness' of the building is one

of its architectural characteristics. The transparency of the building also helps to communicate its purpose to the surrounding community.

While the perimeter walls to the north and south are exaggerated in height to give the library a public presence, the scale of the entrance, next to the principal vehicular access to the site, is compressed, even intimate. This compression in the cross section forms a valley which runs the entire length of the building, and maintains a scale, established at the entrance, along the principal circulation spine. The resultant inward sloping ceiling planes help drive light entering the high side walls deep into the interior.

Robust concrete columns support the valley which marks the central circulation spine of the building. The valley, in conjunction with a complementary pitched attic space above the roof, provides a plenum which houses the major air distribution ducts leading from a mechanical service room located directly above the entrance. The service room, rather than being hidden or concealed, is expressed, forming a jaunty 'penthouse' to the exterior. The cross section of the attic space diminishes, as the number and size of ducts reduce, as it moves away from the penthouse. The changing intersection of attic and valley results in a cross-slope which drains rainwater over large galvanised steel scuppers on to rocky rectangular beds on the ground, to permeate back into the site.

The construction of the building is likened to the natural 'sticks and stones' of the region; a heavy timber (glu-lam) structural frame on a concrete foundation. The construction elements establish the primary character of the building shell.

However, the light of the Vancouver area can be very soft, even weak, under the frequently overcast skies of winter, and the robust, light-absorbing heavy timber and concrete, in themselves, do not distribute light into the deep floor plate. For this reason painted gypsum board on the interior, and stucco on the exterior was overlaid on portions of the building frame. The cladding of ceilings and walls acts to reflect light from the edges to the centre of the building. In addition, this ceiling, in conjunction with the attic of the roof, houses and distributes the mechanical and electrical systems of the building.

Where its luminous and enclosing characteristics are not required, the layer of cladding is feathered out to its own thickness, eventually giving way to exposed construction. Here the tectonic, more durable parts of the building extend outside to form a rain canopy.

The library, set in a suburban area on the edge of forest and agricultural land which has no precedent for public institutions, has chosen an extrovert form to provide a scale for future community and civic buildings, while the finely detailed interior creates intimate spaces for the act of reading.

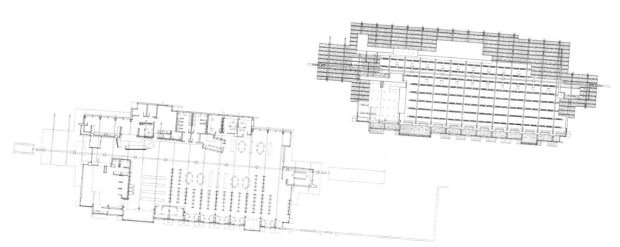

LEFT TO RIGHT: Ground floor plan; reflected ceiling plan

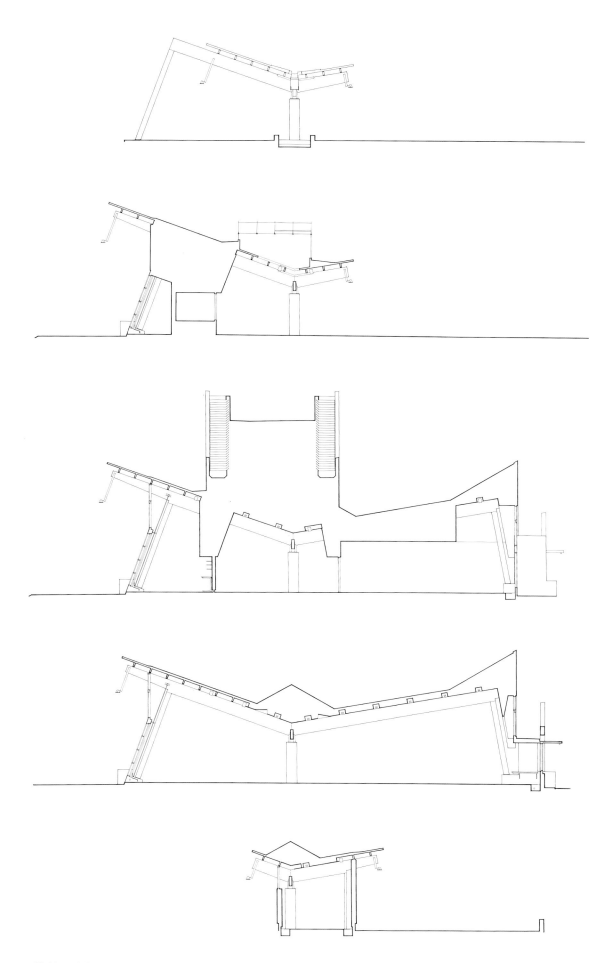

FROM ABOVE: Cross sections, showing progression of 'valley' from entrance to end of building

PEREA, MOSTAZA & VALLHONRAT
GRANADA PUBLIC LIBRARY
Granada, Spain

Founded in the eighth century by the Moors, Granada has a rich and complex history, with many famous examples of Moorish architecture. Granada Public Library, which is also the Library of Andalusia, is built at the edge of the historic centre, on agricultural land belonging to the nearby convents. Recent local planning has recreated the medieval street layout of the city. The imposition of the library on the residential fabric of the city follows the traditional patterns of the large institutional buildings of the city: the Palace of Charles V, the delicate Nasrid texture of the Alhambra, the Renaissance cathedral or the nearby convent of St Jeronimo.

The library thus occupies the entire perimeter of the site, creating residual spaces of restricted dimensions, which produce defined perceptions of the building, in the nature of medieval Mediterranean streets of an Islamic tradition.

A large box, 60 metres by 40 metres, encloses the structural matrix with white concrete, creating a hermetic whole in which light is captured in very specific and localised ways. The ground level is entirely glazed to varying height levels to accommodate the changes in ground level; the glass strips permit the passing public a perception of the interior.

The roof plane of the building is cut by a grid of lattices and skylights which diffuse and tame the strong light of Granada, to give controlled illumination of the library spaces. The floors are organised in concentric rings around the central space which cuts through all levels of the library, and assists in orienting the reader. Beneath this central nave-like space, or 'bowl', is the lecture hall, entered from the ground floor and descending into the basement.

Present-day use of the library incorporates such diverse activities that the whole building has been unified by a spatial simplicity, in which the representative traditions of the library are recognisable. Within the system of superior and lateral illumination, the hierarchy of levels and library functions are complexly articulated, with a 'ritual' route of circulation through the stepped 'bowl' to the different levels. The larger representative spaces – the reading rooms, the lending section and audio-visual material – are gathered around the central space. Within the terraced nature, there is, however, an implied flexibility in the function of the spaces.

Slender, white concrete columns arranged in a series of peristyles line the central space, playing a Western linearity against the Islamic traditions and an interpretation of a singular isotropic reading room. An arcade surrounds the north-eastern perimeter, its exterior wall entirely glazed, and to the south and west corners are similarly illuminated wells that allow daylight into the interior. These spaces reinforce the intentional ambiguity of the relationship between interior and exterior, in a similar way to the architecture, gardens and courtyards of the Alhambra.

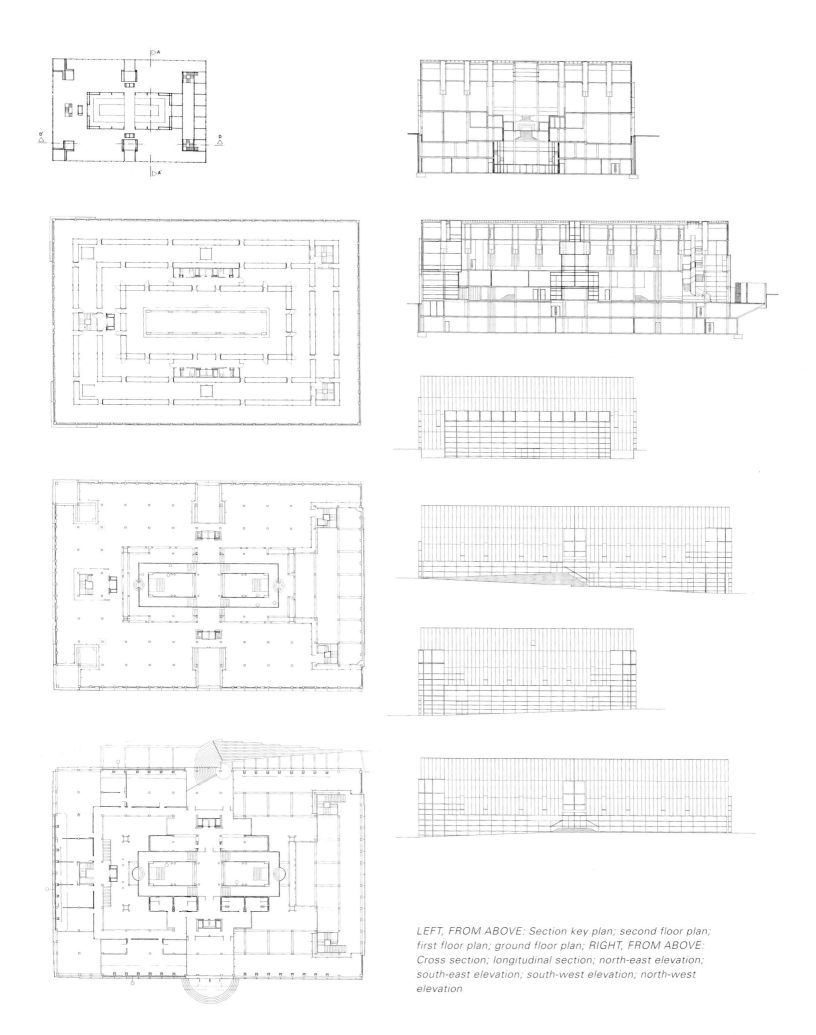

LEFT, FROM ABOVE: Section key plan; second floor plan;
first floor plan; ground floor plan; RIGHT, FROM ABOVE:
Cross section; longitudinal section; north-east elevation;
south-east elevation; south-west elevation; north-west
elevation

DOMINIQUE PERRAULT
THE NATIONAL LIBRARY OF FRANCE
Tolbiac, Paris, France

The brief for the new national library in Paris as part of Mitterrand's *Grands Projets*, stipulated that the building 'should be neither a temple nor a supermarket', but should bring France once more to the forefront of Europe, as the new national library of France. Perrault has created the Bibliothèque Nationale de France, a national monument for the consumer of knowledge, which neither exudes opulence or grandeur nor boldly advertises itself in a brash or populist manner.

Perrault won the international competition for the Bibliothèque de France (as it was originally called) with his scheme of four 'open book' towers around a large sub-merged garden and an esplanade towards the banks of the Seine, which proposed 'a square for Paris, a library for France', drawing upon the precedents of other areas of Paris, the Champ-de-Mars, the Invalides, the Tuileries and the Jardin des Plantes. The glass towers were to take the majority of the collection of books and, around the below-ground garden, were the reading and research rooms, exhibition and reception areas.

It was originally planned to take the collection of post-1944 volumes currently stored haphazardly in Henri Labrouste's Bibliothèque Nationale – a total of some five million volumes – as well as to accommodate an increase in the present level of journals and periodicals, and purchase of contemporary volumes. After a government decision, the brief was reviewed mid-programme to incorporate the greater part of the Bibliothèque Nationale collection, nearly twelve million volumes. With this

the storage of rare books was revised and many of these storage areas are now below ground.

Covering an area of industrial wasteland of some seven and a half hectares, and bordering the Seine for 380 metres, the building is composed of four L-shaped towers on a plinth with a subterranean void in the centre. The plinth, which forms concentric rings around a void is overlaid with wooden boards, forming a public esplanade similar in size to the Place de la Concorde, with large tread boards which step down to the Seine. Visitors enter the building down sloping travelators at either end of the void from the esplanade, to a sunken garden of approximately two hundred and fifty trees – oaks, hornbeams, Scots pine and birch. The garden, over-looked by the researcher's reading rooms and specialised public libraries arranged on mezzanine levels, provides a calm, contemplative environment for concen-trated study. The concentric rings of the basement also have a peripheral ring of technical services – heating, ventilation, electrical and mechanical systems, book circulation – to ensure a continuity of information and to enable connection to be made from any point. Public spaces – currently the auditorium, exhibition space and small lecture and meeting rooms – are also housed in the basement, and these will be supplemented by retail and cafe facilities.

The four towers, 80 metres high, house offices and book stores. They are externally faced in glass but internally screened with mobile wooden shutters. They are intercon-

nected by an internal network of circulation services for the conveyance of books by staff, which is required to be flexible, adaptable and secure.

The wood of the shutters forms part of the rich palette of materials – glass, steel, wood and concrete – Perrault uses to achieve an impeccably detailed interior. The furniture, bookshelves and flooring is also of wood, using the monumental repetition of large-scale elements to effect. Steel mesh is used to exploit its semi-transparent nature, to screen the fire stairs on the book towers, stretched taut against windows and against walls in the four escalator lobbies. Steel sheet metal is used on walls and ceilings in the reading levels, to reflect a cool light and to eliminate any possibility of low light levels. Red carpeting is used powerfully throughout to comple-ment the industrial aesthetic of the steel.

One of the key factors of the National Library of France was the development of existing library technology and resources to improve the status of the national network, strengthening, in turn, interna-tional connections, and the importance of the French archives and catalogue in the transmission of information. Readers in the library have access to computer terminals which enable them to scan the catalogues of the library (seven million records) and the French Union (thirteen million records), and to order documents by way of the automatic document transport system. This is also possible from a distance, reinforcing the library's far-reaching goals for global communication.

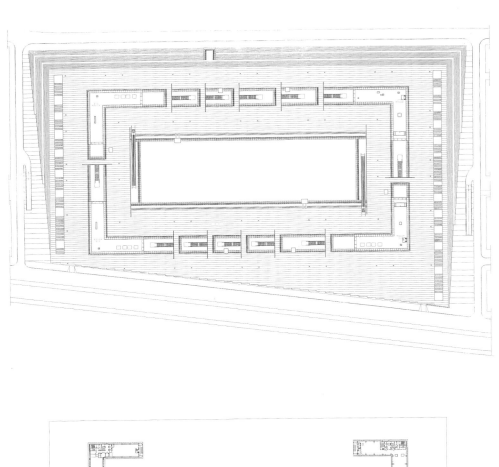

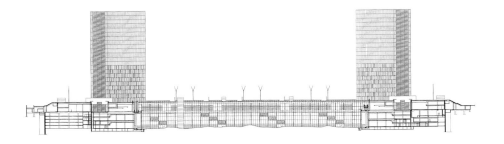

FROM ABOVE: Overall building plan; plan of storage and belvedere level; longitudinal section

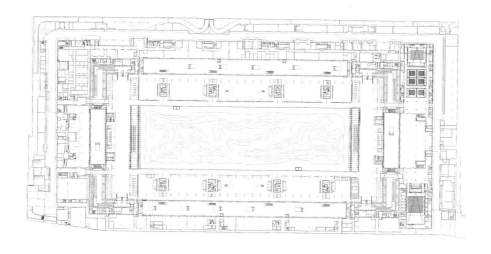

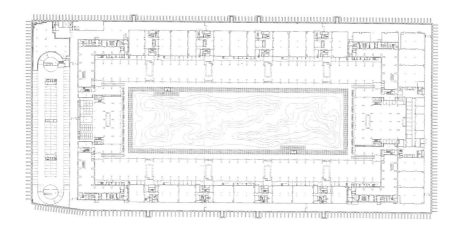

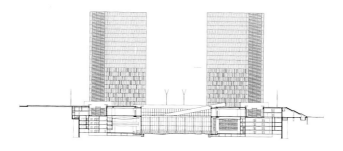

FROM ABOVE: Upper garden level plan with reception, exhibition and public reading rooms; garden level plan with research reading rooms; cross section

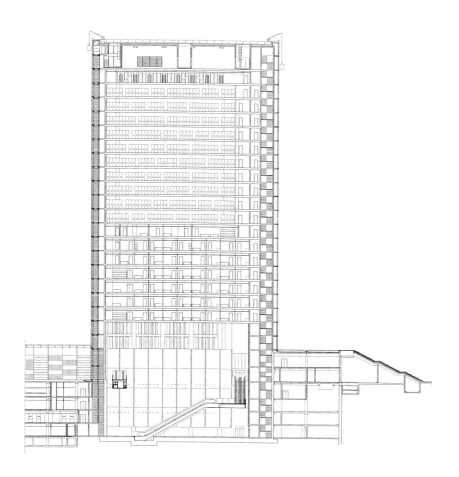

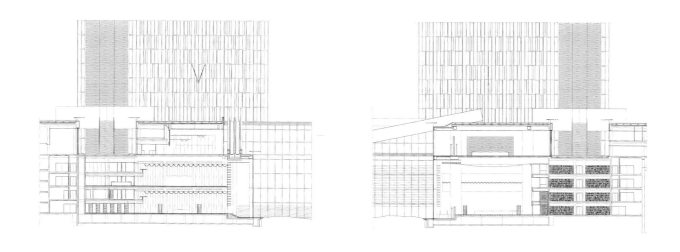

ABOVE: Transverse section through tower; BELOW, LEFT TO RIGHT: Cross section through image and sound reading rooms; section through rare books reading room

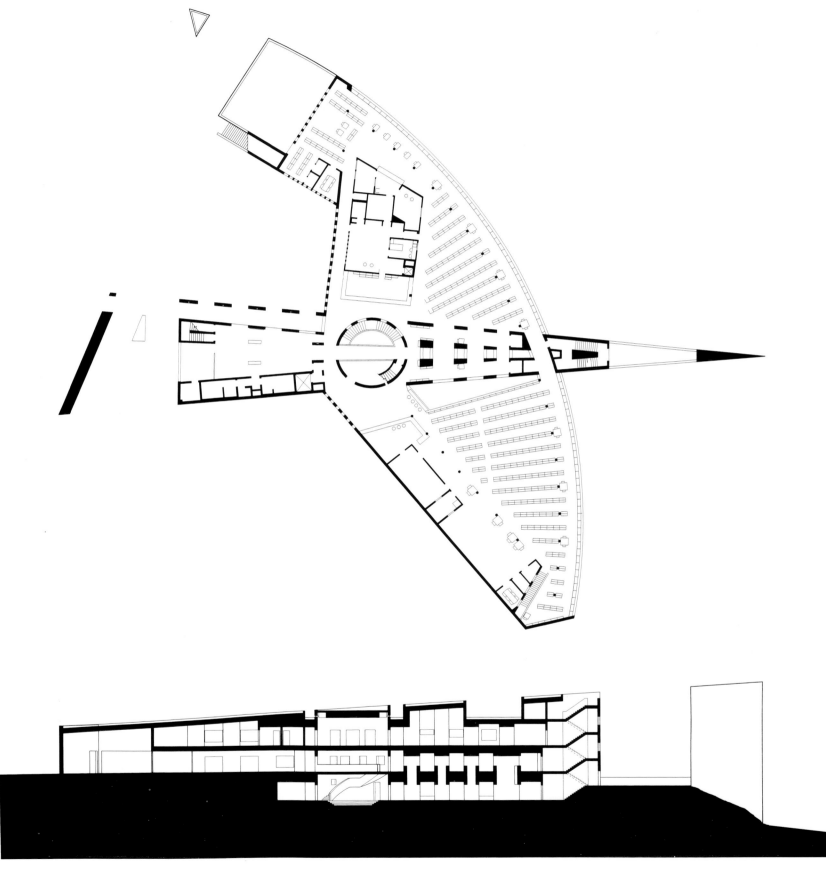

FROM ABOVE: First floor plan; section

ANTOINE PREDOCK
MESA PUBLIC LIBRARY
Los Alamos, New Mexico, USA

Located in the Jemez Mountains, the area is home to rich pine forests, grassy meadows, and dramatic rock formations. The historical cultural development of Los Alamos, New Mexico, has no parallels. This alpine mesa has witnessed numerous settlements: Native Americans from nearby valleys had used the mesa for summer grazing and farming; late nineteenth-century homesteaders established small ranches and farms here; the exclusive boys' ranch school of the town was appropriated by the federal government during World War II to become the home of the Manhattan Project. Most residents of the community today are affiliated with Los Alamos National Laboratory, an outgrowth of the original military research outpost. The new library is a sculptural abstraction of, and a careful response to the surround-

ing natural context. Special care was taken in siting the building to minimise impact on existing trees and vegetation. The library sits low, spreading into a curve on the north side in response to the panoramic views. A tall wedge built of stone, analogous to the nearby Tufa stone ridges in the Los Alamos area, cuts through the building. Where the wedge intersects the building, a warm south-facing courtyard is created and serves as the main entry.

At the point of entry, Mesa Public Library welcomes pedestrians through a garden that links the parking and adjacent municipal building to the entrance. The protective porte-cochere shelters entering visitors from the cold, snowy winter of Los Alamos. The building is characterised by two types of spaces: the cellular organisation of the 'wedge' houses the lobby, meeting rooms,

a bookstore, and private reading areas; the curved portion of the building is large, open-planned and houses the various stacks. The programme required that fiction, non-fiction, reference, young adult and children's areas have a defined presence, while still being linked spatially, to allow for monitoring and assisting patrons. South-facing clerestory windows bring warm, natural light into the stack areas, while the bank of windows on the northern curving wall allows a panoramic view of Pajarito Mountain. The entry courtyard, reading garden, and children's reading deck provide multi-purpose exterior spaces. Within its area of almost 5,000 square metres, specific areas of the building have been identified and designed to accommodate future expansion of the collection.

RICHARD ROGERS PARTNERSHIP
LEARNING RESOURCES CENTRE
Thames Valley University, Slough, UK

The building is situated on the Thames Valley University campus in Slough. The campus contains three dominant sixties high-rise blocks which have determined the pattern of subsequent development.

In addition to locating the site for a new Learning Resources Centre, the architects were required to provide and structure a master plan for the whole campus. This identified areas which would improve the existing landscape and infra-structure, including internal and external routes, parking zones and re-landscaping, and focal points to create a hub for the campus and future phase developments.

The Learning Resources Centre has been developed to fulfil a necessary role as an information centre, housing information in multi-formats – videos, CD-ROM and books. All users of the building will have access to lap-top computers to work on, in a computer-oriented space. This required an open working environment, with a limited number of enclosed seminar rooms.

The form of the building is broken into two distinct segments: a three-storey 'warehouse' of information housed in a simple concrete-framed block and, in contrast, a ground level and mezzanine study area beneath a curving lightweight roof.

The projection of the roof to the south forms a canopy to the entrance. An existing change in level has been removed – unifying the series of buildings and tying the building into the campus.

The building envelope has been designed to be predominantly naturally ventilated, with some mechanical assistance. However, to allow for additional cooling during out of term use, a limited chilling capacity has been included.

The materials are chosen to be simple and robust – a cost-effective approach in which natural finishes (in preference to applied) require minimum maintenance.

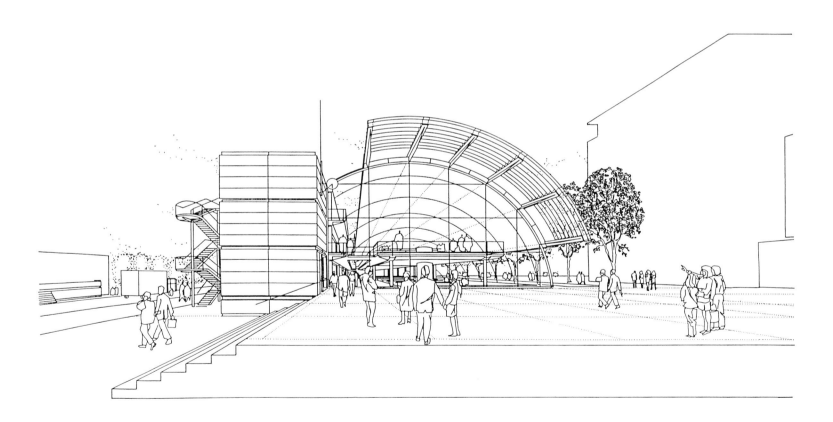

Perspective view

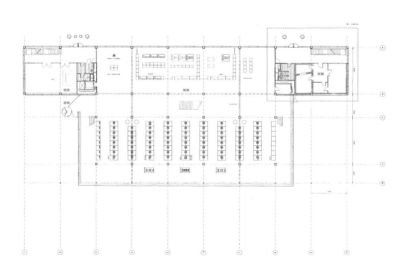 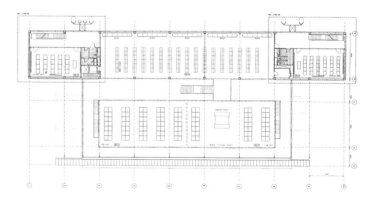

LEFT TO RIGHT: Ground floor plan; first floor plan

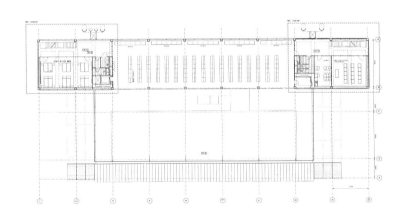

LEFT TO RIGHT: Second floor plan; concept sketch

ALDO ROSSI
UNIVERSITY LIBRARY

Carlo Cattaneo Free University, Castellanza, Italy

The Carlo Cattaneo Library forms one element of the scheme to convert former industrial buildings for university use in Castellanza. This has had two main objectives: the sensitive adaption and restoration of the old Cantoni cotton mill buildings, along with the creation of new structures; and the integration of the complex with the existing urban fabric, linking it to the town centre.

The library, which specialises in titles on economic and political science, is located at the heart of the university. It is situated on a piazza which is accessed from the Corso Matteotti. Around this stand a mixture of adapted and new structures: lecture halls, the Chancellor's building, and a new 660-seat assembly hall/conference

centre. The entrance to the piazza is marked by two newly constructed towers. The reference point for these buildings is the paved courtyard, and the challenge was to obtain an architectural space where the new and the old are balanced in their juxtaposition and integration.

The building to house the library, although already in existence, has been completely redesigned and rebuilt, in terms of both its facades and its internal layout. The library has been thought of as the union between the courtyard at the university's entry and the historic park of Villa Jucker, also part of the campus. It is arranged on three floors: the ground floor, where there are rooms for looking through

and selecting books, a reading room and offices; the lower ground floor, where the storage areas and information services are located; and the first floor, where there are more rooms for studying and reading. All of these spaces relate directly to the park. There are plans to increase the library's capacity by extending it into the building adjacent to the assembly hall.

The materials used for the library's construction are tinted plaster, Montorfano granite and *beola* from Lake Maggiore. Door and window frames are in varnished iron. The internal floors are wood and grey *beola*, while all the internal dividing walls are modular soundproof wood and laminate panels to afford maximum flexibility.

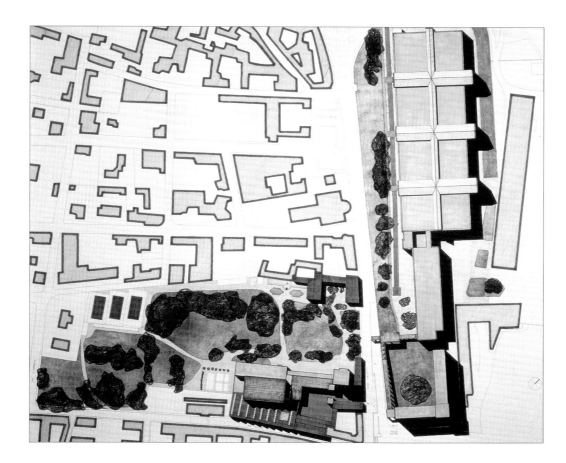

Site plan

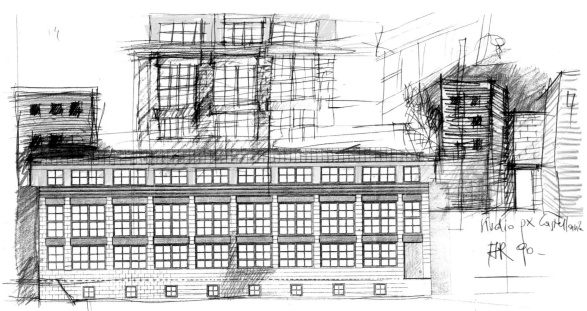

Sketch of elevation facing the park

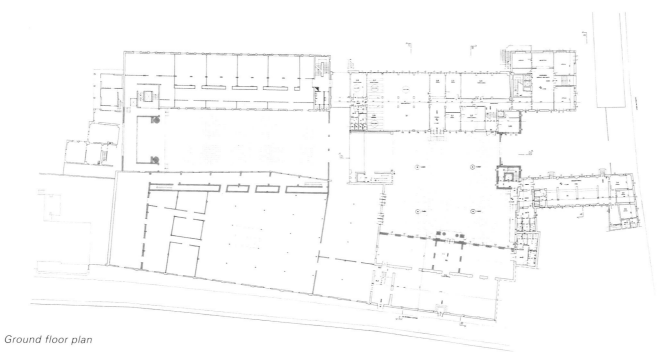

Ground floor plan

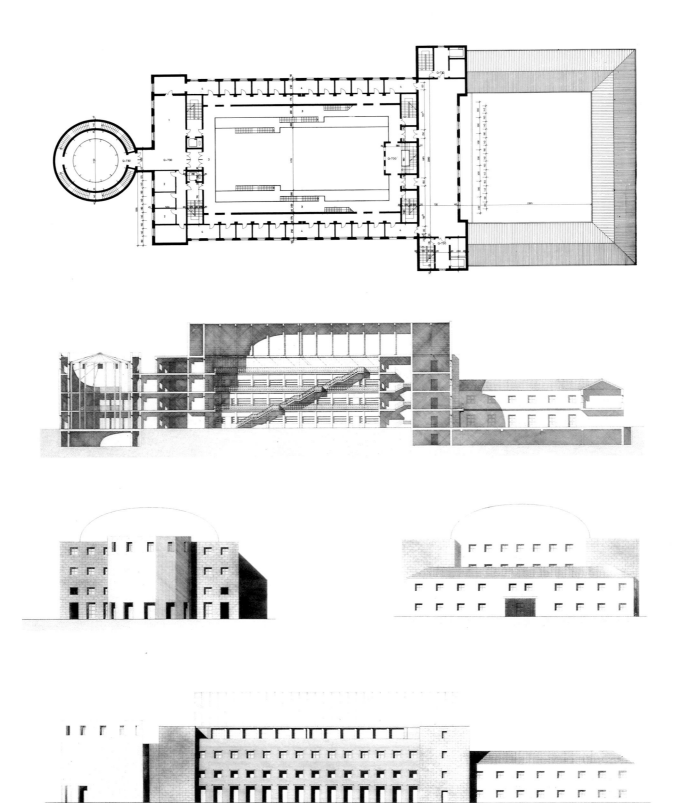

FROM ABOVE, LEFT TO RIGHT: Second floor plan; longitudinal section; rear elevation; front elevation; side elevation

ALDO ROSSI
SEREGNO LIBRARY
Seregno, Italy

Central to Rossi's concept for Seregno Library is the building's civic significance: its place as a centre for the conservation and formation of culture. Acknowledging the seminal influence of Boullée's great project, Rossi stresses that the library represents a 'concordance of different conceptions of the world through knowledge', just as Aristotle and Plato come together in the central space of Raphael's School of Athens.

At Seregno this symbolism is carried through in the great central space where people come to study, while the portico of the courtyard and the terraces above provide places for meeting and discussion. The library also forms a reference point in an area which has lost its nineteenth-century unity; fronted by a small square, it stands between the town hall and two public gardens.

Seregno Library is divided into three distinct parts: the courtyard, the vaulted central space and a cylindrical tower. These correspond to the entrance and gallery; the room for exhibiting and reading books, the meeting rooms and cafe; and the computer and communications rooms (it is significant that these latter are separated from the rest of the library).

The porticos of the courtyard house an art gallery; as Rossi says, 'it is in reality a passageway, albeit an important one'.

The first room, the entrance foyer, is equipped with display panels and signing elements to provide an orientation point for visitors. It also houses a communal information service for the town. In this space Rossi emphasises the importance of *Lichtof*, where the light of the sky becomes an architectural element.

Moving into the great hall, there is a large open area for book information and catalogues (the 'control centre' of the library). Around this are arranged the adult lending and reference areas, and the children's section. The intention was to have a large common reading room where the books constitute the walls and thereby become part of the structure – as they did in libraries of the eighteenth century and more modern works, such as Berlin's library. A system of staircases at each end of the hall leads to the floors above, allowing the public direct access to the books and the walkways of the first floor, and the small rooms for private study and research on the second floor.

The adult lending area is positioned directly after the information area. This displays thirty-five thousand volumes and has thirty chairs and tables for quick consultation of the books to be borrowed. The adult reference area holds eight thousand books, there are fifty table places for study, twenty cubicles for individual study in the open space, ten closed rooms for individual study, and four eight-place rooms for group study. These are organised over all three floors and take into account the different levels of study – from quick checking to detailed research – that readers may wish to make.

In the children's section, five different areas have been planned: lending; reference; audiovisual facilities; lending and reference for pre-school children; and classroom and group work. The closed courtyard is also for children's use.

There is also a periodical library and an audiovisual library which holds ten thousand records and tapes, four thousand videos, films and slides, along with computers. There is a multipurpose room on the first floor equipped for lectures and seminars which has its own entrance to allow use after the opening hours of the library. All offices are placed in areas that don't interfere directly with the movements of the library's users.

Concept sketches

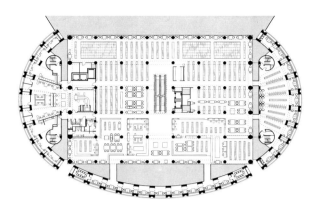

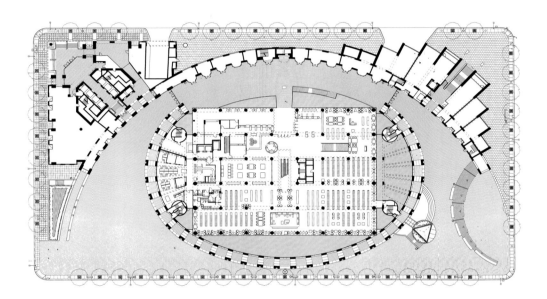

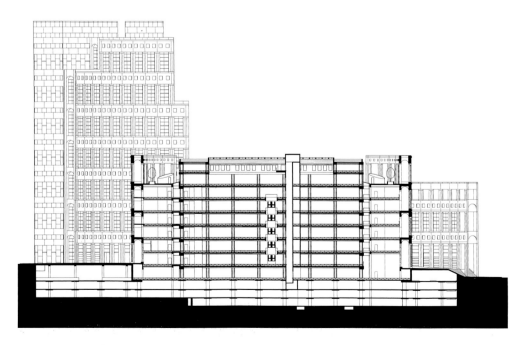

FROM ABOVE: Fourth floor plan; ground floor plan; longitudinal section, with Federal Government Tower to rear

MOSHE SAFDIE AND ASSOCIATES
VANCOUVER CENTRAL PUBLIC LIBRARY

Library Square, Vancouver, British Columbia, Canada

Vancouver's Library Square occupies a block to the east of the city centre. The project includes the Central Public Library, as well as the Federal Government Headquarters, retail and service facilities and underground parking for seven hundred cars. The Federal Government Headquarters' twenty-one-storey tower, to the north-east of the site, overlooks the centrally placed library and has views over the city and harbour to the north and east.

The library has a rectangular core encircled by a freestanding arcade. Interstitial lightwells allow natural light to penetrate the core, which houses the book stacks, library services and information technology points. Library users can select their reading materials and cross steel bridges to study carrels and reading alcoves on the arcade. This move, which takes the study spaces to the exterior of the building, is explained more fully by Moshe Safdie:

> In the traditional library, you have a building in which the heart is the reading room, and around it are the stacks. They face the city, and in the middle is the place where you study . . . This central reading room no longer makes sense. Our way of working and reading today with our lap-top computers, does not require this sort of railway reading room . . . The idea came forward to centralise the stacks – the bulky non-transparent element in the building – and create a reading gallery around them, towards the street and the city. You cross over to the core to pick up your books and then go back to the curved, linear reading room . . . you can look look out towards the city, or in towards the stacks.

A second arcade wall surrounding the library encloses a glazed concourse and rises to the north-east to form the south-west facade of the Federal tower. The sun-filled concourse forms the entry foyer of the library and the internal glass facade of the library allows views between the two spaces, contrasting the lively activities of the cafe and passing shoppers with the quiet and serious study within the library. The surrounding spaces of the block form a continuous public piazza which serves to emphasise the civic qualities of the square. An auditorium and meeting rooms are located under the public promenade.

The forum shape of the building evokes an image of the Colosseum. Elements of classical orders are used to moderate the the difference in levels between the tower and the library. The four-tiered arcade wrapping around the library incorporates large-scale precast concrete elements with a red granite aggregate. These freestanding volumes are constructed of precast panels that double as formwork for the in situ concrete structure. The office tower is clad with matching precast concrete.

In contrast, the core of library stacks is a glass box containing fully accessible mechanical systems. The glazed shafts between the core and the arcade have window-washing equipment, and a raised floor on each level contains cable trays, air ducts and sprinkler systems, which, in conjunction with load-bearing systems that enable reconfiguration of the shelving, allow a fully flexible working environment.

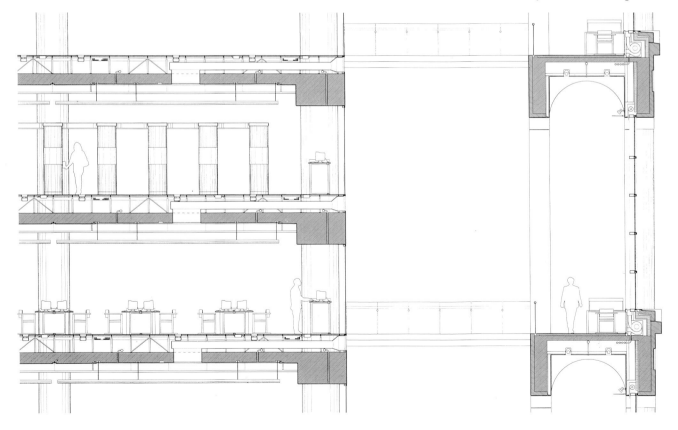

Section detail through library core and arcade

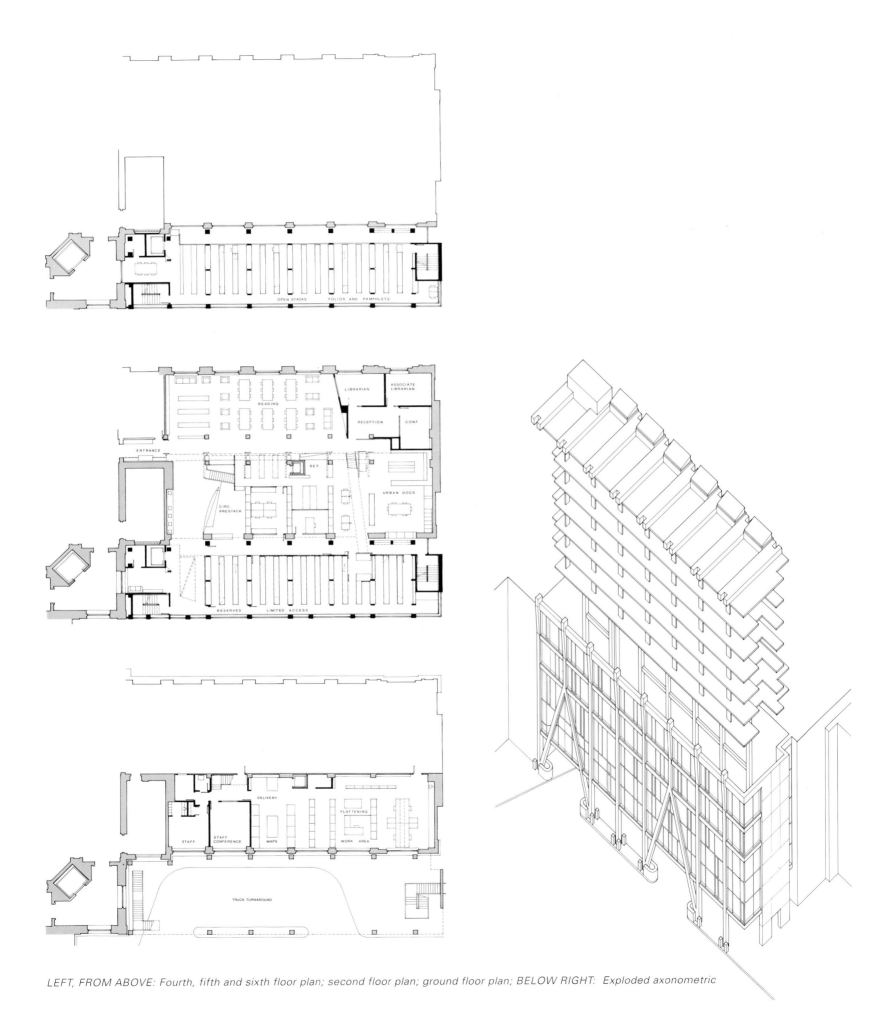

LEFT, FROM ABOVE: Fourth, fifth and sixth floor plan; second floor plan; ground floor plan; BELOW RIGHT: Exploded axonometric

ROTCH LIBRARY ADDITION

MIT, Cambridge, Massachusetts, USA

Founded in 1868, the Rotch Library of Art, Architecture and Planning at the Massachusetts Institute of Technology is one of five divisional libraries. It has the second largest collection of architectural documents in the United States, and serves as an important research centre for the Institute and for the Boston–Cambridge architectural community.

Schwartz/Silver's six-storey extension to the Rotch Library occupies an awkward narrow site in a cramped service court. It adjoins the existing four-storey library building to the rear but sits apart from it; an adjoining two-metre-wide slot allows light and air to circulate between the two buildings. The new extension was not to rise above the skyline of the imposing main building of the complex, and a different floor-to-ceiling height allowed the addition to maintain the same vertical dimension as the original building: only the second floor of each building remains at the same level. The facade of the existing and renovated building has been left almost untouched except where connections are made between the two buildings.

At its base, the library also accommodates the 5.5-metre height of an existing turning circle for trucks and deliveries by raising its powerful concrete frame off the ground at six points, like a bridge, triangulated to enable access to the turning circle. The concrete frame then rises up six floors to the roof where, from huge concrete girders, each floor is suspended. This enables the floor depth to be kept to a minimum, a critical consideration when the building height was so important. As the existing library floors could not hold the weight of continuous stacks, the new building houses the book stacks while the existing interior was remodelled as reading rooms and administrative areas.

In order to entirely glaze the addition, the glazing of the curtain wall was chosen specifically to minimise heat gain and to stop the transmission of ultra-violet rays.

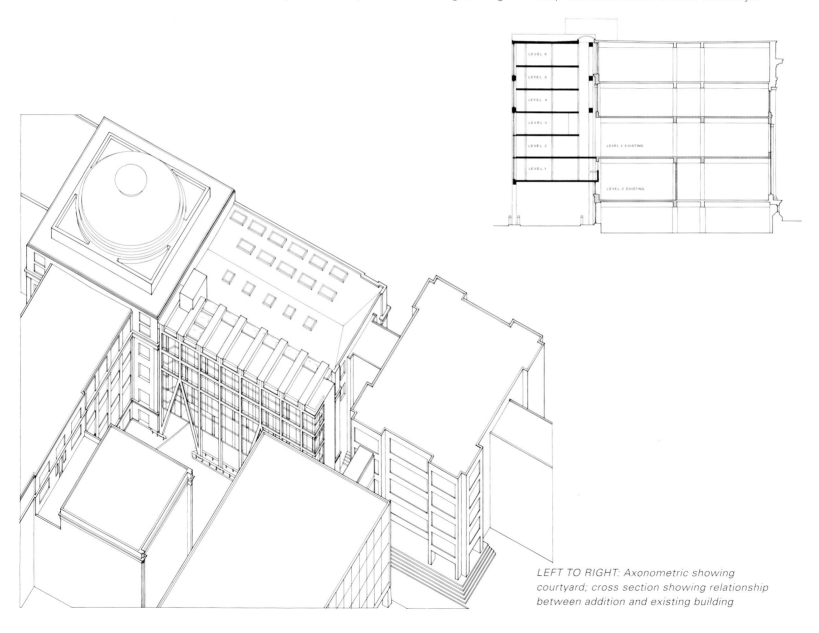

LEFT TO RIGHT: Axonometric showing courtyard; cross section showing relationship between addition and existing building

CLAYTON COUNTY HEADQUARTERS LIBRARY

Jonesboro, Georgia, USA

Jonesboro, Georgia, is wedged in between the south-east end of Hartsfield International, one of the busiest airports in the world and Tara, the mythical home of Scarlet O'Hara. The strip between the two is folksy, hand-painted (not at all mass-produced), a place where one is apt to pull up alongside a pick-up truck with a gun rack and ZZ Top blaring out through the open windows. It is a place where information is sought for practical reasons and history is personal. Scholars will not seek out obscure dissertation-supporting materials here. This library is more like a filling-station, purveying information for living life: a puppet show, a cooking class, a seed catalogue, easy parking – all on offer here. A hypermarket of information . . .

The site is bounded on the north by Battlecreek Road; on the east by Jester's Creek and its associated flood plain, a wooded area lush with hardwoods and pine; and on the south and west by other county facilities. The building is located on the southern part of the site, and is elevated above the car park which is directly in front of the building. The entrance elevation is at the eye level of a seated driver travelling along Battlecreek Road.

The plan is organised on two axes. The north–south axis provides a connecting link between the car park, the entrance, the circulation desk and the board room. The transverse axis, also through the circulation desk, connects the woods and flood plain east of the site, the genealogy collection and a director's office.

The functions are also split into two: the administration facilities and the public areas. The public areas occupy a large open room which is oriented to the woods and creek. A monitor divides the space, emphasising the line of travel to, and the position of, the genealogy collection. The roofs of this space tilt towards the east and the woods. They are arranged so that they fan up towards the south, allowing north light to enter at each 'step'. The children's services are located in the lower space, while the general collection with the tallest stacks is located where the roof is highest.

The structure is steel frame with long span truss joists of wood and galvanised steel, supported on concrete footings. The exterior skin is a combination of metal sidings with a variety of textures and patterns. The general aeshetic is industrial.

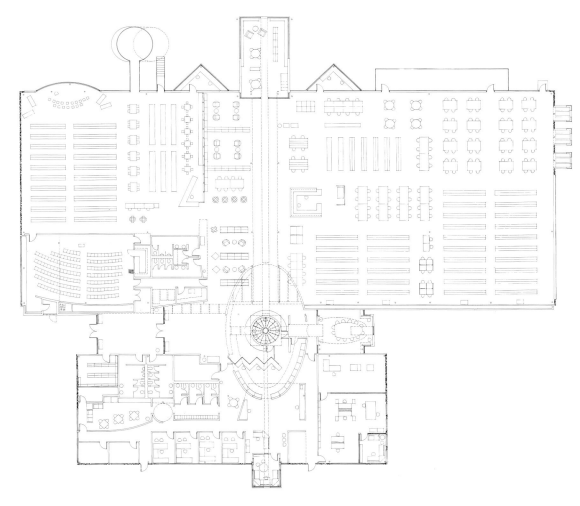

Ground floor plan

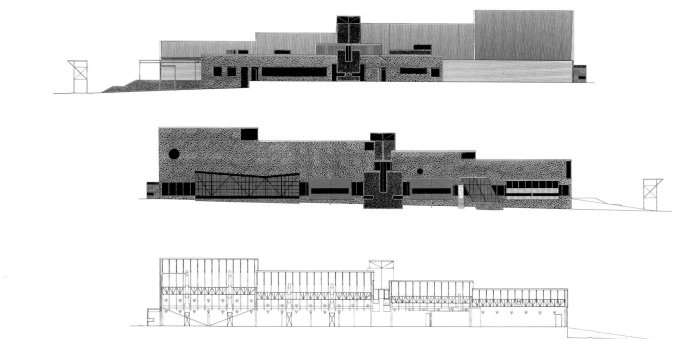

FROM ABOVE: West elevation; east elevation; longitudinal section through public room, looking west

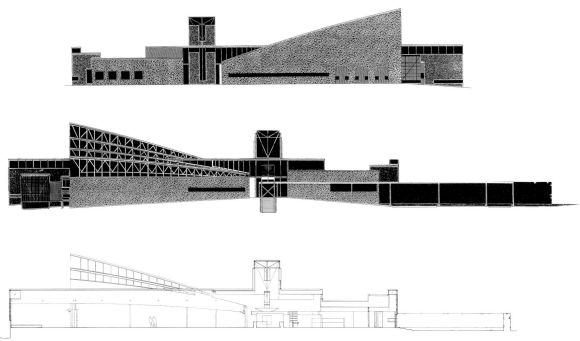

FROM ABOVE: South elevation; north elevation; cross section through light monitor, looking south

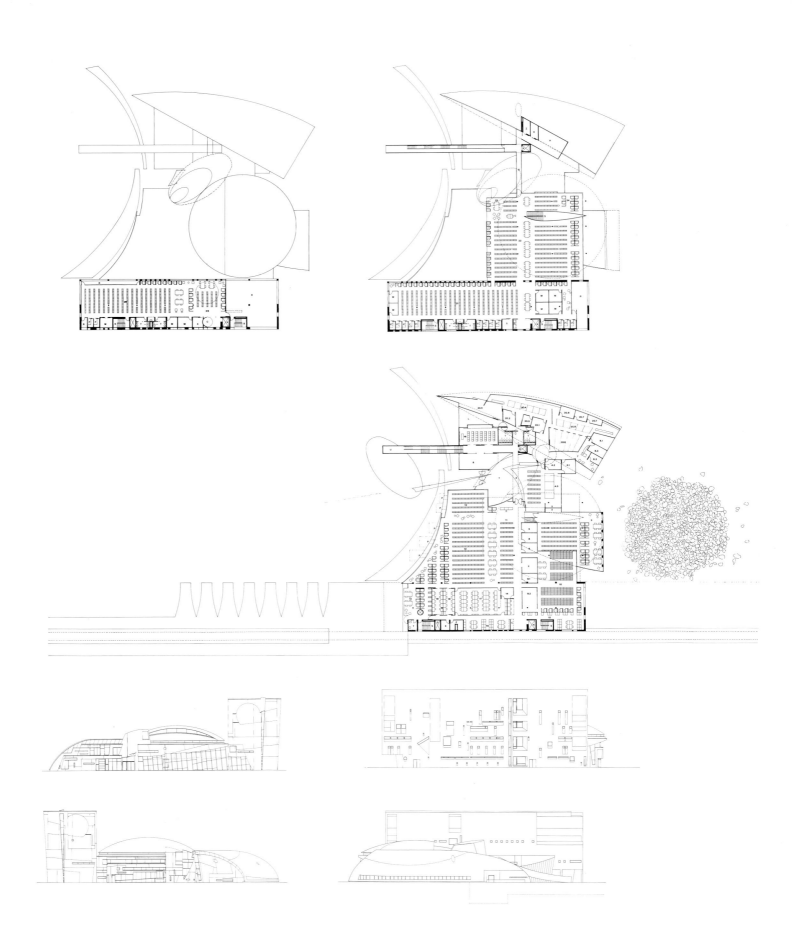

FROM ABOVE, LEFT TO RIGHT: Second floor plan; first floor plan; ground floor plan; north elevation; west elevation; south elevation; east elevation

SCOGIN, ELAM AND BRAY

JOHN J ROSS – WILLIAM C BLAKELY LAW LIBRARY

Arizona State University, Tempe, Arizona, USA

The Arizona desert landscape provokes misreadings. Plants look like animals, animals look like rocks, rocks look like animals, plants look like rocks, animals look like plants, tricking and teasing the eyes. The sun bursts over the horizon, unfiltered by East Coast greenery, immediately filling an enormous sky with incredible light. Textures and colours vibrate. On the ground plane and along the horizon, every form is to excess, incredibly legible and overly important.

The library, which commemorates two prominent Phoenix attorneys, is one of the finest law libraries in the Southwest with a collection of over three hundred and ten thousand volumes and microfilm volume equivalents. The collection includes a broad selection of Anglo-American case reports and statutes, as well as legal treatises, periodicals, encyclopedias, digests, citations and administrative materials. The collection also has growing special

collections in the areas of international law, Native American law, Mexican law, and law and technology. The library is furthermore a selective US Government repository.

The site of the law library addition is on the fringe of Arizona State University's orthogonal campus. The multiplicity of the context – the landscape, the curve of the east property line, the geometrical determinism of the existing law school building and a number of other buildings scattered on the campus fringe – encourages exuberant form-making. The dynamic forms of the new law library building both contrast and complement the existing building, Armstrong Hall. When seen together, neither building dominates the other; rather the two are harmonious, if unconventional, forming a College of Law campus within the greater university campus.

An 'oasis-like' plaza mediates between the existing building and the new building. The forms and spaces of the scheme are

organised over and around the distinct functions of the library: technical services, circulation services, the core collection and the other discrete collections. The collection of exterior forms and interior spaces work in concert to modulate the intense desert sunlight and provide varying architectural experiences.

Accessible shelving for the library's expanding collections and study space at carrels, tables and lounge seating are located throughout the library. It also has a thirty-station computer lab as well as Lexis and Westlaw rooms each containing ten stations, in addition to twenty-seven meeting and study rooms, a microfilm facility and a classroom.

The building's structure is steel frame on concrete foundations. Exterior materials include synthetic stucco, metal roofing and insulating glazing. Interior materials include concrete paint on plaster wall boards and carpets.

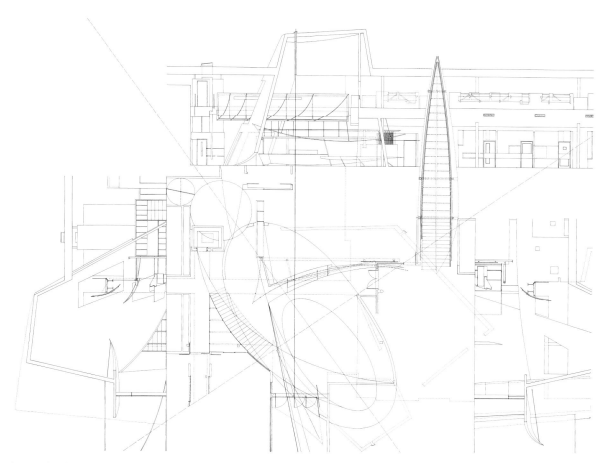

Plan and section projections

SCOGIN, ELAM AND BRAY
CAROL COBB TURNER BRANCH LIBRARY

Morrow, Georgia, USA

The 900-square-metre Morrow Branch library, a fifty-nine thousand volume community facility, is an institutional loner. Set in a horse pasture, it is bounded by a linear shopping centre (which always draws in wet weather crowds), a busy county road and subdivision housing which is sideways-facing and self-contained that refuses to acknowledge the road's existence. Its site is flat, filled with yellow-topped bitter weeds, loblolly pines

and june bug beetles. Its most extraordinary feature is its ceiling of blue sky and bright clouds brushed by pine needles.

The one-acre site is consumed by the programme of building and parking and the best view is upwards. The scheme reflects this, with glass and views high up and enclosing walls down low. Other influences are more abstract, distant connections, such as the headquarters library, the

county courthouse, the nearby neighbourhoods Rex and Ellenwood, and the cardinal points of the compass. Along with the property lines, the lines of influence from these entities give form to the building.

The building plan is an asymmetrical skewed dogleg with a dividing breezeway/corridor with rooms off both sides. To the north of the corridor are the public meeting room, toilets and administrative services.

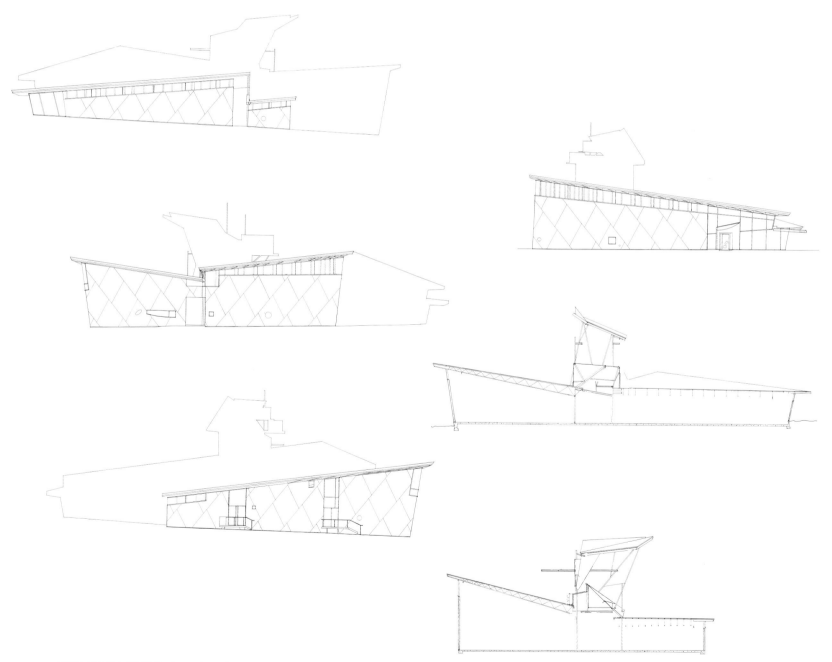

LEFT, FROM ABOVE: East elevation; west elevation; north elevation; RIGHT, FROM ABOVE: South elevation; longitudinal section; cross section

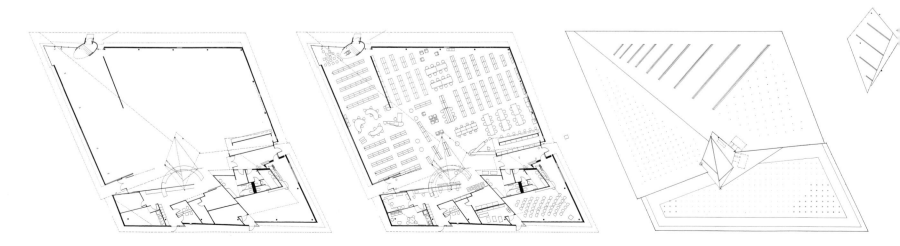

FROM LEFT TO RIGHT: Ground floor plan; ground floor plan with furniture; roof plan

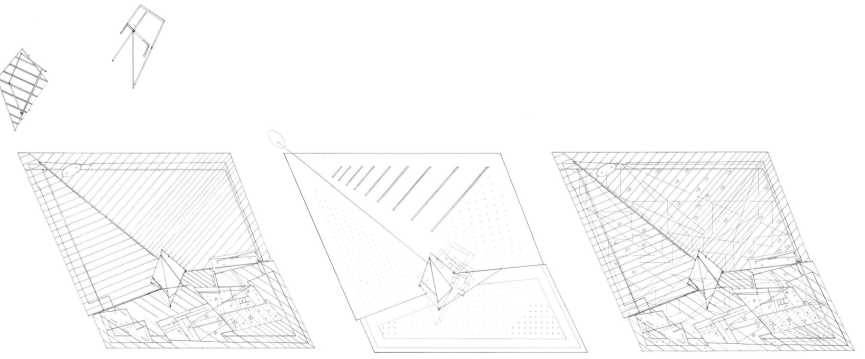

FROM LEFT TO RIGHT: Reflected ceiling plan; roof plan indicating tower; lighting diagram

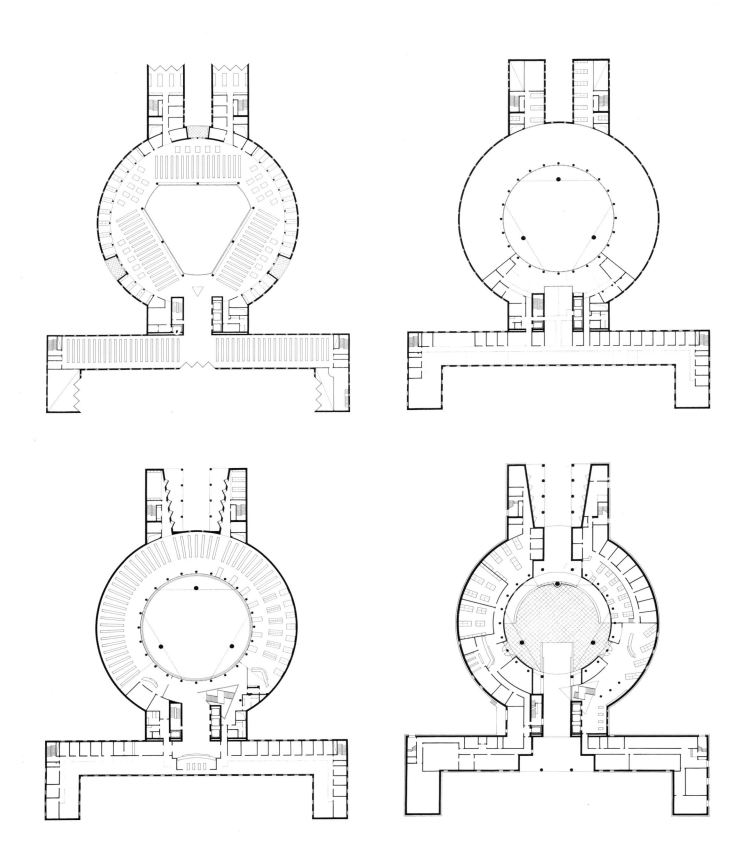

FROM ABOVE, LEFT TO RIGHT: *Third, fourth and fifth floor plan; second floor plan; first floor plan; ground floor plan*

JAMES STIRLING MICHAEL WILFORD & ASSOCIATES
SCIENCE LIBRARY
University of California, Irvine, California, USA

The Irvine campus of the University of California is situated among the rolling hills and canyons of the former Irvine cattle ranch, three miles inland from Newport Beach and forty miles south of Los Angeles. The 1963 Pereira master plan established a large circular park as the heart of the campus with six academic quadrangles and an administrative gateway radiating from it into the surrounding landscape. The outer edge of the park is defined by a ring mall providing pedestrian and cycle connections between the quadrangles. Car parks and service areas are accessed from an outer ring road, confining vehicular traffic to the edges of the campus. Each quad is organised around a linear mall and the Biological Sciences (Bio Sci) mall also connects the Medical School to the centre of the campus.

Future development of the Bio Sci quad will primarily comprise research facilities and the library is therefore likely to be the only non-laboratory building. It will also be used by faculty and students of the Medical School.

Through its function and location, the building is a campus landmark, visible from all approaches. The unique form of the building is in response to the brief which required a logical and coherent organisation, appropriate relationships between departments, and provision of daylight to all reader and staff spaces. It also responds to the long-range campus development plan by providing a sense of urbanity, space identity and a variety of pedestrian experience. The limited space between the Neurobiology building and the quad axis determined the narrow entrance portal facing the ring mall.

The entrance portal and tapered colonnades focus towards the central courtyard and are the first of a sequence of contracting and expanding spaces created by the building to encourage entry and passage beneath it. The circular courtyard, although

enclosed by the library, is a public outdoor space, cool and shaded in contrast to the open landscape surrounding the building. Activity within the library enlivens the mall and makes it a pleasant and safe campus route during the day and night. The mall continues westwards from the courtyard into a tree-lined square incorporating an arroyo and redwood grove. It is intended that this square will eventually form the centre of the developed quad. The spatial progression established by the library begins an attractive promenade between the ring mall and the Medical School.

Unlike a traditional university or civic library the building does not contain a single grand reading room. Instead a variety of reader spaces are distributed throughout the building, offering a choice of location and ambience from centres of high activity to absolute seclusion. Readers are always seated close to windows within small groups rather than within a vast traditional array of reading tables. The accommodation is arranged on six floors.

Visitors enter through an entrance and exhibition hall containing an information desk to supervise the adjacent catalogue area and twenty-four-hour study room. A dramatic stair rises to the lending desk on the second level which controls primary staff–reader contact and public access to all parts of the library. The reference and current periodical areas have separate entrances, opposite the loan desk. Both activities are combined in a double-height reading room which encircles the lower part of the courtyard to allow readers to move easily from one section to another.

On the three upper levels, three stacks, parallel to the triangular sides of the upper courtyard, accommodate bound periodicals and two stacks in the long wing accommodate monographs. Double-height reading rooms with floor-to-ceiling glazing terminate the public levels of the short and long wings overlooking either the ring mall

or square. Study carrels line the outer wall of the central drum with three outdoor reading balconies at each level. Areas between stacks have additional reading tables and lounge seating with views either into the courtyard or across the square.

The librarians' offices are situated on the second level of the long wing with adjacent open work areas overlooking the square. The technical services department controls book and periodical acquisition, indexing and cataloguing for the whole campus. An educational resource facility is situated at ground level with separate entry from the courtyard to allow use outside library hours. Book storage, staff accommodation and a computer suite occupy the remainder of the ground floor. Three passenger elevators, a staff/freight elevator and five staircases distributed across the plan provide vertical circulation. The service yard and truck dock are situated between the drum and long wing on the north side.

The building is of steel framed construction with steel studded exterior walls and internal partitions. The outer facades are of stucco, finished in two colours and delineated with a dark red sandstone base and string course. The courtyard walls and floor are also finished with red sandstone. Clear glazing to the circular reference and periodicals reading room provides views into and from the courtyard. Translucent glazing to the sides of the triangular upper courtyard protect the book stacks from direct sunlight and the clear glazed corner reading areas provide views in and out of the building. The double-height reading rooms in the wings have clear 'saw-toothed' glazing to allow diagonal views across the campus. Reading carrels have small windows to provide exterior views. All clear glazed windows have electrically operated sunblinds controlled by light sensors. The large projecting metal eaves conceal the rooftop air-conditioning plant.

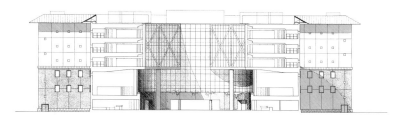

Cross section through internal courtyard

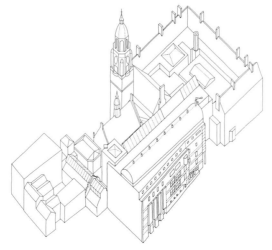

TIBBALDS MONRO
CROYDON LIBRARY

'The Clocktower', Croydon, Surrey, UK

Unlike the museum and arts facilities of the newly redeveloped complex in the Old Town of Croydon, which occupy converted spaces within the listed Victorian town hall buildings, the library is a new building, arranged on four public floors, with an administrative floor above. The vertical configuration was imposed by the council's requirement to set aside a portion of the available site for a commercial development which would contribute towards the cost of the public facility. This caused no problem, however, as the library had already decided to merge reference and lending material. Provided there was good vertical circulation, the subject matter could be arranged in a logical sequence, with popular material below and becoming more specialised in an upwards progression.

Public entry to and egress from the library takes place at ground floor. This level is dominated by the main issue desk and library checkouts. The children's library, which can be noisy at times, is also located on this floor. The glazed screen to the children's library depicts a sea journey to a 'treasure island' framed by two exotic trees adjacent to the entrance. Inside, a performance space and a number of nooks and crannies are provided for the children's enjoyment. The first floor is devoted to popular fiction and large print, the second floor to subject groupings, and the third floor to the more specialised commercial and business library. A substantial local studies library is located at one side of this floor. There is a user education room on the floor below and a dedicated teenage library is housed in a separate suite.

For reasons of security, the vertical circulation for the library is contained within the library envelope, rather than in the glass-roofed court which separates the library from the original building and acts as the circulation hub for the various facilities. Ease of vertical circulation was a major consideration and it was decided to provide escalators and a lift, with stairs confined to staff and emergency use. The escalators are placed on the periphery of the floor so as to provide the librarians with clear uninterrupted space. A dedicated book lift links the returns section of the issue desk to the information desks on each floor and to the administrative floor above. A service lift adjacent to the street loading bay links the receipts/despatch area with the administration floor, where new books and media are processed for distribution to the main library below or to branch libraries throughout the borough. The staff have their own entrance and lift, which doubles as a fire-fighting lift.

The library is designed to provide flexible space and to be at the cutting edge of information technology. Raised access floors are provided throughout, as well as an extensive data riser network. The librarians wanted a bright, accessible environment, with the emphasis on information retrieval systems. Their role model was a department store but without the anonymity associated with so many retail interiors, where the store image has displaced all sense of place. Reference material and behind-the-scenes book stacks are kept to a minimum, while bookshelves are limited to 1.5 metres high for ease of access. Much attention was paid to lighting and acoustics. The library initially sought a lighting level in excess of 600 lux. However, emphasis was placed on quality rather than quantity of light and efficient continental light fittings provide pleasant indirect downlight. Acoustical levels are established by the use of carpet tiles, insulated metal ceiling tiles and sealed double-glazed windows; particular attention was paid to mechanical plant isolation and noise specification of escalators.

The library is air-conditioned. It has a variable air volume fresh-air plant: three small plantrooms per floor supply conditioned air to a pressurised ceiling plenum, with distribution via slot diffusers within the ceiling grid. Energy conservation was an important consideration and the building utilises well-established energy efficiency measures, for example: heating and air-conditioning plant controlled by a building management system; controlled fresh air intake and exhaust air heat recovery; a well insulated building envelope; use of condensing boilers and high frequency fluorescent lighting.

The predominantly off-white walls (enlivened by contrasting partitions adjacent to the enquiry desks), robust oak-veneered doors, a custom-designed speckled grey carpet tile (blue in the children's library), the custom-built issue desk and the selection of furniture, which is predominantly Scandinavian in origin, all further enliven the bright, fresh interior.

The approach to the library beneath the existing Braithwaite Hall, the form of the glass-roofed circulation court, the transparent nature of the curved wall between library and court, the vistas to the Victorian clock tower and the treatment of fenestration to Mint Walk – are all carefully manipulated with the objective of rooting the library firmly in Croydon.

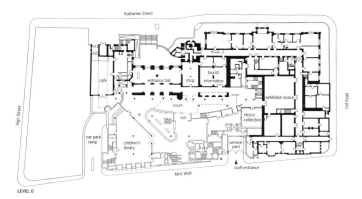
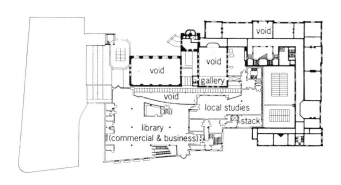

OPPOSITE: Axonometric; ABOVE, LEFT TO RIGHT: Ground floor plan; third floor plan

Street elevation

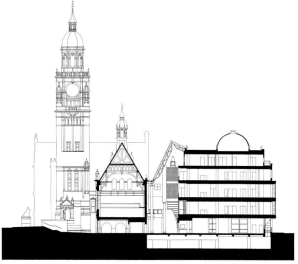

Cross section

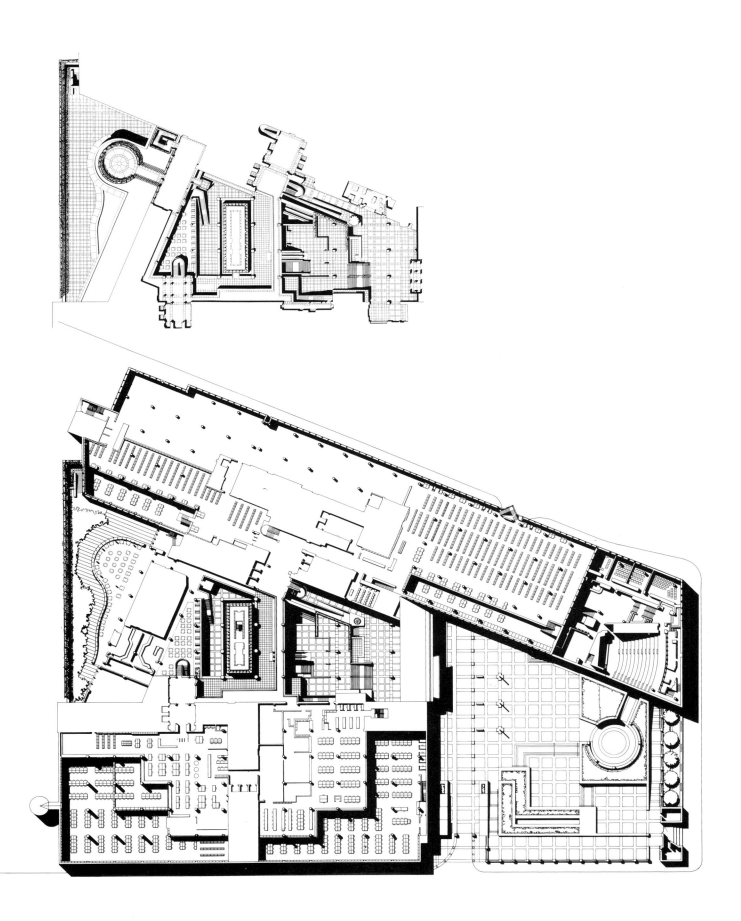

FROM ABOVE: Plan of entrance hall; overall plan

COLIN ST JOHN WILSON & PARTNERS
THE BRITISH LIBRARY
St Pancras, London, UK

Architecture, according to the ancient Greeks, is not a fine art ('which serves only itself') but a practical art ('which serves an end other than itself'). Of the many ends to be served by a library, the deepest inspiration should be drawn from the needs of the reader. The design of the British Library started and ends with the desire and pursuit of that principle.

To an architect the most haunting image of the solitary scholar is the painting *St Jerome in his Study* by Antonello da Messina. Ensconced in a timber shell, the scholar is enveloped in a purpose-made *aedicule* of bookshelf, ledge and desk like an organist's console. The whole structure forms a frame focused upon the act of reading. It is the embodiment of intense concentration in a hierarchy of space and a sympathetic palette of materials.

However, huge contradictions enter into play where it is a case of serving not one but a thousand scholars, particularly since each individual still claims the right to that privileged aura. When, in addition, there is the requirement to exhibit work from the collections to the general public a whole new set of parameters is introduced.

The main objective is therefore to create an easy commerce between the lone scholar and a huge building, to make each feel 'at home' and this task falls within the discipline of architecture.

Here the whole crux lies in the manipulation of scale. For there is a scale that threatens and a scale that invites: and the medium of invitation lies in the creation and sustaining of scale elements that bridge the difference between what serves the individual and what is dominated by 'the others'. Circulation must be channelled to avoid invasiveness; for instance, a balcony edge is given such depth that a reader above cannot peer over and distract or 'threaten' a reader below. Furthermore the visitor should never feel overwhelmed or lost: and so orienting 'porthole' windows offer views back and across the spaces traversed or out onto familiar neighbouring loci. A delicate balance is maintained by threading elements throughout to mediate scale (balustrades, suspended lights, canopies), much as street furniture moderates and mediates between traffic and people.

Daylight is a vital ingredient as the source of ambient light during the day. It both stimulates the attention (artificial light can all too easily dull the senses) and also links the individual to the natural rhythms of the day.

In the great Humanities Reading Room the different readers' tables – at the balcony edge, 'tucked in' below the terrace above or in the tall perimeter vault – offer a choice to the user. In all cases, they offer a long-range view across the room as a stimulating contrast to the focus of close study. Each of the eight reading rooms has an inherently different identity of its own.

The design is grounded in a radical formal asymmetry. This relates to the fundamental duality of functions which entails two very different patterns of use.

In the reading rooms of the Humanities Collections (which occupy the western range of the building) the space is almost entirely occupied by readers. Reference material lines the walls. Daylight pours into the centre by means of clerestory and lantern lights housed in the pitched roofs.

Conversely, the Science and Patents Collections are disposed on 'open-access' shelves, occupying virtually all of the floor space, from which readers are able to consult abstracts, periodicals and books. As the centre of the space is taken up by bookshelves, daylight is introduced from side windows to reader positions around the perimeter of the gallery floors.

The greater part of the 340 linear kilometres of shelving for books, manuscripts, maps and incunabula is buried underground in the most stable environmental conditions, unaffected by season or weather. Material is requested from the storage basement by the reader through the computerised catalogue retrieval system.

The conference centre, with a separate entrance from the courtyard, contains auditoria and seminar rooms. The main staircase in the foyer to the bar (the 'Spanish Steps') spreads to each side into seating nooks.

In the exhibition galleries the nature of material to be exhibited forbids the introduction of daylight, and a cavernous darkness is the ambience against which the jewel-like exhibits are to be displayed.

Libraries are made of the stuff of myth as much as of the methodology of 'information retrieval'. Somewhere within the silent miles of stacks, gallery upon gallery, there awaits the discovery of the Philosopher's Stone.

And so to every scholar the library is a personal realm of secret topography; it is this perception that conditions the propriety of the public image of its architecture. It is no place for the rhetoric demanded by the grand celebrations of opera or theatre. Timeless, massive and withdrawn, it awaits the random arrival of its lonely explorers. Sensitive representation of this ambivalent character urges upon us a certain quietism of the kind described by Adolf Loos in which 'a building should be silent on the outside and reveal its wealth only on the inside'.

The major celebratory monument is the freestanding glass tower – a bookcase six floors high that houses the King's Library and soars out of the basement into the centre of the entrance hall. It will display the magnificent bindings of George III's collection. It is both the jewel in the crown and a heavily used resource for the Rare Books Reading Room.

The sheer size and continuous growth of the collections required that the design should be buildable and inhabitable in self-sufficient stages over time. Such a process can only be matched by means of a free adaptive form of architecture rather than the conventional symmetries of classical form. The solution here is drawn from the tradition of the 'English Free School' and, in the context of Scott's neighbouring St Pancras Hotel, this works well to orchestrate the two buildings together. This integration is carried further by the use of similar external materials – red Lincolnshire brick, Welsh slate roofs, metal and granite facings – which weather well in this climate and require minimum maintenance.

The hubbub of traffic on Euston Road has inspired the construction of a firmly enclosed forecourt that will allow the reader to regain the tranquility lost to the street.

By 2002 St Pancras Station will have doubled in size to accommodate the principal arrival point of the Channel Tunnel rail link. One result of this transformation is that the British Library will be the first building the European visitor will see on arrival in London and the courtyard, the only public open space in the area, will take on a new significance. 'Under the clock tower' will surely become a familiar point of rendezvous.

The building will be completed early in 1997, with first admission for readers commencing in November.

Abridged text from 'Homage to the Reader', Colin St John Wilson, in The Architecture of Information, *catalogue of the British Pavilion, Venice Biennale 1996*

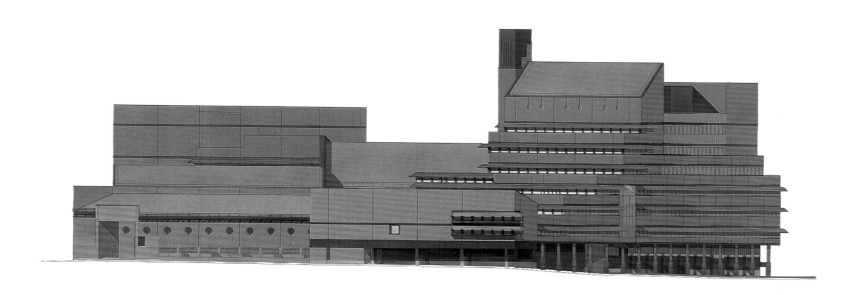

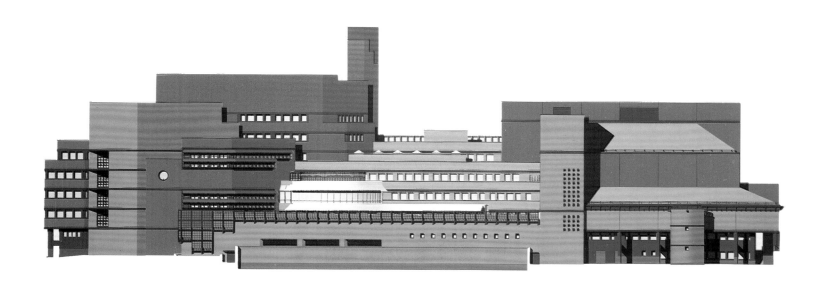

FROM ABOVE: south elevation; north elevation

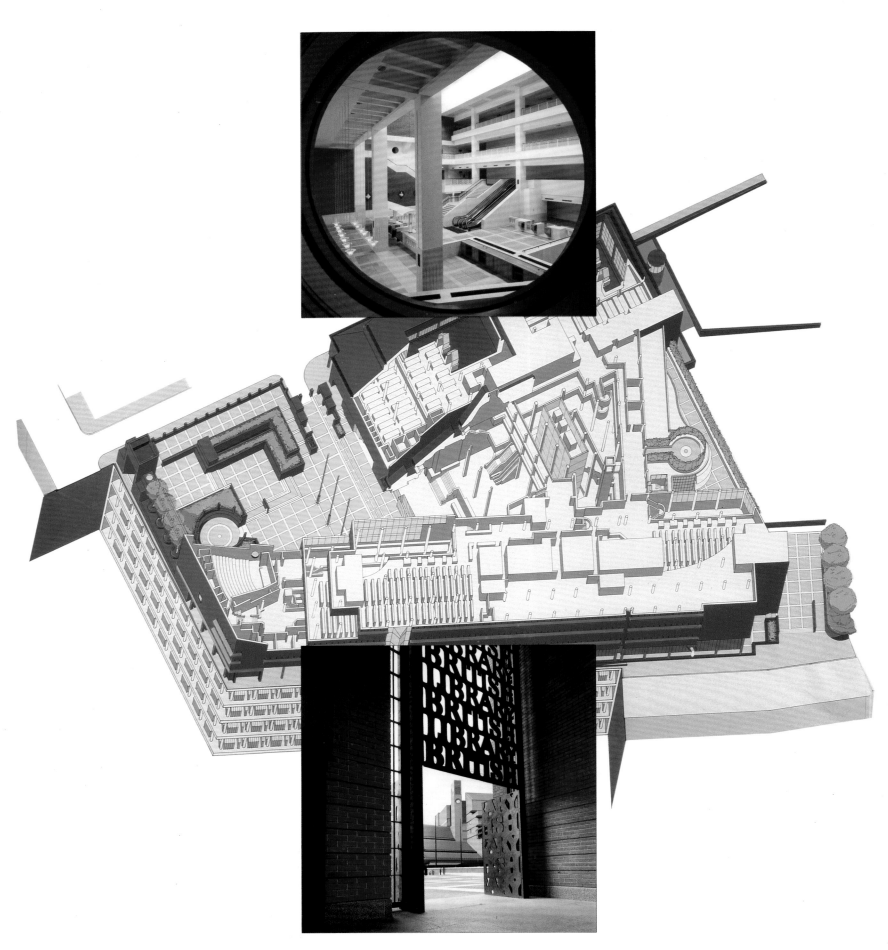

CENTRE: Axonometric

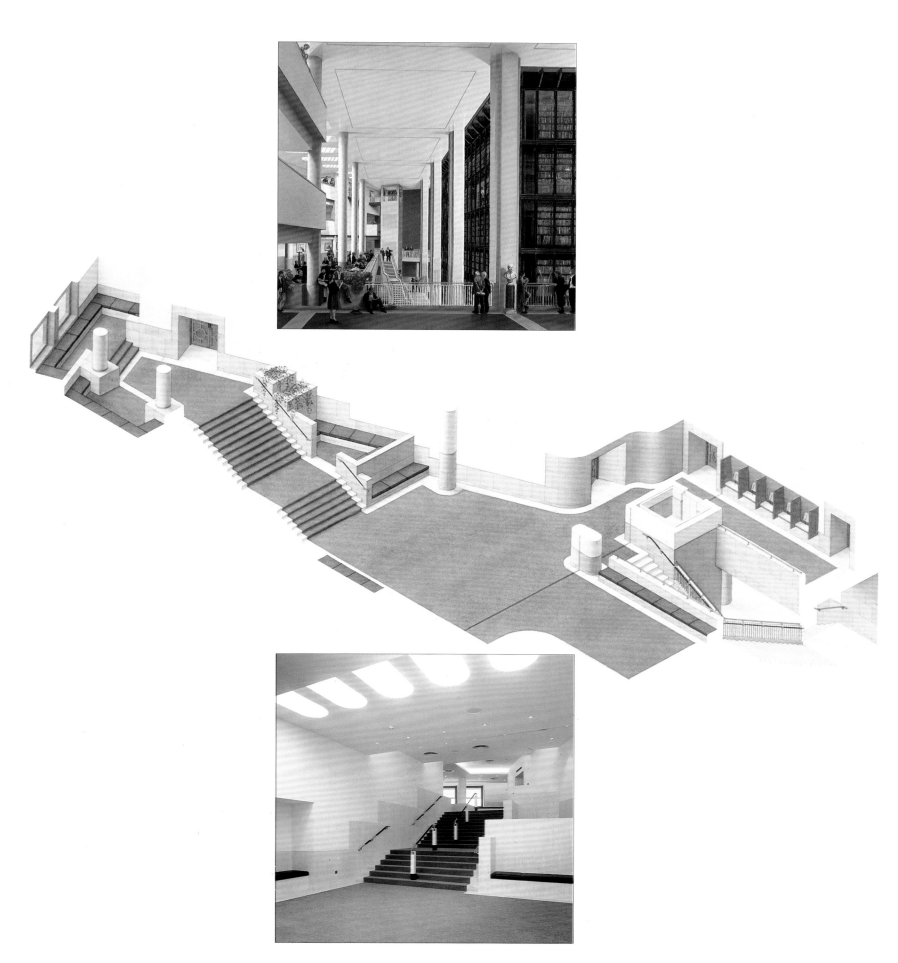

FROM ABOVE: Artist's impression of the King's Library and restaurant; axonometric of the 'Spanish Steps'

ZIMMER GUNSUL FRASCA
BELLEVUE REGIONAL LIBRARY

Bellevue, Seattle, Washington, USA

Over the past two decades, development has transformed Bellevue, Washington, from a bedroom suburb of Seattle into a so-called 'edge city'. The new Bellevue Regional Library was seen as an important catalyst in the implementation of the area's master plan. With a capacity of two hundred and fifty thousand volumes, the 7,400-square-metre, three-storey library houses the largest reference collection in King County's thirty-six-library system. The building also has five public meeting rooms, a large children's area and a gift shop. Underground parking is provided for one hundred and fifteen cars, as well as on-site parking for eighty.

There are two building entrances, one leading to the town centre, and the other from the north, connecting to the car park and the neighbouring areas. Generous outdoor entrance canopies shelter meeting and dropping-off points. The faceted south facade, opening on to a park, has an arcade connecting the library to the future community centre. The arcade also serves as shading for the south-facing reading rooms. Varied roof lines, facade profiles and fenestration reduce the building's

scale. South and east elevations, clad with red sandstone, have exposed ribbed-concrete columns, and the north and west facades a patterned brick veneer, with finer detailing and more domestic scale. Exterior wood overhangs and porches also reduce the institutional appearance. The sloped roofs are of terne-coated stainless steel.

A vaulted public gallery connects the car park and principal entrances, and provides access to the underground parking. The gallery directs patrons through one secure point into the library, and is also used as a lobby space for the public meeting rooms, which have independent access outside library hours. A grand concrete staircase connects the main reading and stack areas. Upper floor reading rooms to the south are provided with overhangs that reflect light on to the interior ceilings. A series of north-facing clerestories and wide stretches of windows create bright and cheerful spaces throughout.

The site, located on a block in the central business district, lacked a sense of place. It is intended that it will eventually have a community centre, a plaza, a small garden, and a future public transit link.

Although the building's forms are unconventional, the structural system is simple and economical; concrete columns from the underground parking extend upwards to support three floors of stacks. Truncated shed roofs introduced over the upper reading and reference areas, with continuous clerestories, provide natural light. Indirect lighting also provides a shadowless and glare-free environment for reading and computer screen visibility.

The building is intended as an image of civic importance and monumentality, which maintains a spirit of intimacy. The ground floor collections are for children and young adults, with the adult and reference sections above. The scale of these zones varies, depending on the specific users: in the children's area, ceiling heights are lower, the furniture and assorted reading areas are all designed at a small scale; the young adult area is furnished with tables and chairs, appropriately larger in scale. Service desks are located to be easily visible to patrons and provide staff with visual control of all areas. The library is equipped with the latest communications systems and computers.

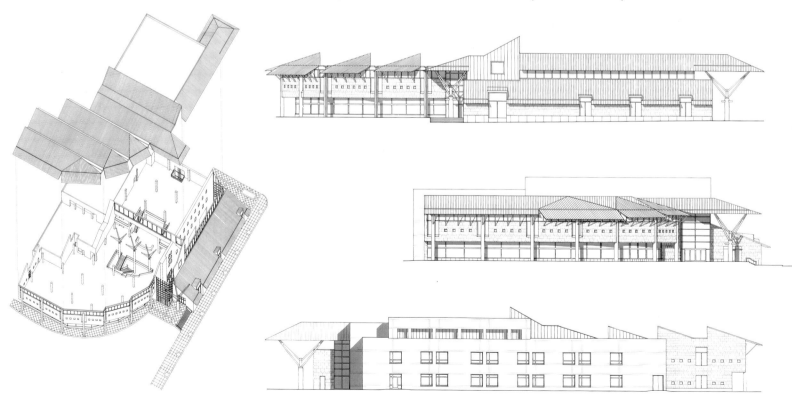

LEFT: Exploded axonometric; RIGHT, FROM ABOVE: East elevation; south elevation; west elevation

INTERIORS IN DETAIL

Michael Brawne

FURNITURE

Henri Labrouste designed two famous libraries in Paris: the Bibliothèque Ste-Geneviève of 1843-50 and the larger Bibliothèque Nationale of 1865-68. Both buildings used exposed iron for their primary structure, although the contemporary critical opinion considered the use of iron as more suitable for railway stations than libraries. In one sense one understands the statement. Looking at an old, slightly blurred photograph of Ste-Geneviève, for instance, one could easily imagine it as a rather noble nineteenth-century railway terminus. What distinguishes it from any train shed, however, is the existence of stacks and reading tables.

It would seem that it is difficult to establish a typology of libraries at the level of the plan and section of the whole building. What makes a building a library is a set of medium- to small-scale decisions which principally involve furniture. When sitting at a desk looking at a book, a computer screen or a microfiche reader, taking a book from a shelf or a journal from a rack, one is most closely involved with a small-scale environment made by furniture. It could certainly be argued that the transformation of a nineteenth-century train shed into a library would require less dramatic action than it did to turn the Gare d'Orsay into the Musée d'Orsay.

If the relatively small scale is so crucial to the proper functioning of a library, this is a reversal of the normal way in which we consider buildings as architects. We tend to leave the design of the furniture – assuming that is in our brief – until late in the design sequence. Yet the creation of particular spaces for small groups of readers might, for instance, very readily affect the structure and, particularly, its spacing. The difference can be seen in two large, roughly contemporary libraries: the Law Library for the University of Oxford of 1964 by Sir Leslie Martin and Colin St John Wilson, and the State Library in Berlin of 1967 by Hans Scharoun. The diagram of the relationship of the reading bays to the open stacks and the study carrels in the original proposal for the Oxford library shows very clearly how structure, space and furniture come together. Moreover, light was to come from above, through deep baffles defining each square group. Scharoun's free flowing spaces, on the other hand, link half-levels to each other and do not seem to suggest any specific sense of place to the reader. The difference between the two designs may stem from different views about the nature of libraries but it also, no doubt, arises from two almost opposing views about space in general.

Nothing in the change from printed material to microforms or electronic storage and retrieval alters the essential one-to-one relationship between a person and the information source. A computer may (at present) be a little more bulky than a book but it still fits on a normal desk in front of the reader. The important difference is that it needs wiring for both power and information. Wire management has thus had serious repercussions on the building section through the provision of hollow floors, and on desk design through providing cable ways from the floor to the desk top. Office furniture has taken aboard this particular problem and provided interesting solutions. The problem may, however, be a temporary one. The idea of a cordless office is being explored vigorously and the transfer of that technology to libraries seems eminently feasible. Certainly the absence of an umbilical cord at every work station would liberate planning.

The general trend of technological development suggests that electronic devices will become less and less rooted and that there will be a resultant greater freedom in placing information sources. Architects will thus have wider opportunities in designing spaces that are conducive to the personal interaction between reader and source or, to put it another way, to deal with those elements which are most characteristic of a library.

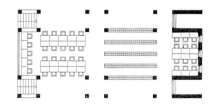

ABOVE: Plan showing stack and reader relationship, Law Library for the University of Oxford, 1964, Sir Leslie Martin and Colin St John Wilson

Michael Brawne & Associates (with Ollertz & Ollertz)
Theological College Library, Fulda, Germany – for this addition to the existing college, Michael Brawne was responsible for designing the furniture to relate to the geometry of the building. The library has a double-height reading room with a central circular rooflight. The reading table echoes the shape of the void above.

De Blacam & Meagher

Cork Regional Technical College – the architects have designed all of the internal beechwood fittings as pieces of furniture placed within the structural shell; stairs, balustrades, desks and the three-storey bookcase galleries. Each reading place is fitted with individual lights and most are wired for computers. BELOW, LEFT TO RIGHT: Details of reading desks – section; elevation; detail; plan

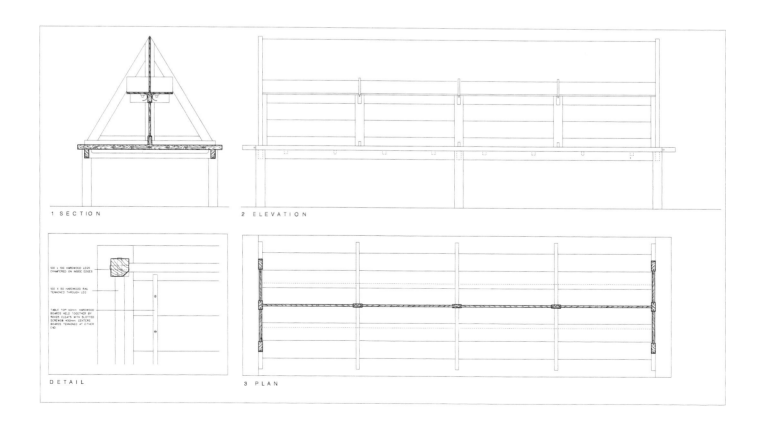

1 SECTION

2 ELEVATION

DETAIL

3 PLAN

Dominique Perrault

The National Library of France – computer visualisations of the interiors of reading rooms and study areas in the lower garden floors. Book stacks are grouped around tables to the edges of the reading rooms.

Evans + Shalev

Quincentenary Library – the book stacks in the library are used to both enclose and divide the space. They are of white painted wood, with traditional simple mouldings. The lightness of the shelving keeps the interior bright and fresh.

bruder DWL architects

Phoenix Central Library – the furniture of the large reading room was designed to evoke memories of the historical reading room. Each reading place on the linear study benches has an individual light. Book stack aisles are lit overhead by lights extended from the tops of the book stacks.

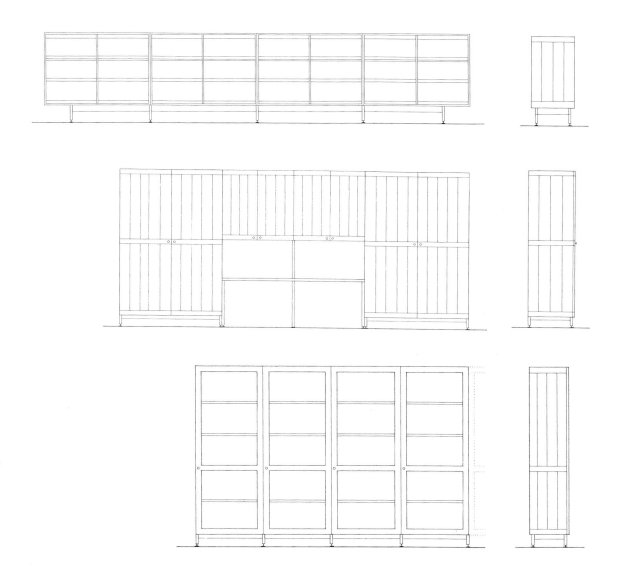

Victo López Cotelo

'The House of Shells' – the interior fixtures were designed by the architect in collaboration with Mark Burkhalter, to form a cohesive insertion into the building shell, using simple lines, different types of display and functional materials. The different styles of storage cases relate to the various media on offer. FROM ABOVE: Details of bookcases in the audio-visual section, cupboards and vitrine cases.

PROJECT INFORMATION

The following information has been correlated from material provided by the architects. All costs and measurements should be taken as a guide only.

Arup Associates
Forbes Mellon Library, Clare College, Cambridge, UK
Type of commission: Invited commission
Structural, mechanical/electrical engineers: Arup Associates
Total area: 825m² (8,880 sf)
Cost: £1.1 million
Design to completion time: Design, 1984

de Blacam and Meagher with Boyd Barrett Murphy O'Connor
Regional Technical College Library, Cork, Ireland
Type of commission: Selection through limited interview
Number of books: 70,000
Project team: Shane de Blacam, Larry Fewer, John Meagher, Mary Laheen, Sandra O'Riordan, Hugh Campbell
Structural engineers: Horgan Lynch & Partners
Mechanical/electrical engineers: Martin Buckley & Associates
Cost consultants: PF Coveney and Associates
Other consultants: Clerk of Works: Bill Cooney; Furniture: Irish Contract Seating
Schedule of main areas
General reading book stacks: 795m²
Reading areas: 560m²
Conference/meeting rooms: 93m²
Reference and periodicals: 115m²
Reserve: 300m²
Technical services: 254m²
Public services: 47m²
Computer areas: Computer access points throughout
Ancillary, support and circulation: 459m²
Total area: 2,672m² (28,760 sf)
Cost: Not available
Design to completion time: Design January 1991, Construction November 1993-October 1994

Architekturbüro Bolles-Wilson + Partner
Münster City Library, Münster, Germany
Type of commission: Direct
Project team: Julia Bolles-Wilson, Peter L Wilson, Eberhard Kleffner, Friedhelm Haas, Martin Schlüter, Andreas Kimmel, Jim Yohe, Manfred Schoeps, Dietmar Berner, Anne Elshof, Cornelia Nottelmann, Jens Ludloff, Laura Fogarasi, Mikkel Frost, Toshi Hisatomi, Dirk Paulsen, Stefanie Schmand
Supervision: Bolles-Wilson + Partner with Harms and Partner
Structural engineers: Ing-Büro Thomas with Ing-Büro Menke und Köhler
Mechanical/electrical engineers: Ing-Büro Albers with the House and Services Department, Building Department, Münster
Acoustic engineers: Büro Stemmer und Tönnemann
Lighting consultant: Lichtedesign
Ground surveyors: Ing-Büro Umpfenbach
Schedule of main areas
General reading book stacks: 3,000m²
Reading areas: 1,700m²
Conference rooms: 250m²
Reference and periodicals: 700m²
Technical services: 550m²
Public services: 500m²
Learning resources: 250m²
Computer areas: Computer access points throughout
Ancillary, support and circulation: 2,800m²
Total area: 9,750m² (104,950 sf)
Cost: £20 million
Design to completion time: 1987-93

Michael Brawne & Associates
The National Library of Sri Lanka, Colombo, Sri Lanka
Type of commission: Commissioned through UNESCO
Number of books: 1 million
Project team: Michael Brawne, Site supervision by Government Building Department
Engineers: Chief Engineer, Department of Buildings, Ministry of Housing & Local Government
Contractor: Muttiah & Son
Schedule of main areas
Closed access book stacks: 2,900m²
Reading areas: 1,900m²
Lecture and conference rooms: 250m²
Periodicals and exhibition: 250m²
Offices: 1,500m²
Ancillary, support and circulation: 700m²
Total area: 11,600m² (125,000 sf)
Cost: Rs50 million
Design to completion time: 12 years
Completion date: April 1990

bruder DWL architects
Phoenix Central Library, Phoenix, Arizona, USA
Type of commission: Direct commission
Number of books: 1.25 million
Project team: Bob Adams, Marc Arnold, Lito Aquino, Will Bruder, Wendell Burnette, John Chopas, Lauren Clark, Mark Dee, Beau Dromiack, Dan Filuk, Michael Haake, Frank Henry, Toni Ann Hindley, Sharon Kraus, Rick Joy, James Lindlan, Dean Olsen, Peter Pascu, Vicky Ramella, Carleton Van Deman, Jeff Wagner
Acoustics, structural and building systems: Ove Arup & Partners, California
Mechanical/electrical engineers: Baltes/Valentino Associates Ltd
Civil engineers: Hook Engineering Inc
Structural fabric: FTL/Happold
Contractor: Sundt Corp
Lighting consultant: Roger Smith; Daylighting Consultant: Tait Solar Company
Landscaping: Martino & Tatasciore
Other consultants: Library Consultants: Mason Associates; Professional Library Consultants pa; Graphic Design: Rowley & Associates
Schedule of main areas
Book stacks, reading areas: 15,150m²
Study rooms: 89m²
Conference rooms: 700m²
Reference and periodicals: 1,163m²
Technical services: 1,292m²
Public services: 409m²
Learning resources: 390m²
Computer areas: 341m²
Ancillary, support and circulation: 6,540m²
Total area: 26,074m² (280,000 sf)
Cost: US $28 million
Design to completion time: 1989-1995

AJ Diamond/Donald Schmitt and Company
Richmond Hill Central Library, Toronto, Ontario, Canada
Type of commission: Direct
Number of books: 170,000
Project team: AJ Diamond, Donald Schmitt, Stewart Adams, Gary McCluskie, George Friedman, Stuart Feldman, Dalibor Cizek,

Shary Adams, Jennifer Stanley, Catherine Benotto, Mary Jane Finlayson, Mike Yuen, Jonathon King
Structural engineers: Robert Halsall & Associates
Mechanical/electrical engineers: Crossey Engineering
Contractor: Buttcon Ltd
Schedule of main areas
General reading book stacks: 1,250m²
Study rooms: 1,000m²
Conference rooms: 225m²
Technical services/office: 1,250m²
Lobby: 325m²
Information: 425m²
Ancillary, support and circulation: 2,500m²
Total area: 7,000m² (75,000 sf)
Cost: Not available
Design to completion time:-

Jeremy Dixon.Edward Jones
Darwin College Study Centre, Cambridge, UK
Type of commission: Limited competition
Structural engineers: Ove Arup & Partners
Mechanical/electrical engineers: Ove Arup & Partners
Contractor: Rattee & Kett
Quantity surveyors: Davis, Langdon & Everest
Schedule of main areas
General reading book stacks: 30m²
Reading areas: 94m²
Study room: 30m²
Technical services: 14m²
Computer areas: 102m²
Total area: 600m² (6,560 sf)
Cost: £1 million
Design to completion time: Commissioned June 1989, construction January 1993-January 1994

Evans + Shalev
Quincentenary Library, Jesus College, Cambridge, UK
Type of commission: Competition, 1991
Number of books: 40,000 volumes
Structural engineers: Anthony Hunt Associates
Environmental engineers: Max Fordham & Partners
Contractor: Coulson & Son Ltd
Schedule of main areas
Book stacks, reading areas: 560m²
Study and conference rooms: 100m²
Technical services: 5m²
Computer areas: 141m²
Ancillary, support and circulation: 394m²
Total area: 1,200m² (12,920 sf)
Cost: £2.1 million
Design to completion time: Competition 1991, construction September 1993-November 1995

Sir Norman Foster and Partners
Cranfield University Library, Bedfordshire, UK
Type of commission: Direct
Project team: Norman Foster, Ken Shuttleworth, Graham Phillips, Robin Partington, Charles Rich, Hugh Thomas, Rodney Uren, Sean Affleck, Tracey Stoute, Nigel Greenhill, Adele Pascal
Structural engineers: Ove Arup and Partners
Mechanical/electrical engineers: J Roger Preston & Partners
Quantity surveyor: Davis Langdon and Everest

Management contractor: Taylor Woodrow Management Contracting
Lighting consultants: George Sexton Associates
Cost: £4.9 million
Design to completion time: 1989-92

Sir Norman Foster and Partners
Squire Law Library, University of Cambridge Law Faculty, Cambridge, UK
Type of commission: Limited competition
Number of books: 120,000+ volumes
Project team: Norman Foster, Spencer de Grey, John Silver, Chris Connell, Michael Jones, Mouzhan Majidi, Giuseppe Boscherini, Angus Campbell, Glenis Fan, Jason Flanagan, Lucy Highton, Ben Marshall, Divya Patel, Kate Peake, Victoria Pike, Austin Relton, Giles Robinson, John Small, Ken Wai, Cindy Walters, Ricarda Zimmerer
Structural engineers: Anthony Hunt Associates
Mechanical/electrical engineers: YRM Engineers
Acoustic engineers: Sandy Brown Associates
Fire consultants: Ove Arup and Partners
Project manager: University of Cambridge Estates Management and Building Services
Quantity surveyor: Davis Langdon and Everest
Cladding consultant: Emmer Pfenniger Partner AG
Landscaping: Cambridge Landscape Architects
Other consultants: Pedestrian Flow: Halcrow Fox
Schedule of main areas
Book stacks (inc reference and periodicals): 12km in length
Computer areas: Computer access points throughout
Total area: 9,000m² (96,880 sf)
Cost: Not available
Design to completion time: 1990-95

Gapp Architects
Sandton Library, Sandton, Gauteng, South Africa
Type of commission: Direct
Number of books: 95,000
Associate architects: Floris Smith and Meyer Pienaar
Project team: Pedro Roos, Glen Gallagher, Karen Wygers, Nina Cohen, Silvio Rech, Therese Christofidis, Cheryl Durham, Candy Soller, John Downie, Adrian Davids, Keith Lambert
Structural engineers: Ove Arup & Partners
Mechanical engineers: Richard Pearce & Partners
Electrical engineers: Everitt & Germishuizen
Civil engineers: Ove Arup & Partners
Contractor: ABCON Construction
Lighting consultant: Paul Pamboukian
Landscaping: EDP
Schedule of main areas
General lending: 1,940m²
(adult: 1,640m²; children's: 300m²)
Study areas: 300m²
Reference and periodicals: 1,144m²
Technical services: 422m²
Ancillary, support and circulation: 152m²
Total area: 4,500m² (48,440 sf)
Cost: SA Rand 17 million
Design to completion time: 3 years, completed 1995

Prof Gerber and Partner
National and University Library of Göttingen, Göttingen, Germany
Type of commission: National competition, 1985

Number of books: 3.6+ million
Project team: Prof Eckhard Gerber, Volker Hachenberger
Structural engineers: Ing.Ges. Neuhaus-Schwermann
Mechanical/electrical engineers: Arge Gruppe Mielchen und Wiechmann, Arge Gruppe Esdorn-Jahn
Lighting consultant: Kress + Adams with Ing. Büro Ernst Schaper
Landscaping: Prof Wehberg, Lange, Eppinger, Schmidtke
Schedule of main areas
Main function area: 4,396m²
Reading and open access areas: 5,213m²
Stacks and technical services: 10,641m²
Administration: 2,352m²
Total area: 23,342m² (251,250 sf)
Cost: DM130 million
Design to completion time: 1985-93

Helin & Siitonen Architects
Joensuu Library, Joensuu, Finland
Type of commission: Competition, 1981
Number of books: 300,000 (Annual lending 1.1 million)
Project team: Tuomo Siitonen, Tuomas Wichmann
Structural engineers: Oy Juva Engineering Ltd
Mechanical engineers: Mäkelä & Jormakka Engineers
Electrical engineers: Veli Hirvonen Engineers
Acoustic engineers: Alpo Halme Architects
Contractor: Joensuu City Building Administration
Lighting consultant: Veli Hirvonen Engineers
Landscaping: Joensuu City Technical Office
Interiors: Studio Simo Heikkilä
Schedule of main areas
General reading book stacks: 1,500m²
Reading areas: 800m²
Study rooms: 100m²
Conference rooms: 200m² (auditorium)
Reference and periodicals: 300m²
Public services: 80m²
Learning resources: 1,428m²
Computer areas: 50m²
Ancillary, support and circulation: 319m²
Total area: 5,715m² (61,515 sf)
Cost: FIM 50.5 million (including furniture)
Design to completion time: 1982-93

Van Heyningen and Haward
Katharine Stephen Rare Books Room, Newnham College, Cambridge, UK
Type of commission: Direct
Number of books: 5,000
Structural engineers: Fogg Associates
Mechanical/electrical engineers: Max Fordham and Partners
Quantity surveyor: Davis Bellfield & Everest
Schedule of main areas
General reading book stacks: 88m² (on 2 levels)
Study space: 18m²
Entrance lobby: 1m²
Total area: 106m² (1,150 sf)
Cost: £54,000
Design to completion time: Constructed summer 1982

Hodgetts + Fung Design Associates
Towell (Temporary) Library, University of California, Los Angeles, California, USA

Type of commission: Direct
Number of books: 210,000
Project team: Craig Hodgetts, Ming Fung, Lunn Batsch, Robert Flock, William Martin, Peter Noble
Structural engineers: Robert Engelkirk Engineering, Inc
Mechanical engineers: The Sullivan Partnership
Electrical engineers: Patrick Byrne & Associates
Civil engineers: AC Martin & Associates
Contractor: American Constructors California, Inc
Lighting consultant: Patrick Quigley and Gary Dvorak, Patrick Quigley & Associates
Other consultants: Steel & Shell Fabricator: Rubb Building Systems
Schedule of main areas
General reading book stacks: 390m²
Reading areas: 885m²
Seminar room: 45m²
Reference and periodicals: 430m²
Technical services: 32m²
Services: 114m²
Computer areas: 81m²
Ancillary, support and circulation: 1,330m²
Total area: 3,250m² (35,000 sf)
Cost: US$2.9 million
Design to completion time: Nine months design and build
Completion date: Autumn 1992

Azusa Kito
Kansai University Central Library, Osaka, Japan
Type of commission: Nomination
Number of books: 2 million
Project team: Azusa Kito Architect & Associates
Structural engineers: Kimura Structural Engineers
Mechanical/electrical engineers: KK Co Ltd Mechanical, Electric and Plumbing Engineers
Contractor: Takenaka Corporation
Lighting consultant: Katori Lighting Consultants
Schedule of main areas
Closed book stacks: 5,835m²
Rare books: 260m²
Reference and periodicals: 2,230m²
Reading areas: 3,340m²
Study cubicles: 100m²
Auditorium: 101m²
Technical and public services: 904m²
Conference rooms: 186m²
Computer areas: 2,739m²
Ancillary, support and circulation: 5,019m²
Total area: 21,750m² (234,115 sf)
Cost: ¥5,000 million
Design to completion time: 1981-1984

Koetter, Kim & Associates
Harvey S Firestone Library Extension, Princeton University, Princeton, New Jersey, USA
Type of commission: Direct
Number of books: 500,000+
Project team: Fred Koetter, Susie Kim, Jack Dobson, Roger Haigh, Craig Spangler, Mark Chen, Carol Nott, Don Semler, William Loftis
Structural engineers: Le Messurier Associates
Mechanical/electrical engineers: RG Vanderweil Engineers
Civil engineers: Van Noté-Harvey
Geotechnical engineers: McPhail Associates

Contractor: Barr & Barr, Inc
Lighting consultant: Powell Lighting Design
Landscaping: Hanna/Olin Ltd
Other consultants: Energy: Tim Johnson; Specs: Todisco Associates
Schedule of main areas

General reading book stacks:	4,095m²
Reading areas:	2,800m²
Small reading areas:	33m²
Ancillary, support and circulation:	723m²
Total area:	5,110m² (55,000 sf)

Cost: $13.8 million
Design to completion time: 1985-October 1989

Henning Larsens Tegenestue

Gentofte Public Library, Copenhagen, Denmark
Type of commission: Invited competition, 1978
Number of books: 600,000
Project team: Henning Larsen, Bjarne F Fredricksen, Lasse Halskov, Pia Wiberg, Bol Fischer, Peter Hancke, Peder Ewald Hansen, Tryggvi Tryggvason, Peter Haugan, Ole Bruhn, Allan Wiinberg, Torsten Thorup, Birgitte von Linstow, Cathlin Holst
Structural engineers: A/S Erik Schmidt, Eric Christian Pedersen
Mechanical/electrical engineer: Tage Kofoed
HVAC engineer: Steen Pedersen
Acoustic engineers: Niels Jordan
Contractor: Højgaard & Schultz a/s
Landscape consultant: HLT a/s and Malene Hauxner

Total area:	7,500m² (80,730 sf)

Cost: Not available
Design to completion time: Competition 1978, construction 1984-85

José Ignacio Linazasoro

UNED Library, Madrid, Spain
Type of commission: Direct
Number of books: 500,000
Project team: Javier Puldain, architect collaborator
Contractor: FOCSA
Other consultants: Santiago Hernan, Juan Carlos Corona
Schedule of main areas

Book stacks, reading, study areas:	4,000m²
Conference rooms:	200m²
Reference, periodicals, technical/public services, computer areas and learning resources:	200m²
Ancillary, support and circulation:	2,000m²
Total area:	7,489m² (80,610 sf)

Cost: 800 million pesetas
Design to completion time: 1989-94

Victor López Cotelo

'The House of Shells' Library, Salamanca, Spain
Type of commission: Direct
Number of books: 42,000
Project team: Victor López Cotelo, Carlos Puente Fernández, Javier García Delgado, José Antonio Valdés Moreno, Clemens Frosch, Ferdinand von Hohenzollern, Rafael Medina Iglesias, José Milla de Marco, Isabel Mira Pueo, Pedro Morales Falmouth, Gustavo Navarro Giménez, José Pascual Izquierdo, Jésus Placencia Porrero, Ana Isabel Torres Solana
Structural engineers: José M Fernández Alvarez
Mechanical engineers: Sefri Ingenieros
Electrical engineers: Cresbo y Blasco
Civil engineers: Cecilio López
Contractor: Agroman SA
Interior design/furniture: Marc Burkhalter with Victor López Cotelo
Schedule of main areas

Ground floor:	898m²

Book store, exhibition, meeting room, catalogue office, network control point, staff facilities

Courtyard floor:	1,150m²

Entrance, reference library, reading room, lending facilities

Mezzanine:	296m²

Lending room, seminar rooms, store

First floor:	805m²

Gallery, music and video, lending, microfilm, research

Second floor:	393m²

Newspapers, periodicals, lending

Third floor:	282m²

Director's office, offices, waiting room

Total area:	3,823m² (41,150 sf)

Cost: 1,013 million pesetas (building restoration), 96 million pesetas (interior fabric and furnishings)
Design to completion time: Design 1984, project 1985-86, construction 1988-93

Lunde & Løvseth

Tønsberg Public Library, Tønsberg, Norway
Type of commission: National competition, 1988
Number of books: 300,000+
Project team: Ivar Lunde, Morten Løvseth, Jon Inge Bruland, Ola Roald
Structural engineers: Dr Techn Kristoffer Apeland
Mechanical/electrical engineers: Harsem Prosjentering a/s, Andersen & Askjem a/s
Contractor: Total Bygg a/s, Willy N Andersen a/s, Elvigs Grass a/s
Lighting consultant: Andersen & Askjem a/s with Lunde & Løvseth
Landscaping: Hindkamar Sundt Thomassen with Lunde & Løvseth
Schedule of main areas

General reading book stacks:	1,900m²
Reading areas:	600m²
Study rooms:	80m²
Conference rooms:	70m²
Reference and periodicals:	200m²
Technical services:	100m²
Public services:	70m²
Learning resources:	100m²
Computer areas:	50m²
Ancillary, support and circulation:	300m²
Total area:	4,900m² (52,700 sf)

Cost: Not available
Design to completion time: Competition 1988, construction 1990-92

Mecanoo

Almelo Public Library, Almelo, The Netherlands
Type of commission: Selection process
Project team: Henk Döll, Maartje Lammers, Aart Fransen, Jan Bekkering, Henk Bouwer, Birgit de Bruin, Johanna Cleary, Renske Groenwoldte, Alexandra Lamboley, Leen Kooman, Anne-Marie van der Meer, Miranda Nieboer, William Richards, Toon de Wilde
Structural engineers: Adviesburo de Bondt bv
Electrical engineers: Brusche bv elektrotechniek
Civil engineers: Raadgevend ingenieursbureau Schreuder bv
Contractor: Aannemersmaatschappij MJ Goosen bv
Schedule of main areas

Book stacks, reading areas, study rooms, reference and periodicals, computer areas, learning resources:	2,596m²
Conference rooms:	132m²
Technical services:	87m²
Public services:	1,135m²
Ancillary, support and circulation:	695m²
Radio station:	135m²
Total area:	4,780m² (51,450 sf)

Cost: NED 11.65 million
Design to completion time: 1991-94

Richard Meier & Partners

The Hague City Library, The Hague, The Netherlands
Type of commission: International competition
Number of books: Library (by the year 2010): 550,000 books, 55,000 CDs, 70,000 videos, 13,000 documentation files, 2,500 journals, 100 newspapers. Archives: 7,000m² of official and private archives from Middle Ages to present, 152,500 objects
Project team: Richard Meier, Thomas Phifer, Gunter Standke, Rijk Rietveld, Diederik Fokkema, Fransico Bielsa, Peter Boche, John Bosch, Patricia Bosch Melendez, Paul Cha, Eric Cobb, Adam Cohen, Susan Davis McCarter, Han van de Eijk, Kenneth Frampton, Stephen Harris, Gordon Haslett, Raphael Justewicz, Gerard Kruunenberg, John Locke, Richard Manna, David Martin, Siobhan McInerney, Brian Messana, Marc Nelen, Alex Nussbaumer, Ana O'Brien, Hans Peter Petri, Hans Put, Greg Reaves, Marc Rosenbaum, Madeleine Sanchez, David Shultis
Structural engineers: Grabowsky & Poort

Mechanical/electrical engineers: BVS Rijswijk
Civil engineers: Peutz & Associates
Contractor: Wilma Bouw BV
Landscaping: Joan Busquets, Alle Hosper, De Kern Gezond
Schedule of main areas
15 km of shelves; 600 individual study seats, 50 study areas
Study rooms: 24 two-person cells, 1 study cell with piano

Public areas:	70,000m²
Total area:	104,500m² (1.1 million sf)

Cost: NLG 275 million/$125 million (for both Town Hall and Library)
Design to completion time: Design 1986-91, construction 1990-95

Moore Ruble Yudell

Humboldt Library, Berlin, Germany
Type of commission: First phase of Cultural Centre for Tegel Harbour
Number of books: 130,000
Associated architect: Abeln, Lubic, Skoda
Project team: John Ruble, Charles Moore, Buzz Yudell, Thomas Nagel, Leon Glodt, Regina Pizzinini, Renzo Zecchetto
Structural engineers: Büro Mannleitner
Mechanical/electrical engineers: Hochbauarnt Reinickendorf
Contractor: Hochtief Construction Company
Lighting consultant: Richard C Peters
Landscaping: Gartenbauarnt Reinickendorf
Other consultants: Colour: Tina Beebe
Schedule of main areas

General reading book stacks:	770m²
Reading areas:	850m²
Study rooms:	60m²
Conference rooms:	28m²
Reference and periodicals:	110m²
Technical services:	37m²
Public services:	200m²
Learning resources:	52m²
Computer areas:	150m²
Ancillary, support and circulation:	212m²
Total Area:	2,469m² (sf)

Cost: US$11 million
Design to completion time: 1984-88

Juan Navarro Baldeweg

Puerto de Toledo Library, Madrid, Spain
Type of commission: Urban planning competition, 1982
Project team: Juan Navarro Baldeweg, Fernando Antón Cabonero, Joaquín Lizasoain Urcola, Franz Bucher, José Maria Gutieerrez de Churtichaga, Enrique Pujano Bambó, Pau Soler Serratosa, Lucrecia Enseñat Benlliure, Rolf Brülisauer
Structural engineers: Julio Martínez Calzón
Cost consultants: Eduardo González Velayos, Pablo Díaz Bucero
Schedule of main areas

Book stacks, reading areas:	1,150m²
Children's library:	480m²
Conference rooms:	83m²
Video room:	8m²
Technical services:	100m²
Ancillary, support and circulation:	910m²
Total area:	· 2,765m²(29,760 sf)

Cost: Not available
Design to completion time: 1990-94

Juan Navarro Baldeweg

Woolworth Center Library, Princeton, New Jersey, USA
Type of commission: Direct
Project team: Juan Navarro Baldeweg, Enrique Pujana Bambó, Leslie Dowling
Structural engineers: Severud Associates and Juan de la Torre
Acoustic engineers: Achentech
Contractor: Barr & Barr
Other consultants: Library Consultant: Michael Keller
Schedule of main areas (Library only)

General reading book stacks:	404m²
Reading areas:	76m²
Study carrels:	100m²
Conference rooms:	68m²
Reference and periodicals:	92m²
Technical services:	42m²

Music and audio-visual areas: 185m²
Ancillary and support facilities: 103m²
Total area: 1,160m² (12,484 sf)
Cost: Not available
Design to completion time: 1994-96

Nurmela – Raimoranta – Tasa
Kuhmo Library, Kuhmo, Finland
Type of commission: Open competition
Number of books: 100,000
Project team: Jyrki Tasa, Tuomo Remes, Antti Luutonen, Timo Kilpiö, Rauli Ukkonen, Hannu Salomaa, Hannu Tikka, Lauri Olin, Elisabeth Pesola
Structural engineers: Pertii Ranta
Mechanical/electrical engineers: Telviconsult
Acoustic engineers: Alpo Halme
Civil engineers: Jukka Syvälahti
Contractor: Alfred A Palmberg
Schedule of main areas
General reading book stacks: 797m²
(adult: 497m²; children's: 119m²; music: 101m²)
Reading areas: 87m²
Reference and periodicals: 63m²
Technical services: 90m²
Public services: 88m²
Computer areas: 29m²
Ancillary, support and circulation: 471m²
Total area: 1,904m²(20,490 sf)
Cost: £2,550,000
Design to completion time: Competition 1984, construction completed November 1988

Patkau Architects
Newton Public Library, Newton, Surrey, British Columbia, Canada
Type of commission: Direct
Number of books: 94,000
Project team: John Patkau, Patricia Patkau, Michael Cunningham, David Shone, Peter Suter
Structural engineers: CY Loh Associates
Mechanical engineers: DW Thomson Consultants Ltd
Electrical engineers: RA Duff and Associates
Acoustic engineers: Brown Strachan Associates
Costing: BTY Group
General contractor: Farmer Construction
Schedule of main areas
General reading book stacks: 397m²
(Adult: 254m²; Childrens: 143m²)
Reading areas: 86m²
(adult: 26m²; browsing: 52m²; children's: 9m²)
Study area: 234m²
Conference rooms: 156m²
Reference and periodicals: 56m²
Technical services: 33m²
Public services: 86m²
Storage: 37m²
Computer areas: 29m²
Ancillary, support and circulation: 217m²
Total area: 1,396m² (15,026 sf)
Cost: CAN$2.4 million
Design to completion time: 1990-92

Perea, Mostaza & Vallhonrat
Public Library, Granada, Spain
Type of commission: Invited to form part of a selection of architects and selected by Ministry of Culture
Number of books: 500,000
Project team: Carmen Mostaza Martínez, Andrés Perea Ortega, Cristobal Vallhonrat Anduiza
Structural engineers: Rodrigo Guarch
Mechanical/electrical engineers: Ofinco
Contractor: Ginés y Navarro, SA
Lighting consultant: Ofinco
Quantity surveyor: Julio Hernanz Cabilla, Carlos Wilhelmi
Other consultants: Extramiana Engineers
Schedule of main areas
General reading book stacks: 1,800m²

Reading areas: 2,300m²
Study rooms: 250m²
Conference rooms: 300m²
Reference and periodicals: 350m²
Technical services: 1,050m²
Public services: 250m²
Computer areas: 50m²
Ancillary, support and circulation: 5,100m²
Total area: 11,750m² (126,475 sf)
Cost: £4.9 million (Furniture and equipment £1 million)
Completion date: April 1994

Dominique Perrault
The National Library of France, Paris, France
Type of commission: Competition, by the Ministry of Culture, Department for Public Buildings represented by the Institute of the Bibliothèque nationale de France
Number of books: 20 million+
Project team: Dominique Perrault, Aude Perrault, Gaëlle Lauriot-dit-Prévost, Daniel Allaire, Gabriel Choukron, Yves Conan, Constantin Coursaris, Maxime Gasperini, Pablo Gil, Guy Morriseau, Luciano d'Alesio, Claude Alovisetti, Emmanuelle Andréani, Judith Barber, Philippe Berbett, Jérôme Besse, Jean-Luc Bichet, Charles Caglini, Jean-François Candeille, Hristo Chinkov, Alexander Dierendonck, Celine dos Santos, Marie-France Dussaussois, Laura Ferreira-Sheehan, Corrina Fuhrer, Catriona Gatheral, Dominique Guibert, Serge Guyon, Dominique Jauvin, Anne Kaplan, Christian Laborde, Maryvonne Lanco, Corrine Lafon, Olivier Lidon, Zhi-Jian Lin, Pierre Loritte, Patrice Marchand, Thierry, Meunier, Brigitte Michaud, Franck Michigan, Rosa Precigout, René Puybonnieux, Martine Rigaud, Hildegard Ruske, Jérôme Thibault, Catherine Todaro, Louis van Ost, Inge Waes
Architectural engineers: Perrault Associés SA
Main contractor: Dominique Perrault, architect-mandataire
Other consultants: Socotec-Appave; ODM; CTFT; Jean-Paul Lamoureux; Setae; Alain Berthaux; Pieffet Corbin Tomasina; Technip Seri Construction; Sechaud & Bossuyt; Syseca; HGM; Sauveterre; ACV; Eric Jacobsen; Bernard Parant
Schedule of main areas 400 kilometres of shelving
Esplanade: 58,811m²
Garden: 10,782m²
Public areas:
Garden, top level: 26,540m²
(1,556 public reading places; restaurant 850m²; lecture halls 3,000m²)
Garden, ground level: 28,680m²
(2,034 reading places for researchers)
Service areas:
Staff areas 2,000m²; workshops, book transit, services 34,103m²
Towers:
Office areas (7 storeys) 16,240m²; storage areas (11 storeys) 26,660m²; technical services, circulation 14,000m²; car parking 19,000m²
Total area: 360,000m²(3, 875, 008sf)
Cost: FF3.6 billion
Design to completion time: Competition 1988-89, design to construction 1990-1995, open to public 1996

Antoine Predock
Mesa Public Library, Los Alamos, New Mexico, USA
Structural engineers: Randy Holt & Associates
Mechanical engineers: P2RS Group
Electrical engineers: Telcon
Civil engineering: County of Los Alamos
Contractor: Bradbury & Stamm Construction
Schedule of main areas
General reading book stacks: 980m²
Reading areas: 260m²
Coference rooms: 143m²
Reference and periodicals: 389m²
Technical services: 130m²
Public services: 125m²
Learning resources: 116m²
Computer areas: 18m²
Total area: 4,933m² (53,100 sf)
Cost: US$5.1 million
Completion date: 1994

Richard Rogers Partnership
Learning Resources Centre, Thames Valley University, Slough
Type of commission: Direct
Project team: Maurice Brennan, Mark Darbon, Michael Davies, Chris Donnington, Michael Elkan, Michael Fairbrass, Marco Goldschmied, Philip Gumuchdjian, Jackie Hands, Avery Howe, Sharni Howe, Amarjit Kalsi, Carol Painter, Louise Palomba, Richard Rogers, Stephen Spence, John Young
Structural engineers: Buro Happold
Mechanical/electrical engineers: Buro Happold
Contractor: Laing South East
Lighting consultant: Lighting Design Partnership
Landscaping: Edward Huthchinson
Cost consultant: Hanscomb Partnership
Computer areas: Computer access points throughout
Total area: 3,500m² (37,670 sf)
Cost: Not available
Design to completion time: April 1994-April 1996

Aldo Rossi
Seregno Library, Seregno, Italy
Number of books: 70,500 (all media)
Total area: 4,410m² (47,470 sf)

Aldo Rossi
University Library, Castellanza, Italy
Number of books: 20,000 (all media)
Total area: 1,900m² (20,452 sf)

Moshe Safdie and Associates with Downs Archambault & Partners, Joint venture
Vancouver Central Public Library, Vancouver Library Square, British Columbia, Canada
Type of commission: International competition
Number of books: 1 million+ (all media)
Project team: Moshe Safdie, David Galpin, Philip Matthews, Ron Beaton, Michael McKee
Structural engineers: Ove Arup and Partners (conceptual); Read Jones Christoffersen
Mechanical: Ove Arup and Partners (conceptual); Keen Engineering Company Ltd
Electrical engineers: Schenke-Bawol Engineering Ltd
Acoustical engineers: Brown Strachan Associates
Contractor: PCL Constructors Pacific Inc
Lighting consultant: Fisher Marantz Renfro Stone
Landscaping: Cornelia Hahn Oberlander
Other consultants: Geotechnical: Cook Pickering & Doyle Ltd; Code: Gage Babcock & Associates; Cost: Hanscomb Consultants Inc; Specifications: J Findlay & Associates; Traffic ND Lea Consultants Ltd; Accessibility: RBO Architecture Inc, Security: Tech cord Consulting Group Ltd
Schedule of main areas
General reading book stacks: 5,280m²
Reading areas: 3,645m²
Study rooms: 160m²
Conference rooms: 570m²
Reference and periodicals: 1,200m²
Technical services: 2,640m²
Public services: 675m²
Learning resources: 125m²
Computer areas: 440m² (all carrels wired)
Ancillary, support and circulation: 10,200m²
Total area: Library, retail and service facilities: 32,500m² (350,000 sf)
Total: 60,400m² (650,000 sf)
Cost: CAN$109 million (for library & Federal Office tower, parking garage, retail, daycare centre and plazas)
Design to completion time: 1992-95

Schwartz/Silver Architects
Rotch Library Addition, MIT, Cambridge, Massachusetts, USA
Type of commission: Client selection process
Number of books: 245,000
Project team: Warren Schwartz, Robert Silver, Randolph Meiklejohn, Anne Pitt, Laura Briggs, Timothy Downing
Structural engineers: Simpson Gumpertz & Heger Inc
Mechanical/electrical engineers: RG Vanderweil Engineers Inc

Contractor: GBH Macomber Co
Schedule of main areas

General reading book stacks:	1,114m²
Special collection:	186m²
Reading areas:	204m²
Study rooms:	232m²
Reference and periodicals:	186m²
Technical services:	279m²
Public services:	93m²
Computer areas:	93m²
Ancillary, support and circulation:	279m²
Total area:	2,787m² (30,000 sf)

(1,950m² new construction, 836m² renovation)
Cost: US$5.8 million
Design to completion time: 36 months
Completion date: January 1991

Scogin, Elam and Bray

Clayton County Headquarters Library, Jonesboro, Georgia, USA
Type of commission: Qualifications-based selection process
Number of books: 129,900
Project team: Merrill Elam, Mack Scogin, Lloyd Bray, Rick Sellers, Isabelle Millet, Tom Crosby, David Murphree, Dick Spangler, Ennis Parker
Structural, mechanical/electrical engineers: Gann Pruitt Womack Davenport & Associates Inc
Lighting consultant: Ramon Luminance Design
Landscaping: Eberly and Associates
Cost consultants: Costing Services Group
Schedule of main areas

General reading book stacks:	930m²

(General: 550m²; Browsing: 28m²; Children's: 110m²)

Reading areas:	600m²

(General: 348m²; browsing: 56m²; children's: 93m²; reference: 74m²; periodicals: 30m²)

Conference rooms:	172m²
Reference and periodicals:	98m²
Technical services:	146m²
Public services:	37m²
Learning resources:	88m²
Computer areas:	92m²
Ancillary, support and circulation:	853m²
Total area:	3,020m² (32,500 sf)

Cost: US$2.1 million
Design to completion time: Summer 1985-June 1988

Scogin, Elam and Bray

John J Ross – William C Blakely Law Library, Arizona State University, Tempe, Arizona, USA
Type of commission: Qualifications-based selection process
Number of books: 310,000+ volumes
Architects: Leo A Daly Company, Architects of Record and Scogin Elam and Bray, Design Architects
Design team: Mack Scogin, Merrill Elam, Lloyd Bray, Jeff Atwood, Susan Desko, Richard Ashworth, Julie Sanford, Denise Dumais, Carlos Tardio, Monica Solana
Structural engineers: Robin E Parke Associates Inc
Mechanical/electrical engineers: Leo A Daly Company
Civil engineers: Coe & Vanloo Consulting Engineers Inc
Construction management: CMX Group Inc
Contractor: Oakland Construction Company
Lighting consultant: Newcombe & Boyd Consulting Engineers
Landscape architect: The Campbell Collaborative
Other consultants: George S Grossman (Law Library Specialist)
Schedule of main areas (New Construction only)

General reading book stacks:	2,188m²

(general: 3,083m²; reserve: 195m²; ref: 111m²; periodicals: 377m²)

Reading areas:	571m²

(general: 395m²; reserve: 74m²; ref: 33m²; periodicals: 70m²)

Study rooms:	139m²
Conference rooms:	130m²
Reference and periodicals:	489m²
Technical services:	297m²
Learning resources:	56m²
Computer areas:	195m²

Ancillary, support and circulation:	2,145m²
Total area:	7,875m² (84,755 sf)

(6,294m² new construction 1,579m² + renovation)
Cost: US$7.37 million
Design to completion time: Summer 1990-summer 1993

Scogin, Elam and Bray

Carol Cobb Turner Branch Library, Morrow, Georgia, USA
Type of commission: Qualifications-based selection process
Number of books: 59,000 volumes
Project team: Mack Scogin, Merrill Elam, Lloyd Bray, Carlos Tardio, Jeff Atwood, Susan Desko, Richard Ashworth, Julie Sanford, Criss Mills
Structural engineers: Pruitt Eberly, Inc
Mechanical/electrical engineers: Sunbelt Engineering Group
Contractor: Lusk and Associates, Inc
Lighting consultant: Ramon Luminance Design
Landscaping: Doug Allen, ASLA
Schedule of main areas

General reading book stacks:	414m²

(general: 232m²; browsing: 149m²; children's: 24m²)

Reading areas:	150m²

(general: 19m²; browsing: 45m²; children's: 53m²; reference and periodicals: 33m²)

Conference rooms:	46m²
Reference and periodicals:	37m²
Learning resources:	26m²
Computer areas:	22m²
Ancillary, support and circulation:	242m²
Total area:	930m² (10,000 sf)

Cost: US$760,000
Design to completion time: Winter 1989-January 1991

James Stirling Michael Wilford & Associates

Science Library, University of California, Irvine, California, USA
Type of commission: Direct commission
Number of books: 458,800
Associate architects: IBI/L Paul Zajfen
Project team: Chris Chong, Felim Dunne, Eilis O'Donnell, Richard Portchmouth, Peter Ray, Mike Russum
Structural engineers: Ove Arup and Partners
Mechanical/electrical engineers: Ove Arup and Partners
Cost consultant: Adamson Associates
Landscaping: Burton & Spitz
Schedule of main areas

General reading book stacks:	3,680m² (2,000 spaces)
Reading areas:	3,300m² (1,625 spaces)
Study rooms:	550 rooms
Reference and periodicals:	1,700m²
Technical services:	1,250m²
Public services:	520m²
Learning resources:	420m²
Computer areas:	110m²
Ancillary, support and circulation:	4,080m²
Total area:	16,150m² (17,380 sf)

Cost: US$ 25.2 million
Design to completion time: 1992-June 1994

Tibbalds Monro

Croydon Public Library, 'The Clock Tower', Croydon, Surrey, UK
Type of commission: Direct
Number of books: 200,000
Project team: Charles Barguirdjian, David Brazier, Chris Colbourne, Jane Dann, Ian Deans, Andy Fifield, Michael Harper, James Harty, Frank Hickson, Robin Johnson, David Leech, Carolyn Maxwell Mahon, Michael Patrick, Mark Richard, Anastasia Saward, Helge Skovbjerg, Joanna Skwarnecka, Francis Tibbalds, Mick Timpson, Robert Tocher, Mark Williams
Structural engineers: Michael Barclay Partnership
Mechanical/electrical engineers: WSP Consulting Engineers
Acoustic engineers: Sandy Brown Associates and Sound Research Laboratories
Contractor: Taylor Woodrow Construction (Southern) Ltd
Cost consultant: Michael Edwards & Associates
Other consultants: Library Fitout: Gresswell
Schedule of main areas

General lending, technical services, reference and study:	2,744m²
Children's area:	806m²
Conference rooms:	57m²
Public services:	84m²
Local studies/archive:	239m²
Ancillary, support and circulation:	1,066m²
Total area:	9,554m² (102,800 sf)

Cost: £13.5 million (£30 million for the whole complex)
Design to completion time: 1988-November 1993

Colin St John Wilson & Partners

The British Library, St Pancras, London, UK
Type of commission: Direct commission
Number of books: Books & serial vols: 12 million; patents: 33 million; map items: 2 million; music scores: 1.5 million; manuscripts: 0.3 million (+ collections of stamps, seals, prints etc)
Project Team: Colin St John Wilson, MJ Long, John Collier, John Honer, Douglas Lanham, Peter Carolin, John Barrow, Peter Brough, Peter Denney, Dennis Dornan, Brian Frost, Rolfe Kentish, Linda Suggate, Fritz Stoll, David Wares, Matthew Barac, Mary Barry, Alison Bell, Alice Brown, John Bushell, John Cannon, Ho Jai Cheung, Andrea Cioccolanti, Hilsie Clelford, Lisa Collins, Hugh Cullum, Mark Davies, Susan Earley, Angus Gavin, David Gibson, Tina Gibson, Neil Godamune, Camillo Gonzalez-Ordonaz, Helen Grassly, Andrew Harper, Glen Harper, Tim Hatton, Dennis Ho, Gavin Hogben, Simon Horner, Krzysztof Jaraczewski, Graham Jenkins, Dennis Jordaan, Andrew Knox, Marcie Larizadeh, Sarah Laycock, Geoff Leffeck, Thomas Leung, Dale Loth, Andrew Matthews, Oktay Nayman, Richard Nightingale, Simon Percival, Tony Pryor, Philip Roberts, Phil Russen, Anwah Salleh, King Siauw, Deborah Saunt, David Spillane, Catherine Stewart, Yann Taylor, Geoff Thomason, Paul Yarker, Helena Webster, Andrew Williamson, Peter Wong
Structural engineers: Ove Arup & Partners
Mechanical/electrical engineers: Steensen Varming Mulcahy & Partners
Project management: Schal Project Management
Contractor: Phase1A: Laing Management Contracting; Completion Phase: McAlpine/Haden
Cost consultant: Davis Langdon & Everest
Schedule of main areas
340km shelving; 1192 reader desks (after completion phase)

Reading rooms:	c13,000m²
Exhibitions:	c1,350m²
Offices:	c12,000m²
Entrance hall:	c2,550m²
Total area: (after completion phase)	112,643m² (1,212,479 sf)

Cost: Not available
Completion date: November 1997

Zimmer Gunsul Frasca

Bellevue Regional Library, Seattle, Washington, USA
Type of commission: Qualifications-based selection process
Number of books: 250,000
Structural engineers: KPFF Consulting Engineers
Mechanical engineers: Notkin Engineers
Electrical engineers: Sparling
Acoustic engineers: Michael R Yantis Associates Inc PS
Contractor: GLY Construction
Lighting consultant: Sparling/Candella
Landscaping: Jones & Jones
Schedule of main areas

General reading book stacks:	3,203 m²
Reading areas:	110 seats
Study rooms:	218 seats
Conference rooms:	309m² (5 rooms)
Reference and periodicals:	1,132m²
Technical services:	1,976m²
Public services:	252m²
Ancillary, support and circulation: (including underground parking)	4,939m²
Total area:	11,811m² (127,134 sf)

Cost: US$19.3 million
Design to completion time: 15 months design, 14 months construction
Completion date: July 1993